Baseball
and Richmond

Baseball and Richmond

A History of the Professional Game, 1884–2000

W. HARRISON DANIEL
and SCOTT P. MAYER

McFarland & Company, Inc., Publishers
Jefferson, North Carolina, and London

Library of Congress Cataloguing-in-Publication Data

Daniel, W. Harrison.
    Baseball and Richmond : a history of the professional game,
  1884–2000 / W. Harrison Daniel and Scott P. Mayer
      p.   cm.
    Includes bibliographical references and index.

    ISBN 0-7864-1489-8 (softcover : 50# alkaline paper) ∞

    1. Baseball—Virginia—Richmond.   I. Mayer, Scott P.   II. Title.
GV863.V82R533   2003
796.357'09755'451—dc21   2002154146

British Library cataloguing data are available

Cover photograph: Broad Street Park, home for Richmond's professional
baseball teams, 1897–1912 (from the Cook Collection, printed by
permission of the Valentine Museum and Richmond History Center)

Manufactured in the United States of America

McFarland & Company, Inc., Publishers
  Box 611, Jefferson, North Carolina 28640
   www.mcfarlandpub.com

To our wives, Kimberly and Margaret,
for their patience and encouragement

Contents

Acknowledgments

A number of persons have kindly and patiently assisted us in the years that we have been researching this project. We are grateful for their help. Among those who have graciously assisted us in researching this project are the following: The library staff at Boatwright Memorial Library, University of Richmond; the library staff at the James Branch Cabell Library, Virginia Commonwealth University, Richmond, Virginia; Thomas Camder and Audrey Johnson of the Special Collections, Library of Virginia, Richmond, Virginia; Mrs. Elizabeth Dementi of Dementi Studio, Richmond, Virginia; Dr. Andrew F. Newcomb, acting Dean of the School of Arts and Sciences at the University of Richmond; Mary Anne Wilbourne and Deborah Govoruhk, administrative assistants, History Department, University of Richmond; Todd Feagans, public relations manager, the Richmond Braves Baseball Club; Charles Saunders, director of library services, *Richmond Times-Dispatch*; Susan Bosseau, *Richmond Times-Dispatch*; Stephanie Jacobe, photo collection, the Virginia Historical Society, Richmond, Virginia; Teresa Roane, The Valentine, the Museum of the Life and History of Richmond.

Preface

The history of Richmond, Virginia's relationship with professional baseball has never been chronicled in detail. The present effort to tell that story is the work of two authors, W. Harrison Daniel and Scott P. Mayer. The account from 1884 to 1932 and the section on the Richmond Braves were written by Mayer; chapter I and the account from 1932 to 1966 were written by Daniel. An earlier version of chapter one was published in the summer 1999 issue of the *Virginia Cavalcade* and the authors are grateful to the editor of that periodical for permission to reuse the material.

This study includes information about the men who played on the field and the men who owned the teams; it also comments on the relationship shared by the team and the city. In many ways, the story of Richmond's history with baseball is a typical example of the development of the professional game. The early period reflects many of the same issues that are seen in modern baseball. There was instability as competing interests fought for control of baseball's fortunes in the city. If the team did not generate enough profit, it was moved to another city or a new ballpark was built. There were frequent changes in ownership as competing interests such as the trolley companies fought to earn not only the profits from the gate receipts of those attending the game, but also the street car fare for getting there.

Even those without a direct financial interest in the baseball team looked to baseball as a representation of the community. Baseball served as a means of promoting the city and its various industries. Baseball in Richmond has very much been about business. The early period was about its growth and was marked by instability. As the game became established, it developed stability in ownership, league affiliation and its place within the Richmond community.

The most reliable source of information regarding early baseball is the local newspaper. A detailed reading of the *Richmond Daily Dispatch,* and the successive *Richmond Dispatch* and *Richmond Times-Dispatch,* was undertaken for this project. While several newspapers have existed in Richmond's history, often competing for readership during the same period, the *Dispatch* was selected for its continuity in publication and for its support and consistent reporting of baseball.

Both W. Harrison Daniel and Scott P. Mayer are long-time baseball fans and both are associated with the University of Richmond—Daniel with the History Department and Mayer with the Office of Admission.

CHAPTER I

Baseball Beginnings
in Richmond, 1866–1883

Although baseball teams were organized and the game was played in some areas of the South prior to the Civil War, it appears that the game was not introduced to the Richmond area until after that war. In an article on August 31, 1866, designed to explain the game to his readers, James A. Cowardin, editor of the *Richmond Daily Dispatch,* stated, "the game of baseball was imported from the North since the close of the war."[1] The first clubs, organized to sponsor baseball teams, were formed in Richmond during the spring and summer of 1866. Interest in the game increased rapidly, and the press exclaimed, "Baseball fever spread more rapidly than cholera." It should be noted that Richmond experienced a cholera outbreak in 1866 at the same time interest in baseball captured the attention of many.[2]

By the fall of 1866, at least fifteen adult and a dozen junior teams had been formed in the city. Among the adult clubs were the following: the Richmonds, Old Dominion, Alert, Olympic, Stonewall, Pastime, American, Lone Star, Spotswood, Independent, and the Confederates. The junior teams, comprised of boys age 15–17, included the Stonewall, Jr., the Richmond, Jr., Morning Star, Atlantic, Rag Muffin, Excelsior,

This chapter is a revised version of "Good Playing and Gentlemanly Bearing: Baseball's Beginnings in Richmond, 1866–1883," which appeared in the summer 1999 issue of Virginia Cavalcade, *©1999 by the Library of Virginia. Used by permission.*

Forrest, and Star. Some of the teams adopted uniforms; for example, the Stonewall uniform included red pants, a white shirt, and red cap. The Pastime uniform featured grey pants with a black belt, white shirt and blue cap.[3] During 1866 there was no fixed schedule for the playing of baseball in the city. Games were played from early spring until mid–December.[4]

The games between the different city clubs and a few visiting teams were played at one of a number of sites. One place where games were played was at the Fair Grounds. Other sites included Rutherford's Field between Grace and Franklin streets near the Fair Grounds, the grounds opposite Elba Park, the area bounded by Twenty-Second and Twenty-Third streets and Grace and Broad streets, the lot at the corner of Twenty-Ninth and N streets, and another at the corner of Decatur and Lawrence streets. Game time was usually in mid-afternoon, around 3:30 to 4:00 p.m. In addition to playing games against each other, some Richmond clubs in 1866 played visiting nines from Washington, D.C., and Baltimore. For example, in October, the Pastime club of Richmond played the National club of Washington in a game at the Fair Grounds that was witnessed by approximately 4,000 persons, including "many ladies." This game lasted over four hours, and the Nationals won by a score of 76–19. Two weeks later, the Pastime nine played the Maryland club of Baltimore at the same site, and the visitors were victorious by a score of 51–36. After each game, the visitors were guests of the Pastime club for dinner at the Ballard House Hotel.[5] The Pastime team was the most prominent one in Richmond during the years 1866–70. Its president and team captain was Alexander G. Babcock, a local ice manufacturer and dealer. Other members of the team included Messrs. Edwards, Davidson, Macmurdo, Smith, McDermott, Tomlinson, and Taylor. Prior to 1870 when the team disbanded, other members included Thompson, Hinchman, Gentry, Duffy, Campbell, Wesley and Redford.[6]

In November 1866, the Olympic club of Richmond traveled to Petersburg for a game with the Cockade club of that city. And on November 23, the press announced that a game for the championship of Richmond would take place that afternoon between two neighborhood clubs, the Spotswood and the Richmond; the Spotswood team won this contest by a score of 102 to 76. By the close of the 1866 baseball season, the editor of the *Daily Dispatch* declared that baseball has "become fashionable from Maine to Mexico and is quite the rage." Its widespread popularity, he exclaimed, was "quite remarkable." One manifestation of interest in the game by Richmonders was the convening of a baseball convention at the Richmond City Hall on December 21. This convention consisted of representatives from baseball clubs in Richmond and the surrounding area.

This gathering named as its chairman Edward Cohen, a local banker and stockbroker and a representative of the Richmond club. The convention also appointed two committees. One was to prepare an invitation to "all the baseball clubs of Virginia" to attend a general convention to be held in Richmond during the first week of February 1867. The other committee was to "arrange for holding the state convention." The invitations issued to the baseball clubs of the state requested that each team appoint three delegates to attend the convention, and it was stated that the "chief object of the state convention was to further the cause of baseball in the commonwealth."[7]

The response of the baseball clubs throughout Virginia to send delegates to the state baseball convention was doubtless disappointing to the patrons of baseball. When the convention met on February 4, 1867, at 8:00 p.m. in Richmond City Hall, there were representatives from nine Richmond teams and from three teams in Alexandria. Clubs from these two cities were the only ones at the state baseball convention. Despite the meager representation of clubs in the state, the delegates at the convention organized or formed the "Virginia Association of Baseball Clubs." Officers chosen for the association were Edward Cohen of the Richmond Club, president; R.M. Latham of the Mt. Vernon Club in Alexandria, vice-president; John E. Davidson of the Pastime club of Richmond, second vice-president; O. A. Glazebrook of the Richmond club, recording secretary; G. Watson James of the Olympic club of Richmond, corresponding secretary; and S.P. Weisiger of the Independent club of Richmond, treasurer.[8]

Although attendance at the Baseball Convention was sparse, interest in and enthusiasm for the game remained at a high level in Richmond throughout 1867. During the summer and fall, at least a dozen adult clubs and an equal number of junior teams engaged in the sport of baseball. Most of the games were between city clubs. However, visiting clubs from Petersburg, Charlottesville, Ashland and Baltimore played teams in Richmond. Richmond was still under military occupation in 1867, but baseball seemed to have been a vehicle for promoting harmony between the people of Richmond and Federal troops stationed in the area. On one occasion, there was a game at the Fair Grounds between a local team and a team of Union soldiers who were stationed at Camp Grant. On another occasion, in a game played at the same site before "several thousand ladies and gentlemen" between the Pastime club and a "picked nine" from other Richmond clubs, the crowd was entertained with music by the "fine band of the Eleventh United States Infantry." The press noted that the band added much to the pleasure of the occasion by their "excellent music."[9]

On several occasions in 1867, special baseball games were played to benefit some charity or worthy institution. At such times, the customary admission fee to the games of 25 cents, plus any additional contributions, was given to the beneficiary. On July 30, the Pastime Baseball Club played a picked nine from other Richmond clubs in a game at the Fair Grounds for the benefit of the Masonic School Fund. On this occasion the weather was fair, and it was reported that several thousand ladies and gentlemen watched the game. On October 15, the same two groups met at the same place and played a game for the benefit of the St. Joseph's Orphanage Asylum. In addition to a large number of ladies and gentlemen, the orphans at the asylum were also present to see the game. Before the close of the baseball season, the Ladies of the Centenary Methodist Church Dorcas Society requested that the Pastime baseball club play a benefit game for their organization. The Dorcas Society was a ladies auxiliary group associated with various churches. The purpose of the society was to provide clothing for and assistance to the poor. In October, a committee from the society appealed to Arthur G. Babcock, president of the Pastime baseball club, to play a game for the benefit of the society, noting that the club had "generously responded to the request of St. Joseph's Orphan Asylum for assistance." Babcock's reply to the society was affirmative, and, on October 25, a game for the benefit of the society was played at the Fair Grounds. At the conclusion of the game, the Reverend Dr. John L. Burrows, on behalf of the ladies of the Dorcas Society, presented Babcock a flag or bunting with white background, blue borders and gold fringe, inscribed on the background, in gold letters, with "Pastime B.B.C."[10]

In September 1867, the Pastime baseball club of Richmond became the first local team to make an extended tour to play teams outside of the area. Between September 15 and 25, the club traveled via train to Baltimore for games with the Maryland and Pastime clubs of that city. From Baltimore, the Richmond club journeyed to the nation's capital where they played the National Baseball Club of that city. The following day, the Pastime nine played the Old Dominion team of Alexandria, and the last game on this tour was with the Randolph Club of Warrenton. The Richmond Pastimes lost to the Baltimore and Washington clubs but were victorious over the ones in Alexandria and Warrenton. At each place the Richmonders were entertained as guests of the home club following the game, and it was reported that the members of the "club had a delightful trip ... that the host clubs made every effort to make their trip pleasant."[11]

These early baseball clubs in Richmond were essentially civic/social organizations which sponsored baseball teams. The officials of these clubs represented a variety of organizations and professions in the city. They

included manufacturers, merchants, bankers, stockbrokers, insurance executives, building contractors, police court judges, printers, wholesale merchants, jewelers, a police captain, pharmacists and physicians. Each club
had its own "meeting rooms" in a local hotel or the building of a business
establishment. These clubs held occasional dinners, dances, parties and
other social functions. It was common practice for the host team/club to
entertain and provide over night accommodations for visiting or out of
town teams. On one occasion, the Stonewall club gave a party for a young
ladies club of Church Hill and later the ladies reciprocated with a party
for the baseball team.[12]

It appears that the closing years of the 1860s witnessed the beginning of a decline of interest in baseball in Richmond. This might have
been a reflection of the lack of support throughout the state for the Virginia Association of Baseball Clubs, which was formed in February 1867.
Perhaps the fact that the people of Richmond and Virginia were experi-
encing drastic social changes as a result of Congressional Reconstruction
legislation was also a distraction. During 1868 and 1869, only a half-dozen
teams were active in Richmond, and, of these, only one, the Pastime club,
pre-dated 1868. During these years, there was slight mention of baseball
activities by the press. It was noted that the local season opened on April
10 when the Pastime club entertained a local nine. A short while later the
Pastime nine traveled to Petersburg for a contest with the Independent
club of that city and later in the season were hosts to the Maryland club
of Baltimore. Despite the decline of interest in baseball, it was during
the summer of 1868 that the press referred to it as "our National game."
It was also during this season that there was the first mention of a college team playing in Richmond. On May 5, there was a game between
the Confederate team of Richmond and the Athletics of Randolph-Macon
College.[13]

The summer of 1869 marked the continued decline of baseball activity and interest in Richmond. The city's most prominent nine was the Pastime, and it was rather active in the summer of 1869. It played games with
several local teams and engaged Baltimore teams at home and in Maryland. The games with the Baltimore club were played in September and
October, and they were for a special benefit. In late August, the press
announced that a series of home and away games had been arranged between
the Pastime club of Richmond and the Pastime club of Baltimore. The
proceeds from these games would be "applied to removing and properly
interring the remains of the Confederate soldiers who fell on the field near
Richmond, and which have not up to this time been attended to." Both
clubs agreed that the funds raised by their games would be used to "employ

a force of laborers…in gathering up and removing to Hollywood Cemetery (in Richmond) the remains of all Confederate soldiers who had not been decently buried and whose graves have not been properly marked."[14]

The decline of interest in baseball, noted in the late sixties, continued into the following decade.. Between 1870 and 1875, there were probably no more than a half-dozen mentions in the local press of baseball activity in Richmond, and the summer of 1870 marked the last mention of Richmond's Pastime club. It was noted that, in the summer of 1872, there was a game of baseball between the Dolly Vardens of Richmond and a visiting team from Arlington. Although this contest was described as a "fine game," it was witnessed by less than 300 persons. Another press item mentioned that in 1874 the Olympic club played a game against the Richmond College club at the Fair Grounds and were victorious over the collegians by a score of 22–21. This was the first mention of a baseball team fielded by Richmond College students.[15]

The year 1875 marks a slight revival of baseball activity in Richmond. During this year, there were eight adult clubs and five junior teams active in the city. The Richmond baseball club was revived after an interval of inactivity, and two of the newly organized local teams were the "Puddlers" and the "Nailers" of the Old Dominion Iron Works. Also this season the Virginia baseball club was organized and would sponsor a team for the next few seasons. The officers of this club were: a printer, John D. Lively, president; a cooper, J. H. Hill, treasurer; and a pharmacist, O. A. Hawkins, secretary. Players included J. H. Tyler, pitcher; William Gypervich, catcher; A. Tomlinson, second base; L. D. Green, first base; Stephen O'keefe, leftfield; J. D. Baker, rightfield; D. F. Lee, shortstop; J. W. Thomas, centerfield; and A. Biglow and P. O. Keefe. Games were played at the Fair Grounds and at other designated areas, and, at some places, seats were constructed for patrons. However, Henrico County authorities warned junior and sand-lot nines that no baseball games were to be played "in the neighborhood of public highways" or "on Sundays."[16]

During the 1875 baseball season, Richmond teams traveled to Fredericksburg, Washington, Lynchburg and Petersburg for games, and Richmond clubs entertained visiting teams from Washington and Arlington. On April 30 and May 2, 1875, the city of Richmond was host to two visiting professional teams—the Red Stockings of Boston and the Washingtonians of the nation's capital. These teams were touring the country, playing a series of games for the "championship of the United States." The two games in Richmond drew approximately 1500 spectators at each contest, including a "goodly number of ladies." Although the Boston team won both games, the press reported that the playing by both teams was excellent and surpassed "anything of the kind ever witnessed in Richmond." It was asserted that these two visiting teams represented "the very best exponents of the National game." The appearance of these teams in Richmond marked the highlight of the baseball season—a season which witnessed its last game on October 8. In this contest, the Virginians defeated another local club, the Pacific, 34 to 5. At this time, all games were worked by a single umpire. A man who was often engaged to umpire contests in Richmond was W.A. Graves.[17]

Although the baseball fever in Richmond did not reach the level it experienced in the years immediately following the war, it did not relapse to the level of the opening years of the seventies. In 1876, eight adults and an equal number of junior clubs were engaged in playing baseball in Richmond. Local clubs, in addition to contesting each other, hosted teams from Baltimore, Petersburg and Hanover County. In August, the Olympic club of Richmond journeyed into the Tidewater area for games with clubs in Norfolk, Portsmouth, and at Fort Monroe. It was noted in the press that the baseball season opened on April 12 and closed following the game for city championship on September 25. This game resulted in a 23 to 10 victory for the Atlantic club over the Virginia club. Two items associated with baseball in Richmond in 1876 were of special interest. One was the game played at the Fair Grounds on August 25 between the Virginia and Atlantic clubs for the benefit of the Lee Monument Fund. At this time, several groups were active in raising funds to erect a statue in the city to General Robert E. Lee. The other was the first mention by the local press of a Negro baseball club in the city. On September 5, it was reported that the "Lone Star Baseball Club (colored) of this city visited Petersburg and played a game with the White Stockings" team of that city. The Lone Star nine was victorious by a score of 31 to 7.[18]

During the 1877 baseball season, six adult teams were active in Richmond and the most prominent team was a newly organized nine named the "Brown Stockings." This club contested others in the city such as the Strikers, the Mutuals and the Athletics. They also hosted visiting teams from Washington, D.C., and Fort Monroe. All games were played at the Fair Grounds. The press stated that the Artillery School team from Fort Monroe "held the championship of the state." At the game on September 26, the Brown Stockings defeated the Artillery School nine 22 to 20, and the following day the score was Brown Stockings 12, Artillery School 6. By winning these two games, the Richmond Brown Stockings claimed the baseball championship of the state of Virginia.[19]

The 1878 baseball season witnessed an increase in baseball activity in Richmond. There were ten adult teams in the city, and two of them, the Richmond club and the Atlantic club, represented revived organizations that had seen little action the past season. During this season, the Richmond and the Atlantic clubs acquired their own park or grounds, Virginia Park which was located at the "head of Marshall Street." This park had an enclosed structure with a special separate seating section "for ladies." This park also featured a covered grandstand section for the seating of more than 400 people. The Richmond club roster included messers, Henry Boschen, Ellyson, Edward Glenn, Herbert Hankins, Wm. Hankins, Hinchman, Paul Latouche, Jonathan Lively, and James E. Powell. Others who became members of the team were Bolton, Graves, Galloway and Napier. The Atlantic club's team consisted of Davis, Sullivan, Merrill, Wesley, Lydon, Challenger, Murphy, Thomas and Dolan. Others who also played for this club included Messers, Sands, Divinie, Barfoot, Crostic and Henry. The Richmond and the Atlantic clubs played all of their games at their park, and other teams were also permitted to use their facilities on occasions when the Richmond or the Atlantic clubs had no games scheduled or were out of town.[20]

The 1878 baseball season witnessed the gradual move toward professionalism in baseball in Richmond. In late June, the press announced that the Richmond baseball club was "making arrangements with one of the best professional curve pitchers in the country and that the club expected him to be in Richmond soon." At the time Richmond was moving toward professionalism in baseball, it should be mentioned that there was at least one dissenting voice in the city. On one occasion, the editor of the *Religious Herald*, the weekly newspaper for the Baptist denomination in Virginia, deplored the emergence of professionalism in baseball. Baseball, he asserted, was a sport which provided "great pleasure" but should not be allowed to interfere "with business" or other important activities. It was a sport that "students, clerks and others" might enjoy. But professionalism in baseball was "going to excess." Professional teams, the editor wrote, "have abandoned the useful pursuits of life and are strolling through the country, to make their living by means very little less injurious than gambling." The "wandering from city to city," he declared, tended to promote "dissipation and vice" and served to "demoralize young men." The Baptist editor concluded his comments by urging the public to stay away from games played by these traveling professionals. The editor of this paper, the Reverend Alfred E. Dickinson, was like a voice crying in the wilderness. The movement toward professionalism in baseball was a dominant feature of the sport throughout the country in the closing decades of the nineteenth century and this trend was manifest in Richmond.[21]

During the 1878 season, Richmond teams entertained visiting clubs from Petersburg, Washington, New Haven, Portsmouth, Binghampton,

New York and New Bedford, Massachusetts. The Richmond club traveled to Petersburg and to Washington for games with teams in those cities. One game in this season was a special contest played between Richmond's two best teams, the Richmonds and the Atlantics. This game was played on September 17, and it was a benefit game to aid "yellow fever sufferers" of the area. This season also witnessed baseball games played in the city between Richmond College and Randolph-Macon College teams. These games were held at the Richmond College grounds, and it seems that the Richmond College students had adopted as a name for their team the Osceola baseball club of Richmond College. Local adult clubs, junior teams, neighborhood clubs and college nines were not the only baseball teams active in Richmond during the summer of 1878. On September 6, the *Daily Dispatch* announced that a visiting Negro club would be in town and that it would play a "picked nine" of the city. The press notice stated that "the Unique Baseball Club (colored) of Washington" would play a Richmond contingent at 3:00 p.m. The game was scheduled at the Richmond and Atlantic enclosed park at the head of Marshall Street, the same site where Richmond's premier teams played their games.[22]

As the decade of the 1870s drew to a close, two new baseball clubs were organized in Richmond: the Pinafore and the Arlington club of Church Hill. Like most of the local clubs, these two experienced short tenure and their players moved to other clubs. However, the Richmond baseball club was active and continued to host an occasional visiting team. It also appears that teams from Richmond College and Randolph-Macon College had established the practice of scheduling games annually with each other.[23]

Among the teams representing Richmond during the 1880 season, the two most prominent were the Richmond club and the Atlantic club. Each played local teams at their park located at the head of Marshall Street. They also hosted teams from Petersburg, Washington, and Baltimore. It was noted by the press that teams from the latter two cities were "professional clubs" and contained some "of the very best players." Clubs from these cities won games played in Richmond and doubtless helped to foster the idea that if Richmond was to be represented by competent teams, they would also have to become "professional" by recruiting and hiring players from elsewhere. During this season, the local press also noted activity by the Richmond College baseball club and by Negro teams in the city. On July 15, the *Daily Dispatch* announced that the Hannibal baseball club of Baltimore was in town to play the Swann club of Richmond. It was noted that both of these were "colored teams." The editor declared that one could "look for a good game" between these two clubs, and the public was encouraged to see the contest. The game was scheduled for 4:30 p.m. at the Richmond and Atlantic Baseball Park. The game resulted in an 11 to 1 victory for the Swann club of Richmond.

Just prior to the beginning of the baseball season in 1881, the local press declared "the National game of baseball, after a quiet interlude...is asserting its claims on young men and boys as a source of healthful exercise and amusement." The premier baseball club in the city this year was the Richmond one. This club had recently been reorganized and was described as the strongest nine ever organized in the city. There were also a number of local nines; for example, there were two new teams composed of the cigar makers of the city—they were the I.C. and the Model teams. Richmond was also represented by at least one black baseball team. The local team was the "Black Swans," and, on one occasion, they hosted a club from Petersburg. Visiting clubs which appeared in Richmond included teams from Lynchburg, Old Point Comfort, Baltimore, Washington, Providence, Rhode Island, and Detroit. The teams from Baltimore, Washington, Providence and Detroit were described as "professional" ones; that is, they were composed of players who traveled throughout the country playing baseball for a living. After each game, the visiting club was treated to a dinner by the host team. The 1881 season witnessed a continuation of the trend toward professionalism in local baseball. In early August, the press noted that the Richmond club had engaged the service of a "professional catcher," and, later in the season, it was announced that the Richmond club had secured the services of a player who was formerly a member of a professional club in Detroit.[25]

In 1882, the principal adult baseball team in Richmond was the nine of the Richmond baseball club. This year the club was advancing toward becoming a "professional club." It was noted early in the season that the team had acquired a player from Baltimore, and later it was announced that the Richmond club had "acquired the services of several new players," one being a "first class catcher." On one occasion, the press noted that Henry C. Boschen, a shoe manufacturer and the president of the Richmond club, was active in the city soliciting donations for the team to acquire new players—specifically a catcher, pitcher and a third baseman.[26] He hired Charley Ferguson of Charlottesville, a pitcher and Wm. Nash, one of his employees as a third baseman. As the Richmond club was moving toward being a professional team, several new local clubs were formed in the city. For example, the printers of Baughman Brothers formed a team and adopted the name "Printers" and the employees of West, Broach and Company organized a team and took the name of "Tinners." Other local or sand-lot teams included the ones formed by the employees of D.M. Lee and Company and R.H. Whitlock Company.[27]

As the Richmond club acquired better players, its record against visiting "professional" clubs improved. During the 1882 season, the Richmond club's record against visiting professional clubs was eleven victories and three defeats. The wins included three game series against clubs from Baltimore, Washington and Philadelphia. In September, the Richmond club made a week long excursion into Pennsylvania and New Jersey where they played clubs in Philadelphia, Pottsville, Reading and Camden, New Jersey. The Richmonders won five games on this tour, and, on another occasion, they defeated the Artillery School nine from Old Point Comfort, Virginia. During the last week of July, the Richmond club played a three game series with the Alexandria baseball club. This series was described by the press as being for the state championship. Each game "attracted a large crowd," and the local club swept the visitors from Alexandria three games to zero. It was also claimed by the press that the 1882 season witnessed a significant rise in the number of persons who attended baseball games in the city. The *Daily Dispatch* asserted that "an astonishing number of persons were attending local baseball games." The fans were seeing a better quality of baseball; during the 1882 season, the Richmond club played forty-one games; thirty-one were victories, eight were losses and two games resulted in ties.[28]

Shortly after the close of the baseball season in 1882, the game lost one of its principal boosters. On November 21, 1882, James P. Cowardin, editor and founder of the *Daily Dispatch*, died. Cowardin had devoted much attention to the emergence and growth of baseball in the city and had done more perhaps than any other individual to publicize the game, its clubs and personnel. His demise came practically on the eve of Richmond fielding its first professional team and joining official league play.[29] Richmond's two other newspapers, the *Daily Whig* and *The Enquirer*, both practically ignored baseball.

On February 20, 1883, there was an announcement in the press that the Richmond Baseball Club was "making preparations for a lively season." It had scheduled some of the "best teams in the country" to visit Richmond, including clubs from Cleveland, Washington, Boston, Baltimore and Philadelphia. It was also noted that the team hoped to better its 1882 record of 31–8 and 2 by adding a "few foreign players" to its roster. The Richmond club was one of approximately a dozen clubs active in the city in the spring and summer of 1883. A number of teams were local nines such as the Fulton club, the Brown Stockings, Our Boys, the employees of Randolph and English, the employees of Rose, W.E. Simmons and Brothers, Montague's Shop and the Old Dominion Tobacco Factory. Juvenile teams included the Clippers, the Athletics, the Star and theOlympics.[30]

In June 1883, baseball in Richmond began moving closer to professionalism. On June 20, the press reported that "a number of gentlemen in the city had organized the Virginia Baseball Association" and had elected the following officers: a stockbroker, William C. Seddon, president; a police captain, Charles H. Epps, vice-president; an insurance executive, Frank D. Steger, secretary; and an insurance executive, Thomas L. Alfriend, as treasurer. It stated that the association would apply to the state for a charter and that capitol stock would not be less than $5,000 or more than $20,000. A committee of three was appointed to secure "suitable grounds" for their team. Shortly after this association was formed, the Richmond baseball club changed its name to the Virginia baseball club, and it became the association's representative. The committee to secure grounds announced on July 5 that facilities, including grandstand, had been arranged for at the head of Franklin Street. The Virginia club was composed of the best players in the city, and some of them had formerly been associated with other teams. Among those on the Virginia roster were the following: Glenn, Powell, Latouche, Hankins, Nash, Schaff, Fore, Morgan, Mills, Ferguson, Smiley, Quinn and Kain. The Virginia club played the schedule arranged earlier by the Richmond club and was aggressive in scheduling on their own. During the season, the Virginians played "professional teams" from Baltimore, Washington, Philadelphia, Newark, Pittsburgh, New York, St. Louis, Trenton, Wilmington, Boston and Detroit. The Virginia club also made a ten day northern tour which extended from late August into September. They played teams in Washington, Wilmington, Philadelphia, Brooklyn, Kingston and Middletown, New York. On this tour, the Virginia team played eight games and were victorious in five of them. When the baseball season ended on October 20, the Virginia club's record was thirty-three victories and fourteen losses. Nine of the losses were to "professional" or "league teams."[31]

The reorganized team with a new name and ballpark elicited much interest in the city. During the summer, the press declared "baseball interest is now at fever heat." This "fever" manifest itself in the attendance at the Virginian's games—several reported 3,000 or more spectators to games that charged admission of 25 cents.[32] One practice/custom that the Virginia club inaugurated in the summer of 1883 was one which professional baseball would later adopt: that of admitting ladies free to certain games if they were accompanied by a gentleman. Although this was not called Ladies Day, it evolved into this practice. On July 8, 1883, the *Daily Dispatch* announced that at the game between the Virginia baseball club and the National club of Washington, D.C., "Ladies will be admitted free when accompanied by a gentleman."[33]

About a month prior to the close of the baseball season, the press announced the formation of an organization which would virtually bring the Richmond team into the ranks of professional or league teams. On September 14, the *Daily Dispatch* noted that, at a recent meeting in Pittsburgh, a new baseball association was formed. Delegates at the meeting were from Chicago, Philadelphia, Baltimore, Scranton, Washington, Pittsburgh and Richmond. Richmond's representative was William C. Seddon, president of the Virginia baseball club. At this meeting there was formed a new baseball association "under the name of the Union Association of Baseball Clubs." Officers were chosen for this organization, and a constitution and by-laws were adopted. After discussion as to which cities would be represented by teams in the new organization, a decision was postponed until a later date.[34]

CHAPTER II

Professional Baseball
Comes to Richmond, 1884

Richmond was not asked to become a member of the league formed under the auspices of the Union Association. This, however, was a momentary setback for baseball supporters/enthusiasts in Richmond. Seddon and others felt that a city of 63,600 people was ready and eager for professional baseball. At a meeting held at the Bingham House in Philadelphia on January 4, 1884, representatives from Richmond, Baltimore, Wilmington, Harrisburg, Allentown, Reading, Newark and Trenton became charter members of the Eastern League. W.C. Seddon of Richmond was elected league president, S. Reineman of the Trenton club was chosen vice-president, and Henry B. Diddlebock of Philadelphia was selected as treasurer.[1]

The Eastern League adopted the rules of the American Association, one of two major leagues, but with a few changes of its own. For example, in the Eastern League the pitcher was to deliver the ball from a point below the shoulder rather than being required to deliver the ball from a point below the hip. The Eastern League required the home team to remove disorderly persons from the grounds within fifteen minutes or the game would be called in favor of the opponent. The Eastern League also established that a game would be considered complete if the side that batted first had completed its fifth inning and the team that had batted four times was ahead in runs. League officials agreed to hire four regular umpires and two substitutes. The salary would be $100 a month for the regulars and $5 a game for substitutes. The annual membership fee for clubs in the Eastern League was $100.[2]

There was much anticipation among the citizens of Richmond for the home team's inaugural season in a professional league. The Virginians, as the team was called, opened the baseball season hosting the Providence club of the National League for a three-game set beginning April 3. The Virginians also conducted exhibition games with other National League clubs, including Cleveland and Philadelphia. The Eastern League schedule did not begin until May 14 when the Harrisburg team came to Richmond. The exhibition games drew large crowds despite cold weather. The first game with Providence was witnessed by approximately 1,000 fans. A similar attendance witnessed the game with Philadelphia.[3]

Prior to the opening of the 1884 season, the Virginia club experienced a controversy concerning a manager. In October 1883, the Virginia baseball club had agreed to a verbal contract with Ted Sullivan to manage the team. Sullivan had managed the St. Louis Browns of the American Association and had led the club to a second place finish in 1883. However, he decided to leave the Browns because of constant interference with the team by the owner, Chris Von der Ahe. Despite the verbal contract, by February 1884, Sullivan had decided not to honor the agreement with the Virginia club. He came to Richmond and requested release from his agreement with the Virginians. The directors of the club refused to honor his request, and he departed Richmond, promising to return no later than March 25. However, shortly after returning to St. Louis, he telegraphed the directors of the Virginians to see if they still insisted that he arrive for the opening of the season. When they responded that they did, he wrote that he would not come to Richmond, because he was staying in St. Louis. Henry Lucas, founder of the St. Louis Maroons, offered Sullivan the opportunity to earn $1,000 more than the Richmond club contract. With Sullivan otherwise employed, the Virginia Baseball Club's directors brought M.S. Allen from Roundout, New York, in to serve as manager and pitcher for the Virginians. In 1883, Allen had pitched for the Leader club of Kingston, New York.[4]

The player roster of the 1884 Virginians included the Dugan brothers—Edward, a pitcher and William, a catcher. The roster also included Doyle a pitcher; Bill Morgan, a catcher; Jim Powell, first base; Billy Nash, third base; Smiley, second base; and Dick Johnson, shortstop. The outfield included Eddie Glenn, David Cain and Stratton. Paul Latouche was an alternate or utility player. Several articles from the April and May *Daily Dispatch* indicate that the citizens of Richmond had a growing interest in baseball. One article noted that "the baseball flag may be seen flying over 609 Broad Street every day that a game is to be played by the Virginians." It was also noted that every game would be followed on W.J. Manning's bulletin board at his place of business on Broad Street. Andrew Krouse also informed the public that all of the Virginians' away games would be reported, inning by inning, on the score board at his restaurant on Broad Street near Brook Avenue. That same day's *Daily Dispatch* printed for those "not familiar with the game in detail" an explanation of the abbreviations listed in the box score. The clarification was written in response to a letter sent to the paper by T.E.P. of White Hall, and ran under the heading "For the Uninitiated."[5]

Although the fans in Richmond were developing a growing interest for baseball, many spectators at the Virginia baseball park were gaining a reputation for poor behavior. In an article describing the crowd's "howls, hoots and hisses" after a poorly called game by umpire William Hoover, the *Daily Dispatch* admonished both the fans and management: "A Richmond crowd thinks it their right, if not their duty, to ratify or disapprove the decisions of the umpire; but they ought nonetheless, always to remember the presence of the ladies. A repetition of the doing of yesterday will be very injurious and will drive people away. Better management should prevail."[6] The *Daily Dispatch* also reprinted an article from the Wilmington, Delaware *Sunday Critic*, which claimed that "the audiences in Richmond are beyond description for rowdyism…treating all the visiting clubs to the vilest abuse."[7]

The Eastern League experienced its first disruption before the season was two months old. On May 27, the Monumental club of Baltimore announced that it had disbanded. The Ironsides club of Lancaster, Pennsylvania, was chosen to complete the Monumental's schedule. In early July, the Harrisburg club disbanded. On July 16, 1884, officers of the Eastern League met in Philadelphia and granted full membership to the Lancaster and York, Pennsylvania clubs.[8] In August, the Reading club withdrew from the Eastern League, citing poor attendance as the reason for the team's demise. Two other teams also left the league and moved to other affiliations. The Wilmington, Delaware club moved to the Union Association and the Richmond Virginians withdrew to join the American Association. The Eastern League was able to finish the season as a five-team league; the following year, 1885, the league was reorganized as the New York League.[9]

Richmond's foray into the American Association began on August 5, 1884. In 1882, the American Association had started as a six-team circuit that rivaled the six-year-old National League for major league status. The league expanded to eight teams for the 1883 season. In the

1883–84 off-season, the American Association directors voted to expand to twelve teams for the 1884 season. Brooklyn, Indianapolis and Washington were immediately chosen; shortly thereafter, the league was completed when the Toledo club was accepted into membership.[10] The Washington ball club struggled through the early portion of the season. By the first of August, they had a record of 12 wins and 51 losses, and the club officials announced that the club was disbanding. The American Association then invited the Richmond Virginians to take the place of Washington. On August 5, 1884, the *Daily Dispatch* announced that the Virginians were moving from the Eastern League to the American Association and that the first game for the club as a member of a major league was scheduled that afternoon with the Athletics of Philadelphia. The paper also noted that Mr. Seddon had been dispatched "up North to secure the services of several good players."[11]

The other members of the Eastern League were quite upset with the Virginia baseball club for leaving the league. Henry Diddlebock, the Eastern League treasurer, threatened to reject the resignation of the Virginia club and instead would expel the club on the grounds of financial indebtedness to the league. The Eastern League contended that the Virginia club owed $24.50 for Seddon's expenses when he visited Philadelphia in July for a special meeting of Eastern League officials and another $20 in fines levied against players Powell and E. Dugan. Seddon's reply, as printed in the *Daily Dispatch*, claimed that the $24.50 was league expenses, as his travel was conducted in his capacity as Eastern League president. In the case of the player fines, Seddon explained that the $10 assessed against Powell for arguing with an umpire should be negated. Powell's role as captain of the club gave him the right to do so. Seddon agreed that Dugan was out of line in his argument and the amount of his fine would be deducted from his salary and forwarded to the league's treasurer.[12]

Seddon and the directors of the Virginia Baseball Club realized that the club needed more funds to complete in the American Association. The stockholders met on August 8, 1884, and announced that they would seek to increase the stock from $5,000 to $10,000. Two hundred shares of stock, with a value of $25 each, were made available for purchase. It was announced to those wishing to invest in the Virginia club to "call at the office of Thomas L. Alfriend, the treasurer, at number 1117 East Main Street." Club directors appealed to "lovers of the game" not to "allow the Virginia Baseball Club to go down now that it was on the eve of a most brilliant career."[13] The Virginians completed the season in the American Association and finished with a 12–30 record, ahead of the Indianapolis Hoosiers and the Pittsburgh Alleghenys.[14]

The Virginians late season entry into the American Association helped bring large crowds out to the Virginia baseball park, located at the west end of Franklin Street, where later a monument to Robert E. Lee would be erected.[15]. The first game versus the Athletics of Philadelphia drew nearly 2,000 spectators. A September game against the St. Louis Browns brought over 2,000 fans to the park.[16] The Richmond fans, who had been chastised by the press for rowdyism early in the season, continued to cause problems as the season came to a close. This time the issue was race. Late in the season, the Toledo Blue Stockings were scheduled to play a series in Richmond. On Toledo's roster was the African American catcher Moses Fleetwood "Fleet" Walker. Walker was well-educated and had played baseball for the Oberlin College nine. In 1883, he was with the Toledo club in the Northwestern League. When the Blue Stockings became a member of the American Association, Walker became the first African American to play in the major leagues. The controversy started when Charlie Morton, manager of the Toledo club, received a letter from "seventy-five determined men" in Richmond stating that Walker would be mobbed if he appeared on the field in Richmond. A rib injury kept Walker from playing and there was no mention of the threat or of Walker in the Richmond press when Toledo came to town for a series of games.[17] Despite the absence of African American players in the American Association, African Americans often attended games at Virginia Park. According to the *Daily Dispatch*, the "colored spectators always hurrah for the visiting team. They yell with delight when the home team gets a set-back."[18]

At the winter meeting of league officials in December 1884, the American Association decided that of the four new clubs, only the Brooklyn entry would be retained for 1885. Thus, Richmond's only experience with a baseball club in the Major Leagues ended after less than a half season. In order to remain at the professional level, the Virginian Baseball Club was forced to seek affiliation with another league. Later that same month, W.C. Seddon joined other "baseball men" for a meeting in Philadelphia to discuss the formation of a new Eastern League of Baseball Clubs. At this meeting, clubs representing Richmond, Norfolk, Washington, Lancaster, Trenton, Newark and Jersey City were selected for membership; a vacancy was reserved for a Baltimore club. When the Monumental Club of Baltimore was unable to join the new league, the Quaker Club of Philadelphia moved to Wilmington and was selected to fill the vacancy.[19] At this meeting, Henry H. Diddlebock was elected president, with a salary of $1,000, and George M. Ballard of Newark was selected as vice-president. The board of directors included Michael Scanlon of

Washington, J. Henry Klein of Trenton, John Copeland of Lancaster, and Mr. McCarrick of Norfolk. Each club deposited $250 in a reserve fund, which would be divided by the club still active in the league at the end of the season.[20]

There was a new excitement for baseball in Richmond as the 1885 season dawned. The press was predicting good things for the team and their manager, Joseph Simmons. Simmons had managed the Wilmington team in 1884. The Virginia club directors had much faith in Simmons' ability; they granted him "full authority to employ and discharge any of the men of his own will." That trust seemed justified—Simmons made no personnel changes throughout most of the season. The July 21, 1885, edition of the *Daily Dispatch* reported, "Manager Simmons started with eleven men and he has not signed nor released a player this season."[21]

The Richmond fans shared the excitement displayed by the press. The exhibition season began with the 1884 National League Champion Providence club before a crowd of 1,200. The Virginians shut out the Champions 4–0. The three-game series drew 3,000 spectators, including a "large number of ladies." When the Norfolk club came to Richmond to open league play, a crowd of 1,500 saw the Richmond club win 8–1.[22] Although fan support was strong for the Virginians, the rest of the Eastern League was not as successful. On June 20, the Wilmington club suspended operations and the franchise was transferred to Atlantic City. This move was short-lived, lasting only four days. The Atlantic City club disbanded, and the same day the Jersey City club announced its decision to disband.[23]

The failures of the Wilmington (Atlantic City) and Jersey City teams prompted the Eastern League Board of Trustees to meet in Philadelphia on June 29, 1885. The directors voted to expel the Wilmington (Atlantic City) for failure to pay financial obligations to the league. The Trenton club was granted permission to play out the remainder of the season in Jersey City. Clubs in Albany and Hartford were extended invitations to join the Eastern League, but both declined. League directors then voted to continue as a six-team circuit with Richmond, Norfolk, Washington, Trenton, Lancaster, and Newark; the scheduling committee rearranged the schedule for the remainder of the season.[24]

In addition to the financial trouble of some clubs, the 1885 season presented other woes for the Eastern League. The umpiring situation in the league was a source of constant trouble. Early in the season, the Richmond press supported the umpires and criticized the fans for their behavior. On one occasion, the press declared, "Whether the decisions of the umpires are correct or not, the umpires fill a position which makes their decisions final and obligatory." We hope that "our boys will never fall into the habit of criticizing every decision of the umpires" but will always strive to gain success by "good honest playing" and not by "kicking and bull-dozing" the umpires. Throughout the season, the *Dispatch* urged players to continue playing "good honest ball." Manager Simmons also, on occasion, criticized the fans for "hissing and hooting" unfavorable calls.[25] On one occasion, the league sought to allay criticism of the umpires by suspending for a week one of the most unpopular umpires, William Quinn, for "unjust decisions" he made in a game involving Richmond and Jersey City.[26] According to the *Dispatch*, "The Eastern League finds it hard to secure good umpires. Nobody seems to be able to please the audiences and clubs, and therefore good men declined to serve." Because the league was forced to consistently use replacements, the inability to secure professional umpires only exacerbated the problems on the field. The *Dispatch* often lamented the league's failure to have an official umpire sent to Richmond for the Virginians' games. The umpire problems grew so great that league officials met in Baltimore in late July and voted to depose President Diddlebock. George M. Ballard of Newark was chosen as his successor.[27]

Manager Simmons' boys opened the season with a flourish and by July 21, 1885, the Virginians had a 46–11 record and held a nine game lead over the second place Washington Nationals. While the prospect of winning the league championship was appealing to management, the Virginians' easy victories began to have a negative effect on the fans. The early season crowds had regularly been between 1,000 and 2,000; but by the end of July a game with the Trenton club brought only 500 fans to the ballpark. Public outcry reasoned, "Who wants to see a one-sided game? We know who will win without going to the grounds."[28]

The dwindling fan support forced Thomas Alfriend, president of the Virginia baseball club, to gather the club directors and friends of the club for an August 7 meeting. Alfriend announced that the club needed to raise $1,500 to carry it through the remainder of the season. At this meeting, the club gathered subscriptions totaling $200. A subscription committee was formed to "call on the businessmen of the city for contributions." A formal statement encouraging public support to save the team was printed in the *Dispatch*.[29]

Immediately after the club's announcement, the second place Washington Nationals came to Richmond for three games. The series drew large crowds and the Virginians took all three games, with 1,500 fans watching the home team win the final game 5–4. The enthusiasm seems to have vanished when the Nationals left town. Norfolk next visited

Virginia Park for four games. The home team won the first three, but there were only 500 fans in attendance for one of these games.[30] With fan support declining and the campaign for funds not producing the hoped-for results, club officials decided to sell some of their best players. On August 22 officials announced that Billy Nash and Dick Johnson, two of the team's best players, were sold to the Boston Beaneaters of the National league for $1,250. Nash, a Richmond native, went on to enjoy ten years in Boston. He played with the Beaneaters from 1885–89. In 1890, he signed with the upstart Player's National League team in Boston but returned to the Beaneaters in 1891. He remained with the club through the 1895 season and was traded to Philadelphia to finish out his major league career. His final year in baseball was in the minor leagues in 1899.[31] The sale of these two players proved disastrous for the Virginians. They lost the next five games and their grasp on the Eastern League pennant was in jeopardy. There was some speculation in the press that Richmond might not have a ball club the next season.[32]

The Richmond Virginians fell apart in September 1885. The players were a month late in receiving their salary and threatened to disband the club. Instead of quitting, they voted to withdraw from the Virginia baseball club management and attempted to complete the season on their own. The club tended the treasury to the players; the sum amounted to approximately $7.50 per man. While pride propelled the players to want to finish the season, the fans did not support their efforts. About 250–300 fans came out for the Virginians' first game without management. Only 200 came the following day. After that game two of the Virginians' players accepted offers to join the Newark club and left town on the evening train. The team could not finish the season, and the pennant was taken by the Washington Nationals. Richmond's entry into the ranks of professional baseball came to an inglorious end. After the collapse of the Virginians, the city of Richmond would have an eight-year drought without a professional baseball team.[33]

CHAPTER III

Richmond's Second Venture into Professional Baseball

With the Virginia baseball club no longer in existence, the spring of 1886 did not hold the same excitement for the Richmond fans that 1884 and 1885 had held. The Richmond fans did not have a team of their own for the coming 1886 season. April of that year provided the "lovers of the game" in Richmond with the only opportunity to witness professional ball games in the city. The Boston club of the National League had leased the Virginia ballpark for the last two weeks of April for a series of exhibition games and workouts before the National League season began. The Boston club promised a game every afternoon, announcing two games with the Rochester club, one with Newark, and split squad matches on days when other teams were not scheduled. The Boston team featured three players who were prominent players on the Virginia baseball club: Billy Nash, Dick Johnston and Edward "Pop" Tate. The first game played by Boston and Rochester was held on April 19, 1886, and brought about 600 spectators to Virginia Park.[1]

The practice of National League teams venturing south for preseason exhibition games began in 1870 with both the Chicago White Sox and Cincinnati Red Stockings. Each club made a trip to New Orleans that spring. Throughout the 1870s, other professional clubs began to experiment with exhibition games with minor league teams in the South. It soon became custom that the clubs would head south for a short stay in training camp followed by an extended exhibition season visiting different minor league teams throughout the region. The minor league

25

teams welcomed the major league clubs and enjoyed the profitability created by the large crowds wanting to see baseball's best players. In Richmond, some of the largest crowds and most significant revenue days were earned when the Virginians hosted traveling major league teams at Virginia Park. By the end of the 1890s, southern spring training was practiced by all major league teams.[2]

On March 9, 1890, the *Richmond Dispatch* printed an article entitled "BaseBall Players: How the Knights of the Diamond Pass the Winter." The article highlighted a life of luxury filled with "expensive meals, the finest cigars, exotic beverages" and little physical conditioning. In the spring, "it is no easy task for the trainer of a base-ball team to get his men into proper form and condition after five or six months of luxury and idleness." The poor conditioning of the players added to the club owners' interest in southern spring training. The warmer temperatures were viewed as a way to prevent "muscular colds and rheumatism," while working off the winter's inactivity.[3]

Without a professional team of its own, Richmonders, from 1886 to 1894, had to satisfy their baseball interest with the occasional exhibition game, local amateur and semi-pro teams, and college baseball. Interest in baseball on college campuses began to develop in the Northeast in the late 1850s. The first intercollegiate game was played July 1, 1859, between Amherst College and Williams College. While the Civil War slowed some of the growth of the college game, southern colleges were quick to catch up with their northern counterparts. At the University of Virginia, where townball had been played before the war, several baseball clubs were formed by 1866. By the end of the 1870s, clubs were also formed at Washington and Lee, Randolph-Macon College, and Richmond College. These early teams were student organized and controlled, supplying their own equipment and raising funds to cover expenses. They played intercollegiate games as well as games with various amateur and professional teams.[4]

During Richmond's years without a professional team, the *Richmond Dispatch* helped keep its readers interested in baseball by regularly printing scores and game summaries of local college teams, including the University of Virginia, Randolph-Macon College, Wake Forest, Georgetown College and Richmond College. The April 18, 1886, *Richmond Dispatch* article that announced the Boston club's lease of Virginia Park also included a game summary of the Richmond College and Randolph-Macon College match that entertained about 300 spectators on the Richmond College grounds. The Richmond College boys easily won 13–3, scoring at least one run in every inning.[5]

Mayo Island Park/Tate Field (courtesy of Dementi Studio in Richmond, Virginia).

The prospect for professional baseball in Richmond brightened in March 1890. On March 1, City Circuit Court Judge Beverly R. Wellford recognized the charter for the Richmond Athletic Association. "The purposes of the company are to organize, manage, control and operate a baseball club or clubs, to encourage athletics sports and exercise, and to do other things as may be proper in the conduct of its business." The club's officers were B.C. Metzger, president and manager; V. Donati, vice-president; C.B. Neal, secretary-treasurer; and Messrs. Levin Jones and P.M. Courtney, directors. The capital stock was to "not be less than $2,500 nor more than $25,000 divided into shares of $25 each. Real estate may be held, not exceeding $10,000 in value." The association had obtained a three-year lease on Mayo Island for the development of a ballpark.[6]

The site of Mayo Island was chosen for its geographic location. Being in the middle of the James River and separating the cities of Manchester, on the southern bank, and Richmond, on the northern bank, an island ballpark provided access for the residents of both Manchester and Richmond, being "easily reached from the post office of either city within ten minutes."[7] While many thought that the island would prove too small for a ballpark, the *Richmond Dispatch* reported that the grounds were to "have an average width of 380 feet." The distance from the gate to center field was reportedly 515 feet. In order to prevent balls from being hit into the James River, "the grounds were enclosed with a high, almost air-tight fence, and to the left of home plate, where is the narrowest part of the field, there is stretched above the fence a wire gauze about seven feet high."[8]

Mayo Island Park featured a grandstand that was 100 feet long and 28 feet wide. The grandstand contained "800 chairs taken from the Exposition building" with a network of gauze wire designed to protect the occupants from batted or thrown balls. Between the grandstand and the outdoor seating areas, the park had a seating capacity of 3,000. Fans attending games would enter through a "passimetre which would register and keep an accurate record of the entire number of visitors each day." A tiered section of the grandstand was designed especially for the "colored fans."[9]

In the construction of Mayo Island Park, the Richmond Athletic Association renovated an old house "fronting the bridge avenue" to provide dressing rooms for the players and lockers for the uniforms and equipment. The building also afforded "the provision of other necessaries." Constructed next to this building was the team's ticket office. Here fans could purchase general admission or grandstand tickets. Tickets were 25 cents for the general admission and an extra charge for grandstand seating.[10]

The team assembled by the Richmond Athletic Association consisted mostly of local talent. Charles W. Householder, a player with the old Virginia baseball club, was chosen as the captain and first baseman. Other members of the infield included Alexander D. Hill of Patterson, New Jersey, at second base; Richmonder Charles "Barley" Kain at shortstop; and A.W. Stanhope of the Metropolitan Club of New York City at third. The outfield had two Richmonders in Paul Latouche, also a Virginia baseball club player, in left and "Reddy" Foster in center. Right field was played by W.C. Kelley of Lafayette, Indiana. The team featured two experienced batteries in Hurte and McCaffrey from Philadelphia and Quarles and Widgins from the 1889 Roanoke club. The team was outfitted in dark blue uniforms with white stockings, belts, and caps. "Richmond" was spelled in white letters across the chest. The team was known in the *Dispatch* as the "Richmonds."[11]

The first opponent for the Richmonds was William Barnie's Baltimore Orioles, a member of the American Association. The Orioles arrived in Richmond on March 21, 1890, and planned for an entire week of spring training with the Richmonds. The series was much anticipated by Richmond fans, as the Orioles featured the beloved Pop Tate. Tate had started his career with Boschen's Richmond club, then played for the Virginia baseball club before being sold with Nash and Johnston to the Boston Bean-Eaters at the end of the 1885 season. The Richmonds and Orioles first game was canceled due to wet weather. A prolonged rain kept the Mayo Island field from being ready for play. As of March 22, 1890, the field had been "top-dressed with red clay" but had not been rolled or sodded. The Orioles did play a five-inning practice game with the Richmond College ball club at the open field on Franklin Street that was once the site of the Virginia Baseball Park.[12]

The Richmonds and Orioles finally met on the field at Mayo Island Park on March 24, 1890. The first game drew nearly 1,000 patrons to the new ballpark. The crowd included "quite a number of ladies" and a "large colored contingent." Despite not having sod, the field was described as firm. The "heavy city street roller, with six mules hitched to it" worked the field the entire day, and the area behind the plate was "well covered with sawdust." Although Richmond lost the game 8–6, the fans were excited that professional baseball was back in Richmond. At the end of the week, Barnie was impressed enough with the Richmond ball club that he took their application for admission to the American Association with him. He promised to deliver it himself. However, he expressed doubt that the Richmonds would gain acceptance.[13]

Despite not having a formal league affiliation, the Richmond club planned a full exhibition schedule for April. Most of the games were scheduled for Island Park, but the team also scheduled a two-week road trip for the last half of the month. The wet weather that hampered the readiness of the field for the first game caused the cancellation of many of the home exhibitions. The team's miseries continued while on the road trip. The weather cooperated but their batting and fielding did not. Although the club lost most of the games, Manager Metzger felt that the competition with "well-drilled and strong clubs" would help his team. While the competition may have improved the players' skills, the club's poor play dampened the excitement that was generated by the prospect of having professional baseball back in Richmond. On May 1, 1890, fewer than 250 fans attended the Richmonds' first home game after a two-week

Charles "Squire" Donati (courtesy of Virginia Historical Society).

northern trip. Although the Richmonds defeated the Marylands of Baltimore 15–4, an even smaller crowd came out to the park the next day to watch the home team win 17–1. The Saturday game was canceled due to the low attendance on Thursday and Friday.[14]

The Richmonds played only a few more ball games before management decided to disband the team. The Richmond Athletic Association's failure to secure a league for its baseball team seemed to verify the *Washington Capitol's* opinion posed in 1883 that in order for a professional team to be profitable, it must be in a league.[15]

After the Richmond Athletic Association club was disbanded, several players formed the Player's club. Charles "Squire" Donati, vice-president for the disbanded Richmonds and an Eighteenth Street restaurateur, served as the new club's manager. The *Dispatch* described Donati as being "very anxious to see a ball club kept here." The club continued to play local teams and hosted exhibition games with traveling professional teams. However, Donati's "Giants," as the club was known, struggled to maintain its existence. "They barely earned enough money to buy baseballs." Despite the struggles, Donati attempted to keep the team in the field for two more seasons. Finally, in 1892, Donati's endeavor ended, as the club did not last through March.[16]

Richmonders once again had baseball games to attend in 1893. Semi-professional teams in Richmond, Petersburg, Forest Hill and the squad from Richmond College regularly met for games. While there was not an organized professional league in 1893, the interest in these games helped encourage the creation of the Virginia State League in 1894. The Virginia League was a six-team league comprised of teams representing the cities of Richmond, Norfolk, Petersburg, Lynchburg, Staunton, and Roanoke.[17]

There were actually two separate plans proposing the formation of a professional baseball league in Virginia for the 1894 season. Mr. T.K. Sullivan of Washington advocated the formation of a league that would incorporate teams from across the state. The other proposal came from W.B. Bradley of South Richmond and Tim West of Richmond. These two men were involved in the management of the Manchester (Forest Hill) and Richmond teams that competed in 1893. Their proposal was for a quad-city league that featured their two clubs plus teams from Norfolk and Petersburg.[18]

Mr. Sullivan scheduled a meeting with the purpose of organizing a state league on the afternoon of March 6, 1894. Bradley and West decided to hold a similar meeting that morning. Mr. Perkins of Petersburg and Mr. C. Sommers of Norfolk joined them at the Ryall Hotel in Richmond. Mr. Apperton and Mr. Morris, representing Staunton and Roanoke, were also in town but did not join the morning meeting. At the early meeting, the original foursome decided to expand their league and invited Apperton and Morris to an evening meeting. The second meeting convened at 8:00 and ended with the formation of two committees, one to establish rules, regulations, and bylaws; the other to study transportation and schedules. Sullivan's meeting was canceled. The *Dispatch* announced that Sullivan left Richmond that night and accepted the position of manager for the Atlanta team in the Southern League. The Southern failed to complete the season, ending play during the first week of July 1894.[19]

Each of the representatives at the March 6, 1894, meeting agreed to enter a team in the proposed Virginia State League Association. The league's board of directors featured a representative of each club, and C. Sommers of Norfolk was selected as president. The VSL voted to accept the National League rules of play for the 1894 season and made successful application to the National League for recognition and protection under the National Agreement.[20] The Executive Committee selected an umpire from each city to conduct games and represent the league. The umpires' salaries for the first year were $50 per month. By 1896, the league would have a chief umpire employed at $150 per month and two assistant umpires earning $100. The league decided to restrict player salaries to $5,000 per club. Each team was to hire an official score-keeper who was responsible for reporting on all games played in its home city. Gate receipts were to be shared by the home and visiting club, with forty percent going to the visitors and a guarantee of $33.33. With his gift of three dozen balls and the promise of $50 to the pennant winner, Albert Spalding's baseball was selected by the Virginia State League as the official league ball. The schedule committee was forced to draft a second schedule for the 1894 season. Before the 1894 season started, the Richmond and Manchester teams were merged, and Lynchburg was admitted as a third team from the western part of the state.[21]

W.B. Bradley, owner of the Richmond club, and Timothy West, its manager, leased the 360 by 380-foot lot on the corner of Vine and Main Streets for the construction of West End Park. The ballpark featured a 600-seat grandstand and "bleachers enough to seat every fan in the city." A roof, designed to cover the bleachers, was added in early June 1894. The grounds were built to front Main Street with the grandstand, directly behind the diamond, built at the Vine Street corner. The site was selected with transportation for spectators in mind. The lot was located on a stop of the Main Street car line. It was speculated that the Clay Street line would also service the park on game days. The combined car lines promised service that would arrive and depart every two and one-half minutes. West End Park would serve as the home of Richmond's professional baseball team for three seasons, 1894–96.[22]

The Virginia State League team that represented Richmond during those years carried a variety of nicknames onto the field. In the late nineteenth century it was common for teams not to have an official nickname. Rather, the team was known by its full name (much like the original Virginia baseball club of 1883) or the team went by the name of the ball club's home city (such as Henry Boschen's "Richmonds" also of 1883). Newspaper reporters took great liberties in creating nicknames for ball clubs, often utilizing several names for the same team.[23]

The baseball writer for the *Richmond Dispatch* was an obvious proponent of this style, as a variety of names were utilized to describe the 1894 Richmond entry in the Virginia State League. At the beginning of the season, the team was simply known as the "Richmonds." But by the end of the first week of the season, the *Dispatch* was referring to the team as "Tim West's Colts," using colts to symbolize a group of strong, young men. The "Colts" moniker was soon dropped in favor of "bloody-shirts" or "Richmond Reds," both references to the team's red jerseys. The *Dispatch* writer also utilized the name "Legislators," drawing upon the city's status as the seat of state government. On June 24, 1894, the *Dispatch* began an article by referring to the team as the "Richmond Reds" in the first sentence and then used the name "Legislators" in the second. Later in the season, the team was given an official nickname, "Crows," when Bradley replaced the red shirts with a custom-made black uniform. This uniform featured black pants and shirts with "Richmond" across the chest in large white letters. When management outfitted the team in blue uniforms for the 1895 season, the nickname was changed to "Bluebirds." This name would prevail into the 1896 season.[24]

As evidenced by the large crowds that routinely flocked to West End Park in 1894, Richmonders heartily welcomed the Virginia State League. Attendance for games in 1894 varied from 600 to 6,000 persons, with the average attendance being nearly 1,500 patrons. The *Dispatch* writer noted that, in the latter half of the season, the "accommodations at West End Park frequently proved inadequate for the crowds that thronged it." Regulars who attended included Virginia governor Charles T. O'Ferrall, his sons, and members of the governor's staff.[25]

Richmond fans did more than attend home games in large numbers. The *Dispatch* dubbed one group of regular spectators as the "Grand Amalgamated Order of Rooters." The recognized leader of this group was "General" John C. Small. This group attended home games in large numbers, jeering the opposition and supporting the home team. The group also made frequent arrangements with the Chesapeake and Ohio Railroad to attend games in Norfolk and Petersburg. The group's support for the local boys extended beyond their hurrahs at the ball games. In the middle of the season, they established a purse of more than $100 to be shared among the players if Richmond should win the Virginia League championship.[26]

The Richmond club's fan support was also able to ease some of the racial tension that existed in the stands at the Virginia baseball club's games in the earliest period of professional ball in the city. When the Virginians played, it was routinely noted in the newspaper accounts of the game that the African American fans supported the visiting teams. At West End Park their support was decidedly for the home team. The *Dispatch* even gave special recognition to "Buck" Spotswood on July 19, 1894. At the July 18 ball game, John Small was not in his usual place leading the "Order of Rooters," and the crowd was not in its typical fervor. Spotswood was able to arouse the African American fans to lend the missing support. The *Dispatch* noted, "In everything but color 'Buck' is eligible for membership in the amalgamated association."[27]

By placing a strong team in the field, the Richmond management gave fans every reason to lend their support. Formed as a combination of the 1893 Forest Hill and Richmond semi-pro teams, the Richmond Crows featured many players with local ties. The team also featured the return of Edward "Pop" Tate. Tate's major league career had ended with the Baltimore Orioles, but the Crows provided him the opportunity to continue playing baseball. Joining Tate on the crows roster were Charles "Barley" Kain; Tim West, manager and first baseman; "Baby-face" Phillips, who had made a name for himself while playing with the Richmond College ball club; "Reddy" Foster; and Jake Wells. These men formed the nucleus of a ball club that started the season strongly and was in contention for the pennant until the last week of the season. The final tally placed Petersburg with Spaulding's flag with a 72–44 record and a .6207 winning percentage; Norfolk in second with a 66–45 record and .5946; and Richmond in a close third with a 67–48 record and .5826.[28]

League officials were pleased with the success of the Virginia State League. At the end of the season, three of the six teams—Petersburg, Norfolk, and Richmond—reported earning a profit. Although all three declined to publicly divulge the amount of the earnings, the figures were estimated to be several thousand dollars. Attendance at league games varied by locality with Richmond's game low of 600 being equal or higher than the estimated average at four of the other club's home parks. Exact attendance figures were not recorded, but Richmond was guessed to have the highest average attendance at nearly 1,500 fans. Norfolk's had the second highest average with nearly 1,300 to 1,400 persons attending each ball game. Petersburg averaged between 600 and 700, Lynchburg, approximately 400, and Roanoke, 350. Staunton, with just under 300 per game, was forced to fold late in the season and the state league moved the franchise to Newport News–Hampton.[29]

At the year end meeting, the Virginia State League owners decided to submit to the National League its intention to sponsor a state league for the 1895 season. The league would once again be a six-team circuit composed of the same clubs that had concluded the season with Newport News–Hampton being a minor exception; the franchise was transferred to Portsmouth. One significant change for the 1895 season involved financial prospects of the ball clubs. Mr. Smith, manager of the Roanoke club, proposed a change in the distribution of gate receipts, especially for games played in Richmond, Petersburg, and Norfolk. His plan, which was adopted, was an attempt to help the clubs from the smaller cities have the same fiscal opportunities as the clubs from the large cities by sharing the revenue a bit more equally.[30]

Public interest in the 1895 season of the Virginia State League was noticeably strong. At the beginning of the 1894 season, the state league was viewed as a mere expansion of the semi-pro ball that had been played in Virginia for the previous several seasons. For the most part, the players were local boys or unknown professionals who could not catch on with an established league. During the season, the state league was able to earn the respect of fans and baseball men as a competitive professional league. With the strong enthusiasm and a new plan to share gate receipts equitably, the state league owners hoped to capitalize on popular support. At this time baseball, like many other business ventures, was illegal on Sundays, leaving Saturday as the only weekend game. Without games on Sundays, the summer holidays and Saturdays usually produced the largest attendance. The schedule makers planned for Richmond, the largest city and the team with the greatest 1894 attendance, to play at home on all three holidays and seventeen of the twenty-two Saturdays during the season.[31]

Richmond fans did not disappoint the state league directors. The first game of the 1895 season brought 5,000 spectators to the West End Park to see the Bluebirds defeat Petersburg. The Richmond club continued that success by winning the first five ballgames, and did not suffer a defeat until the sixth game on Saturday, April 21, 1895, when the crowd was once again over 5,000. The Bluebirds continued to dominate the Virginia League throughout the season, not only winning the pennant, but also maintaining possession of first place for all but one day of the season. Richmond ended the season with 78 victories and only 45 losses for a winning percentage of .634. Lynchburg was the closest rival finishing 69–51 (.575). No other team in the state league finished with a winning record.[32]

It was no surprise that the Bluebirds started the season as strong as they did. The Richmond management had made a conscious effort to strengthen the team for the 1895 season. Tim West, who had served as both co-owner and field manager in 1894, selected Jake Wells to be the team's manager for 1895. Wells brought back many of the same players, including "Reddy" Foster and "Barley" Kain. But perhaps Wells' most important addition to the Bluebirds was pitcher Jesse Tannehill from Cincinnati. Tannehill became the star pitcher for the club in 1895 and 1896. He won twenty ball games in 1895 while losing only seven. In the 1896 season, Tannehill posted a 23–17 record in Richmond. Tannehill later enjoyed a thirteen-year career in the major leagues, playing for the Cincinnati Reds, Pittsburgh, Washington, and Boston.[33]

After the close of the season, Richmond and Lynchburg, the first and second place teams of the Virginia State League, began a series of seven games to compete for the Nowlan Cup. The cup series was originally called the Green Cup, as Mr. Green, a jeweler in Roanoke, proposed the idea for the contest. He created a beautiful silver cup that he would present to the winner. However, when Richmond and Lynchburg declined to play any of the games in Green's hometown of Roanoke, he rescinded his offer. The Nowlan Company, jewelers in Lynchburg, offered a new cup. The victor would have possession of the Nowlan Cup until the end of the next season when the first and second place teams would compete for the nineteen-inch-tall silver and gold trophy. The first three games were played in Lynchburg. After the series shifted to Richmond the Bluebirds won the cup with a 5–3 victory in the sixth game, played before more than 5,000 fans.[34]

The Bluebirds' season included one more series of games. Nashville, the Southern League pennant winner, challenged Richmond to a five-game series for the "championship of the South." All of the games were played before large crowds in Richmond's home ballpark. Although the Bluebirds won the first game 16–3, Nashville rebounded for a 7–0 shutout of Richmond in game two and captured game three by a score of 14–9. Richmond won game four 6–4 to set up an exciting fifth game. Nashville captured the crown with a 13–4 drubbing of the Bluebirds.[35]

The success of the Virginia League in 1895 prompted baseball men in Danville and Hampton to file for franchises for 1896. League operators, however, denied these bids and decided to keep the league a six-team circuit. John C. Small, who gained fame as Richmond's chief rooter, was selected by the owners to serve as league secretary and treasurer. J.L. McLaughlin of Lynchburg was chosen as league president. The schedule committee awarded Richmond with home dates for all three holidays and every Saturday of the season. It was decided to continue the Nowlan Cup series. The 1896 season was to be divided into halves, and the winner of each split season would play for the cup. League officials were expecting a banner year in 1896.[36]

In the first half of the 1896 season, Richmond was not able to duplicate its 1895 heroics. The Bluebirds won their first game against Roanoke but lost the second game. On July 1, the club finished the first half of the season with a 35–29 (.547) record and earned second place behind Lynchburg 44–29 (.603). The second half season returned Richmond to its winning ways, with the team taking the standings lead on August 11. Although the 1896 season was a financial success for the Richmond club, the rest of the league was not as fortunate.[37]

At the close of the first half, the Petersburg club was about to expire under the burden of debt. Money from spring exhibition games was still owed to the Baltimore and New York National League clubs. Several businessmen raised money to continue a club in Petersburg. These men understood that they would not incur the debts created by the previous club's management. In August, National League president Nick Young ruled that the Petersburg club owed the money to the National League franchises. Virginia League directors replaced the Petersburg club with a team in Hampton.[38]

On August 20, the Roanoke team announced that it was disbanding. Management cited financial concerns and poor attendance as its reasons. The remaining league owners met and decided to continue the Virginia League schedule with only five teams. The following day, the Lynchburg baseball club decided to end its club's season despite being second in the standings and after winning the first half crown. This action was precipitated by the fact that the club was scheduled for nine games against the defunct Roanoke team. Management realized that nine idle days in the season would be financially disastrous. The club paid the players' salaries in full and sent them home. The remaining clubs reorganized as a four-team circuit for the remaining twenty-two games of the season. Richmond was declared the champion of the first half of the season, and the victor of the remaining twenty-two games would be crowned the second half champ. The two champions would then play for the pennant and the Nowlan Cup.[39]

The quest for the cup did not contain the same excitement as in the previous year. With only a week to play in the season, Richmond and Norfolk accepted bids to join the Atlantic League for the 1897 season. This league was composed of teams in Hartford, Connecticut; Newark and Patterson, New Jersey; and Reading, Lancaster, and Philadelphia, Pennsylvania. With teams in larger cities, this league was able to draw larger crowds. In turn, teams could earn stronger profits and would be able to field much stronger teams than the Virginia League. Naturally, the other two Virginia League teams found little interest in the last few games of a soon to be defunct league. Norfolk won the second-half championship. However, the Bluebirds were able to halt Norfolk's late season charge for the title and defeated the Crabbers in five games to capture the Virginia State League pennant and the Nowlan Cup.[40]

The Atlantic League had been formed in the fall of 1895. In its origin, the AL was a six-club circuit, with teams in Hartford and New Haven, Connecticut; Patterson and Newark, New Jersey; Wilmington, Delaware; and New York City. The New York club, called the Metropolitans, was owned by Andy Freedman, who was also owner of the National League's New York Giants. Halfway through the first season, Lancaster replaced New Haven. League owners expelled the New York Mets because of Freedman's habit of transferring players between his two clubs. Philadelphia was brought in to replace the Mets. After the first season, the Atlantic League decided to expand to eight ball clubs for 1897 and extended the invitation for Richmond and Norfolk to join. At the same meeting, Ed Barrow, the owner of the Patterson franchise and future general manager and president of the great New York Yankee ball clubs of the 1920s, 1930s, and early 1940s was selected as president of the league.[41]

Throughout professional baseball, there was optimism for a strong 1897 season. The Sunday, March 21, 1897, *Richmond Dispatch* printed an article titled "Base-Ball Outlook for 1897." The article was written by O.P. Caylor, a long-time writer for the different newspapers in Cincinnati, an instrumental founder of the American Association in 1882, and a National League ball club owner. Caylor's article expressed high expectations for the season. In 1896, there were seventy-two cities represented by teams that subscribed to the National Agreement and more were scheduled to operate in 1897. Caylor noted that even in periods of a financial downturn, much like the financial panic that began in 1893 and continued into 1896, baseball not only prospers, it usually records banner seasons. He reasoned that when compared to other forms of entertainment, baseball is significantly less expensive. During a depression, theaters and racetracks, with admission fees ranging from $2 to $5 become a costly outing, while baseball at 25 cents or 50 cents is very affordable. With that in mind, the major leagues were looking for a strong season. Caylor noted that the minors should do so as well since "the rule has been that success or disappointment for the major body affects the minor leagues and associations in a similar manner."[42]

The fans in Richmond shared the optimism that Caylor expressed for the game. Jake Wells was returning for his third year as manager of W.B. Bradley's Bluebirds. Wells re-signed some of the Bluebirds' stars of 1896, with Kain and Foster returning. Joining them would be Bob Pender, Paddy Boyle, Cooper Hargrove, and Norman "Kid" Elberfield, a youngster at twenty-one years of age from Cincinnati. However, Wells' greatest challenge for 1897 was to improve the team's pitching. Jesse Tannehill had signed a National League contract with Pittsburgh. To replace Tannehill, Wells signed Jack Chesbro, who had formerly pitched for Roanoke in 1896, and Sam Leever, who was being scouted by several National League teams but preferred to have more time in the minor leagues. After leaving Richmond both of these men enjoyed successful major league careers. In 1899, the Richmond club sold Chesbro to the Pittsburgh Pirates for $1,200. He had a twelve-year major league career with the Pirates, Yankees, and Red Sox. He was one of the first spitball pitchers. He compiled a record of 198 wins and was elected to the Baseball Hall of Fame in 1948. Sam Leever had an eleven-year major league career with the Pittsburgh Pirates. In 1903, he won twenty-five games—six of which were consecutive shutouts. He compiled a career record of 193 wins and a winning percentage of .656.[43]

With a strong team in place and a new league, Bradley acquired a new ballpark. The grounds, named Broad Street Park, were built on land leased from the Richmond, Fredericksburg and Potomac Railroad near where Allen Avenue dead-ends with Broad Street. The northern fence overlooked the R.F. & P. Rail Yard. The park was built with a seating capacity that exceeded 6,000. The field at Broad Street Park was enormous with "over the fence homers being few and far between." The left field line was the shortest, measuring 295 feet. Straightaway center measured 560 feet. The line down right was 340 feet, and the right field wall actually incorporated the side wall of a house that was adjacent to the grounds. The location provided occupants of the building with a view of the game in both the upstairs and downstairs windows. With eighty feet between home plate and the grandstand, the area in foul ground behind the plate was increased over the measurements at West End Park. The field itself was slightly elevated to assist in drainage after a rain.[44]

Bradley's Richmond baseball club began the season wearing the Bluebird uniforms from 1896. After the first ten games, Bradley outfitted his team with new gray uniforms and the team's name was changed to the Johnny Rebs. On September 3, 1897, Bradley, the sole stockholder in the Richmond Baseball and Athletic Association, sold the ball club, the rights to the Atlantic League franchise, and the lease on the Broad Street Park to Charlie Donati and Clarence Boykin. Donati, known to Richmond baseball fans for his semi-pro teams in the early part of the decade, eliminated the name Johnny Rebs and the club played the remaining two weeks of the schedule under the name Giants. Donati created an environment of entertainment at the ballpark. For the first game under new management, the club hired the Stonewall Band of Staunton to perform a concert during the time between the games of the Labor Day doubleheader. He also popularized the practice of players engaging in throwing and running contests before games.[45]

On the field, the Richmond ball club earned the respect of the other Atlantic League franchises and enjoyed the support of the Richmond crowds. The Bluebirds opened the season against Lancaster with a 9–7

victory before nearly 4,000 spectators at Broad Street Park. After their first game playing under the name Johnny Rebs, the Richmond club had posted a 7–4 record and held control over second place in the league standings. By July 6, the Johnny Rebs were wallowing in sixth place with a .475 winning percentage, yet continued to attract large crowds at Broad Street Park. The day before, the club played two games in honor of the Fourth of July holiday. Despite losing both games, 5,580 people came out for the morning game, and 6,747 attended the afternoon match. After Donati took over the team, the club began a small climb in the standings. On a Labor Day doubleheader, the Giants took both games from the Norfolk Brooms and attracted over 7,000 spectators for the second game. The Richmond club finished the season in fourth place with a 73–58 (.557) record. Lancaster won the pennant, finishing 90–44 (.667).[46]

Atlantic League owners met at the end of the season to contemplate plans for 1898. All eight clubs decided to remain in the league with Manager Scharsig given permission to move his franchise out of Philadelphia. Allentown became the new league city for 1898. The league offered the two Virginia clubs a four-year contract to remain members of the Atlantic League. While Richmond finished fourth in the standings, the club, along with Hartford and Newark, was one of only three that posted a profit in the season.[47]

While the Richmond ball club's future for 1898 in the Atlantic League was secure, its ownership was in dispute. On September 24, 1897, the *Richmond Dispatch* reported that the Richmond Railway and Electric Company was planning to purchase a controlling interest in the Richmond Baseball and Athletic Association. Their intention was to abandon the one-year-old Broad Street Park and return the club to the West End Park on Main Street. When Bradley's team played at the West End Park in 1894–96, the railway company prospered from the fans attending ball games and riding the Main Street Line. However, the company refused Bradley's attempts to have it invest in the club. At the end of the 1896 season, Bradley entered into a five-year contract with the Traction Company that ran the Broad Street car line and built a new ballpark. The move to Broad Street Park meant an end to a significant revenue source

Opposite: Broad Street Park, home for Richmond's professional baseball teams (1897–1912). The park was built on land leased for the Richmond, Fredericksburg and Potomac Railroad. It was located on Broad Street between Allen and Lombardy Avenues and incorporated a house in the outfield wall. (Photograph from the Cook Collection. Printed by permission of the Valentine Museum and Richmond History Center.)

for the Richmond Railway and Electric Company. They now wanted it back.[48]

The Richmond Baseball and Athletic Association was capitalized at $12,000 with 120 shares of stock. When Bradley sold the organization in early September 1897, Donati, C.T. Boykin, and P.B. Shield each purchased one-third interest. Within a few weeks, Boykin sold his shares to Donati. Donati was willing to sell sixty of his shares to the Richmond Railway and Electric Company, with the understanding that he would remain the baseball director and that Jake Wells would be the team's manager. Shield was the counsel for the Traction Company, and the company threatened a legal challenge if the ball club attempted to rescind its contract to remain at the Broad Street Location.[49]

Through the legal difficulties, the Traction Company emerged victorious. After the courts ruled that the ball club was legally bound to the Broad Street Park, the Richmond Railway and Electric Company withdrew their offer. Mr. John Skelton Williams, president of the Richmond Traction Company, purchased all of Donati's shares in the baseball association. Williams then hired W.B. Bradley as the general manager, renewed Jake Wells as the field manager, and restored the nickname Bluebirds for the Richmond ball club. The team kept its gray uniforms but added blue stockings, belts, and caps and blue and white striped sweaters.[50]

The Richmond Railway and Electric Company was not about to let the Traction Company have all the baseball profits to themselves. The February 13, 1898, *Richmond Dispatch* reported that throughout the late winter, the Railway and Electric Company had begun construction of a ballpark on Vine and Main Streets. They were proposing the development of another Virginia League throughout the state. However, this new league would not be able to apply to the National League for protection, as the Traction Company owned recognized rights to Richmond. It is uncertain what the fate of the Railway Company's efforts were, for this was the only mention in the *Richmond Dispatch* about the proposal. It is likely that without the protections accorded in the National agreement, no other parties responded to the company's plan.[51]

The legal disputes concerning team ownership that occurred in Richmond in 1897 were the first indication in Richmond that baseball was more than just a game; it was business. Factors leading to this conclusion had been evident in other levels of the sport for decades. Business interests created the concept of the American Association. Many of the team owners were brewers by profession. When the National League prohibited the sale of alcohol at game and expelled Cincinnati prior to the 1881 season, brewers in several cities formed the American Association, a league that had become known as the Beer and Whiskey League. It was only natural for the railroads and trolley companies to become involved in baseball. In *Baseball, the Early Years*, Harold Seymour presents several examples of associations formed between the rail companies and baseball owners. Many were limited arrangements such as the excursion trains run by the C&O Railroad to Petersburg, Norfolk and Hampton during Richmond's tenure in the Virginia State League. Other examples include outright ownership, such as the Richmond Traction Company's 1897 purchases of the Richmond BaseBall and Athletic Association.[52]

Excitement was high in Richmond as the opening of the 1898 season approached. Not only did the *Daily Dispatch* have strong pre-season praise for Wells' Bluebirds, but the paper also noted that correspondents from other league cities were impressed with the Richmond squad. A grand parade was planned to begin the festivities for the opening game. Special seating arrangements were made for Virginia governor J. Hoge Tyler and his staff, and Richmond mayor Richard M. Taylor was to throw out the first ball. Despite the hopes of league fans for a banner season, international events would soon cast a shadow over the entire 1898 season.[53]

On February 3, 1898, the USS Maine, anchored in Havana Harbor, suffered a tremendous explosion. The incident increased the tension that already existed between Spain and the United States. War seemed imminent. A week before the Atlantic League was scheduled to commence season play, the *Dispatch* noted that "as soon as this war excitement cools off a little and good old steady times settle, the fever of 1895, 1896 and 1897 will return to the ballpark greater than before." However, the "war excitement" would not cool off. The day before the season opened, the paper announced that President William McKinley issued a call to arms. The proclamation issued the order for the assembly of a volunteer army of 125,000 men to be organized to aid in the war effort against Spain in the fight for Cuba's independence.[54]

The Spanish-American War of 1898 was relatively short, lasting about the length of the baseball season. While the war provided limited impact upon daily life in the United States, it produced a major effect on minor league baseball. Attendance at minor league games was down. In Ed Barrow's memoirs, he quotes an article from *Spalding's Baseball Guide* for 1898: "The Atlantic League, like all minor leagues in that year of our war with Spain, had to suffer financially, only one club in the circuit of eight escaping heavy loss. That was the Richmond club, which won the pennant." Ed Barrow was president of the Atlantic League, and later manager of the Detroit Tigers and Boston Red Sox. From 1921–45, he was general manager of the New York Yankees. He was elected to the Hall of Fame in 1953. Despite winning the pennant with a record of 78–43 (.644), the Richmond team did report ending the season with a debt. The loss was largely attributed to interest in the war, the chief cause for the decreased attendance figures.[55]

After the financial results for 1898 were made public, the *Richmond Dispatch* printed an editorial that advocated abandoning the Atlantic League and reviving a Virginia League. The very next day, E.H. Cunningham, manager of the Norfolk club, and W.B. Bradley, president of the Richmond club, announced that they would withdraw from the Atlantic League and announced their intention to revive a state league. However, M.M. McGuire, as representative of the Richmond Base-Ball and Athletic Association, the controlling body for the Bluebirds, announced that the franchise rights to Richmond belonged to the Atlantic League and that the team would participate in that league. During the off-season, the Richmond paper printed articles speculating which league would be home for the Richmond ball club. Bradley advocated a Virginia League franchise and the association wanted to continue in the Atlantic League.[56]

Richmond and Norfolk were not the only cities questioning future affiliation with the Atlantic League that off-season. A late fall *Richmond Dispatch* headline read, "DECAY OF LEAGUE, The Atlantic Now Seems Likely to Go to Pieces." By spring the paper's outlook had changed, proclaiming, "NOW FOR BASE-BALL. The Prospects Are Bright For Atlantic League Success." The Atlantic League decided to drop Hartford and allowed Norfolk to leave. Scranton and Wilkes-Barre were admitted. The Richmond press noted that interest in the national game had revived since the end of the war and that the city was anticipating a great season in 1899.[57]

The 1899 season opened with little fanfare, and, for the first time, the Richmond club opened the season with an away game. Also for the first time, the club lost its first game. However, the club did not endure a long losing streak and soon posted a 5–4 record, good enough for third place. The Bluebirds won their first home game by a score of 7–1 against the Newark club before a large crowd of over 2,000 fans, including the governor. Behind the solid pitching of Jack Chesbro, the club had attained the top spot in the Atlantic League standings by July 1 with a 41–14 record (.746). The nearest competitor was the Wilkes-Barre team that was playing a .592 percentage with 33 wins and 22 losses.[58] Richmond's interest and support of baseball was not shared throughout the Atlantic League. On July 5, Scranton officials announced that they were disbanding their ball club. President Edward Barrow called a meeting of club officials to plan for the second half of the season. The *Dispatch* expressed grave doubts about the season continuing. Up to that point, most of the league's teams were continuing the financial losses that had started in the previous season. The Paterson club existed only with the help of the other league teams; Wilkes-Barre had begun to sell players; and Newark owners had openly expressed dissatisfaction with the league.[59]

At the meeting of the owners, the league decided to drop the Paterson club and continue as a six-team league for the second half of the season. A new schedule was devised and Richmond, with a 50–16 record, was proclaimed winner of the first half of the season. The new season was short-lived. On August 5, it was reported that Ralph Seybold, a Richmond outfielder, was sold to Cincinnati, and Joseph Dolan, the club's second baseman was going to Philadelphia. The same day it was revealed that the Wilkes-Barre franchise was sold to Charles H. Manning, president of the Kansas City baseball club. His aim was to send the best players from Wilkes-Barre to his Kansas City squad. The following day, Atlantic League officials announced that the league was disbanding. Jake Wells was able to make an agreement with P.T. Powers, president of the Eastern League, to take the remainder of his club to Syracuse, New York, to complete the season as a replacement club. At this time, Richmond was leading what was left of the Atlantic League with a 13–9 record. (.590). In his five seasons with Richmond, Wells had led the team to five pennants.[60]

After the Atlantic League folded, plans for a revived Virginia League for 1900 were begun. Jake Wells returned to Richmond, but this time as the team owner. During the winter of 1898–99, Wells and Edward Barrow, Atlantic League president, entered into a joint business venture. They opened a vaudeville theater in Richmond. An unusually large snowstorm delayed the opening of the theater for several days, costing the pair substantial capital. During the first few weeks, the theater continued to lose money and Barrow sold his interest to Charles McKee from Pittsburgh. Soon thereafter the theater business began to pick up, and within three years McKee and Wells had twenty-one theaters and summer amusement parks throughout the South. One of the amusement parks was in Richmond. The partners built a pavilion at Reservoir Park near the junction of the two trolley lines. The booming theater business allowed Wells to buy into the Virginia League. He employed Mr. Charles Boyer as the field manager for the team.[61]

Wells continued the Bluebird name for his team and continued to utilize Broad Street Park. Harry Berte, who had played for Wells in the nineties, was brought in as shortstop and to serve as infield coach. Barry Kain and Reddy Foster returned to play for Wells, who was also able to sign Lee Tannehill, younger brother of former Bluebird Jesse Tannehill, to play third. Other members of the club, while new to Richmond, had playing experience in other minor leagues.[62]

The Bluebirds opened the 1900 season by shutting out Petersburg 6–0 on the first day, winning 5–3 the second day, and winning the third game 12–23. They continued their streak for the first six games, not succumbing to defeat until Portsmouth won 4–0 in the seventh game of the season. Richmond finished the first month of the season with a 15–10 record (.600) and was in third place behind Norfolk (.826) and Hampton (.708).[63]

Jake Wells must have found the summer of 1900 to be very frustrating. His team was playing well, and, on June 1, he was selected to assume the presidency of the Virginia League after E.H. Cunningham of Norfolk resigned. His amusement business was booming. However, despite having a solid ball club, the fans were not coming to the games. His team was losing money, and the public's interest in baseball seemed to be fading. His wildly popular amusement businesses required him to focus his energies on the theaters full time, and he announced his resignation as league president. He turned the ball club over to the players and volunteered to serve as an advisor to his baseball club.[64]

Four days after Wells withdrew from the league, the Richmond ball club was forced to do the same. When the Petersburg club announced that it financially could not survive and decided that it was withdrawing, the Richmond club was left with limited options. The other members of the league, all centered in the Tidewater-Peninsula region, decided to drop Richmond and continue the season as a four-team league, consisting of Norfolk, Portsmouth, Hampton and Newport News. The Richmond players received the news during the fourth inning of their June 12 game against Newport News and made no attempt to win. The club finished with 21 wins and 13 losses (.600).[65]

After the failure of the Virginia League in 1900, baseball officials in Virginia looked to add some North Carolina teams to the league rather than attempt to add weaker Virginia cities. Discussions of forming a Virginia-North Carolina League began in January 1901. Several cities were being considered for admission to the new league. At times, a league of as many as eight or ten teams was considered. However, on February 18, the league was formally organized, teams included Norfolk, Portsmouth, Newport News, and Richmond. The Richmond franchise had been acquired by Charles Donati, a Richmond native who had been involved in baseball earlier. Raleigh was the only North Carolina franchise secured at the time, but within a month Wilmington was admitted as the sixth club.[66]

Donati hired Barley Kain as team manager and employed a number of the 1900 squad. The league recognized Richmond's past support of its teams and awarded the franchise home games for the season opener and all of the summer holidays. Nearly 1,000 fans came out for the first game of the season at Broad Street Park. The Grays, as the Richmond club was named, battled Wilmington to a thirteen inning 4–4 draw. The club then shut out the visitors the next day. The excitement generated by the first two games did not last long. Richmond became one of the worst teams in the league.[67]

Trouble began for the Virginia-North Carolina League before the end of June. On June 21, the Newport News and Portsmouth franchises both announced that they were withdrawing from the league. These two franchises were moved to Charlotte and Tarboro, North Carolina. League directors decided to split the season and rearrange the schedule to accommodate the new locations. Richmond ended the first half with an unimpressive 19–38 record (.333). The Grays started the second half of the 1901 season winning seven of their first twelve games and were third in the standings. However, the club was on shaky financial ground, and, on July 6, management offered to allow the club to continue as a cooperative. The players refused and the team was forced to disband. Norfolk followed Richmond's lead and withdrew. The North Carolina teams attempted to continue, but the entire league was declared a failure on August 17, 1901. With the third consecutive season aborted before its conclusion, Richmond fans and baseball managers became weary of the sport. Once again, Richmond was about to endure an extended absence from the ranks of professional baseball. A team did not play in Richmond until 1906 when the Lawmakers represented Richmond in a new Virginia League.[68]

CHAPTER IV

The Revival and Demise of the Virginia State League, 1906–1914

    Richmond was not alone in its struggles to maintain a professional baseball club at the turn of the century. The experience of Richmond was reflective of the national interest in the game. The failures of the Atlantic and Virginia Leagues were typical of many small minor league circuits. Even the National League, America's only major league in 1899, went from a twelve-team league to one of only eight ball clubs. The league eliminated teams in Louisville, Cleveland, Baltimore and Washington in hopes of restoring profitability to the venture.[1]

    Baseball owners were primarily responsible for their own troubles. Many entrepreneurs attempted to capitalize upon baseball's increased popularity in the 1890s by establishing teams and leagues of their own. Most teams and leagues joined the National Agreement, thereby recognizing the National League's premier status as the only major league in exchange for territorial rights and protection from raiding of players by wealthier teams. In the late 1890s, several minor leagues attempted to challenge the National League's sole claim to major league status, and a costly baseball war erupted. By August 1901, the National League's competition with the American League forced owners to announce that protections accorded by the National Agreement were abrogated, and the minors were threatened with significant player and geographic disputes.[2]

Thomas Jefferson Hickey, president of the Western League, quickly responded to the nullification of the National Agreement. He sent a telegram to all minor league presidents notifying them of the league's actions. He urged the men to meet on September 5, 1901, at Chicago's Leland Hotel. All eleven of the organized minor leagues were represented in person or by proxy. The first order of business was to establish the National Association of Professional Baseball Leagues, an organization that still governs minor league baseball today.[3]

The intent for the formation of a National Association was to bring the minor leagues into a cohesive group that could prevent the major circuits from raiding their rosters. In the organization's second meeting on October 24–25, 1901, the association established rules and regulations in order to stabilize minor league baseball. The most important was a classification system. Minor leagues were divided into four classes: A, B, C, and D. This system was designed to provide equal competition among teams in a given league. Leagues composed of smaller cities with lower operating budgets were labeled as Class D. The team rosters were to be composed of players with limited experience. Class A, the highest classification, contained the most experienced minor league players. The classification system was altered in 1908 to include an AA rating. In 1946, AAA ratings were introduced. In 1963, the B, C, and D ratings were discontinued and "rookie league" and "instructional league" circuits were formed for the least experienced players.[4]

The National Association's organizational system became known as Organized Baseball. Professional leagues or teams that did not join the association were labeled as "outlaw leagues." Under the old National Agreement, leagues that did not sign the agreement were simply referred to as "independent leagues." It was these independent leagues that necessitated the formation of the National Association. They challenged the stability that the agreement had provided. With the recognition that the preservation of the association was paramount to the individual league's survival, Organized Baseball sought to create a negative image for outsiders, hence the use of the term "outlaw."[5]

In January 1903, the two competing major leagues came to agreement that both the National and American Leagues could share status as major leagues. The end of hostilities between the two leagues paved the way for a Major-Minor League Agreement within the framework of the National Association. With stability restored to Organized Baseball, the American public once again welcomed the sport as the national pastime. While the major leagues entered a profitable era, the minor leagues saw an explosion of popularity. The expansion of the minors began with thirteen leagues in 1903, and, by 1914, there were forty leagues party to the National Association.[6]

With baseball's popularity restored nationwide, it did not take long for the game to return to Richmond. In 1904 and 1905, three semi-pro leagues thrived in the city. The Twin Cities League was apparently the strongest of the three. All Twin Cities games were played at Broad Street Park, and the *Times-Dispatch* included detailed game summaries and complete box scores in the papers. The league featured four teams: the Richmonds, the Manchester Colts, the Brownies, and a team representing the Northside known as Barton Heights. The league's most significant player was Charles "Barley" Kain, the star of Richmond's professional ball clubs of the late 1890s. On April 23, the first Saturday of the 1905 season, nearly 4,000 spectators came out to witness all four teams of the Twin Cities League participate in a pair of games at the ballpark. Barton Heights defeated the Colts in the first game 3–2, and the Brownies conquered the 1904 league champion Richmonds by a score of 9–6.[7]

The Twin Cities League shared the baseball spotlight in Richmond with the Suburban League and the Capitol City League. The Suburban League was also a four-team circuit and featured the Northside Stars, the West End Angels, the Chestnuts, and the Knoxalls. The Capitol City League was comprised of six teams: the Brooklands, E.E. Blues, Monroes, Hobos, Elban, and White Swans. These two leagues played their games in various local or neighborhood fields in Richmond. The *Times-Dispatch* reported scores for all games and published league standings but rarely provided complete box scores or game summaries.[8]

Interest in professional and semi-professional baseball had seen a resurgence in other parts of the state by 1905. Danville was the lone Virginia representative in the Virginia–North Carolina BaseBall League. Danville's competition consisted of a team in Greensboro, one in Charlotte (the Water Drinkers) and a team that, by the end of the season, was simply dubbed the Orphans. The Orphans began the year in Salisbury-Spencer, later moved to Winston-Salem and by the end of July were without a home. The team struggled for three weeks after leaving Winston-Salem, but the Orphans' financial situation had created too much hardship for the club and the league. Both the team and the league announced disbandment plans on August 20, 1905. The Danville club, league pennant winners, continued to play for the remainder of 1905 by staging exhibition games throughout the state of Virginia.[9]

The local amateur leagues created a new enthusiasm for baseball, and the travels of the Danville club generated interest in a revival of the Virginia State League. On September 2, 1905, the Danville BaseBall

Association was created as a joint stock company capitalized at $2,000 in anticipation of a new league. Two weeks later, a *Times-Dispatch* headline announced that the Virginia State League would begin play in the spring of 1906. Teams in the league would be required to feature at least eight men that were local or at least Virginian. Richmond baseball hero Jake Wells was directing the league's organization.[10]

On October 25, 1905, the league was officially organized as the Virginia League of Professional Baseball Players. Jake Wells was elected to serve as president for the six-team circuit. Ball clubs representing Richmond, Roanoke, Portsmouth, Norfolk, Danville, and Lynchburg were scheduled to begin play on April 26, 1906. Charlie Donati and W.B. Bradley, known in Richmond for their efforts at maintaining the city's professional baseball franchise in the 1880s and 1890s, controlled the lease of the Broad Street Park and set about planning for the team to represent Richmond in the new state league. The men chose Charlie Schaffer to be the team manager. Although play would start in April, Schaffer would not need to have his roster within the league's salary limit of $800 a month until June 1. He planned to bring many players to Richmond for tryouts with the intention of settling on thirteen or fourteen players by June 1, 1906.[11]

Richmond's entry in the Virginia League was officially known as the Richmond club. However, the local press assumed the initiative to provide a nickname for the club. The sports editor of the *Times-Dispatch* conducted a contest, allowing its female readers to submit "appropriate names for the aggregation that is to represent the capital city." The contestant submitting the winning entry would receive a season pass that would allow her and her escort to have grandstand seats at all of the Richmond club's home games. Entries included "White Stockings," "Dixie Trotters," "Eagles," "Commanders," "Old Dominions," and "Sprinters." None of these suggestions captured the editor's attention. Entries, however, by Minnie Dickenson and Miss A.T. English won both ladies season passes. Their suggestion "Lawmakers" was declared the winning entry by the press.[12]

After one season, however, the press dropped the nickname "Lawmakers" and began referring to the team as the "Colts." It was common for the paper to utilize both names in the same article. "Colts," being the shorter of the two, was the name most often written in the headline. "Lawmakers" was sometimes utilized in the subheading, and both names were written in the text of the article, often in the same sentence. By 1911, the *Times-Dispatch* had dropped the name "Lawmakers" altogether and referred to the Richmond ball club exclusively as the "Colts."[13]

The city of Richmond was eager to welcome Virginia League play in 1906. The season opened on April 26, amidst a celebratory atmosphere. The players for both the Lawmakers and the visiting Lynchburg Hill-climbers were marshaled to the game in a grand parade that featured a band seated in a wagon pulled by mules and the players riding in the back of "all of the automobiles in town." There were eight automobiles in the town. The parade was the first motorcade in Richmond's history. As the procession wound through the main streets of the city, onlookers hung out of windows and crowded on street corners to cheer the return of professional baseball to the city. As the caravan passed Richmond College, the students greeted the ball players with cheers of encouragement. When the procession ended at the Broad Street Park, the Reverend Dr. J.B. Hawthorne, pastor of Grove Avenue Baptist Church, threw out the first ball to start the season.[14]

The 2,000 fans that came out to root for the Lawmakers left Broad Street Park disappointed as the Hillcilimbers won 6–3. Although the team assembled by manager Charlie Schaffer was not strong enough to capture the Virginia League pennant in 1906, they were popular with the Richmond fans. The Lawmakers entered the final week of the season with a 50–53 record, and in a Labor Day doubleheader with the Danville club, more than 7,000 patrons came to the park. Richmond ended the season in third place with a final record of 57–54 (.513).[15]

Although the Lawmakers did not win the Virginia League pennant, the season was a financial success for the club. While exact figures were not revealed, officials acknowledged that the team made a profit of "several thousand dollars." The team had been accorded by the schedule makers home games every Saturday, and the Richmond fans did not disappoint league operators. The Saturday attendance averaged several thousand spectators and was reported to nearly equal the attendance at many American League games. The season was such a success that all teams in the Virginia League reported a profit. With such a strong first year, the league magnates were looking forward to the future.[16]

In 1907, each of the Virginia League clubs once again turned a profit. The *Times-Dispatch* did not report financial figures, but it was reported that Richmond once again was the leader in terms of dollars earned, despite finishing fourth in final standings. The Richmond club had started the season with a winning streak, but, by mid-season, the Lawmakers were last in the six-team circuit. In early July, owner Bradley released manager Schaffer and made several player changes that helped improve the team. Shortstop Ralph Reeve finished the season as manager. The most important acquisition came from the Portsmouth club in the form

1908 Richmond "Lawmakers," Virginia State League Champions (courtesy of Virginia Historical Society).

of pitcher Robert "Dutch" Revelle. Revelle proved to be Richmond's ace hurler over the next several seasons. After the July personnel shakeups, the Lawmakers made a push for respectability and finished the season with a 62–62 record. In addition to the strong pitching of Revelle, Bill Heffron led the league in stolen bases with fifty-four and Guy Titman led the league by scoring sixty-seven runs.[17]

The 1908 season is remembered as one of the most exciting in Richmond's baseball history. At the conclusion of the season, the *Times-Dispatch* reported that the city had "never supported the team as well as they did the 1908 pennant winners." The attendance for Lawmaker home games averaged more than 5,300, with a season total of 442,622. The average attendance for Lawmaker games exceeded that of several major league teams, including the New York Yankees, St. Louis Cardinals, the Brooklyn Dodgers, Washington Senators, and Boston Braves.

The attendance pinnacle for the Lawmakers came on Labor Day in a doubleheader with Danville. The clubs were in a tight pennant race with only a few weeks to play. A large crowd of approximately 10,000 saw the Lawmakers take the morning game 2–0. Over 15,000 fans packed into Broad Street Park for the afternoon game. The fans saw an exciting 1–1 game that was ruled a tie after ten innings. The Lawmakers' victory in the first game pushed them ahead to stay. The pennant was officially clinched on the evening of September 12 when the Lawmakers' Quinn and Revelle pitched the team to victory in both ends of a doubleheader against Roanoke.[18]

The 1908 Lawmakers did not experience any of the personnel problems which afflicted the 1907 team. Prior to the opening of the season, Bradley acquired a new manager, Perry Lipe, formerly of the Southern League. He was manager and

Jack Quinn (courtesy of *Richmond Times-Dispatch*.

also played third base. He led the league in runs scored with sixty-five. Lipe built a strong team that featured Jake Kanzler at first, Jimmy Ison at second, and Sandy Sandherr at shortstop. The outfield returned the starters from the 1907 team: Guy Titman, Bill Heffron, and Doc Sebrie. The stars on the mound were "Dutch" Revelle, who led the league in strikeouts with 199, and the mid-season acquisition Jackson Quinn, who finished the season with a record of 14 victories, no defeats, and three ties. The only player on this remarkable team who would see playing time in the major leagues was Quinn. He was drafted by the New York Yankees near the end of the 1908 season. He enjoyed a twenty-three-year major league career and was one of the seventeen pitchers allowed to use the spitball after it was banned by major league baseball in 1920. He compiled a career record of 247 wins.[19]

The success of the 1908 87–41 (.608) season did not continue into 1909. The Richmond club played well but suffered long slumps in the early and middle parts of the season. As the season entered its final week, the Colts narrowly held third place and ended the season at Broad Street Park with a doubleheader against league-leading Roanoke. Although Richmond had no chance of overtaking Roanoke, approximately 12,000 fans attended the final games. The Colts lost 7–1 in the first game, but the fans were rewarded in the second with an 8–0 victory by the home team. The highlight of the season occurred in the Colts' final game when Colts' second baseman and leadoff hitter, James Ison, sent the first pitch over the left field bleachers and out of the park. Ison's homerun was the only ball hit out of the Broad Street Park all season.[20]

The Colts finished the 1909 season in third place 63–61 (.508). Roanoke and Norfolk finished in a tie at 73–49 (.599). Rather than having a playoff to decide the champion, the Virginia League directors ruled that the pennant belonged to Roanoke. Norfolk's final day victory was overturned by a technicality. The game was originally to have been played in Petersburg earlier in the season. The teams decided to play the postponed game as part of a doubleheader to end the season. However, league rules stated that "no postponed game shall be played on any field other than that on which it is regularly scheduled." In the ruling, the directors reasoned that Norfolk had an unfair advantage by having an extra game on its home field, and Roanoke was declared league champion.[21]

The Colts' mediocre season of 1909 was repeated in 1910. The club finished the season fifth in a six-team league with a record of 50–67 (.427). By the end of the season, public interest in baseball was in serious decline. The *Times-Dispatch* proclaimed that as the losses piled up "interest began to die, and it has been dying in carloads ever since." At the next to last game of the season, less than 100 patrons sat in the 10 cent bleachers, with a similar number in the grandstand and no one in the 25 cent bleachers. Despite the poor season, nearly 4,000 fans came to witness the season's final game. The large attendance was attributed to custom rather than actual support for the club as "enthusiasm was about as slow as a narrow gauge [rail] road in the Virginia mountains." The press noted that the crowd, which "normally yells themselves hoarse urging the home team to its best efforts, breathed a sigh of relief when the agony was over."[22]

After two disappointing seasons, the *Times-Dispatch* became more critical of the Colt's ownership. Since the beginning of the professional game in Richmond, *Times-Dispatch* writers were ardent supporters of the team and its ownership group. While an article might criticize the team's owners or its players for a particular action, the overwhelming attitude was of unflagging support. Despite the team's record, the paper consistently urged fans to go to the games and support the home team. This unwavering support had helped professional baseball become a financially profitable venture in the city. Now that the game was firmly established and "as fat as Standard Oil for the owners," the paper began to openly challenge the Colts' ownership.[23]

The ire of the press was sparked by more than poor performance in the box scores. In August 1910 it was announced that the Montreal franchise in the Eastern League was to be sold for $40,000. It was reported that an unnamed Baltimore man was interested in buying the club and bringing it to Richmond. He intended for W.B. Bradley, the Colts owner, to be a financial partner. The *Times-Dispatch* thought that this was good news; the paper was in favor of Richmond moving to a higher league rather than "plodding on as the leading town in a small one-state circuit, whereas its rightful place is with cities of its size and larger." The press maintained that Richmond's leaving would not destroy the Virginia League. It argued that the level of play in a higher classification league would "inspire baseball fans throughout the state and would increase interest in all local franchises." The entire state, it was claimed, would benefit with the Eastern League in Richmond, and Bradley was urged to accept the offer from Baltimore. A month later, it was apparent that Bradley was not interested.[24]

Bradley was criticized as being comfortable in the Virginia League and not willing to spend the money necessary to pay better ball players. The Colts were the only team that earned a profit in each season of the Virginia League. Being in the largest city and enjoying the greatest popular support, Bradley could count on the rest of the league presenting Richmond with a favorable home schedule that included most weekends and holidays.[25] Bradley's financial success made the league viable. The league needed him. With his position secure, he had limited incentive to spend money on higher salaries. As a result, during the 1910 season, many low-salaried players were brought in to try out for the team, but each one failed. Throughout the season, more and more ballplayers were brought to Richmond and released. The *Times-Dispatch* argued that with money spent on the travel expenses of all these players, Bradley could have allowed the club to hire a few quality players. The critics claimed that Bradley owed the city a faster-paced ball club and higher league classification. It was predicted that if he did nothing, the Richmond club would lose money the following season, that the Virginia League would fold, and that Richmond would then be without baseball.[26]

In October 1910, the outlook for baseball's immediate future in Richmond was grim. It soon took a turn for the worse. Norfolk threatened to leave the Virginia League and start an Eastern Virginia League. Charles H. Consolvo, president of the Norfolk franchises, cited that his ball club was in severe financial difficulty, and the league was to blame. In order for him to keep his team in the Virginia League, he wanted the league to increase its competitiveness. To do so, he felt that it was necessary to eliminate Roanoke and Danville, add Portsmouth and Newport News, and increase the salary limit. These moves would remove the least profitable teams, add cities with a potentially larger fan base, geographically centralize teams to reduce travel costs, and increase the level of play, thereby attracting a larger audience. The other league members were reluctant to make the changes. It took the league owners nearly a month to settle the dispute. Amidst the threats and legal maneuvers, the minor stockholders charged that Norfolk's financial woes were more to blame on Consolvo's mismanagement than the structure of the Virginia League. The shares of the Norfolk club stock were placed in receivership, and Norfolk's Virginia League franchise was officially placed on sale.[27]

After the Virginia League stabilized the situation with Norfolk, Bradley attempted to answer his critics by publicly addressing the issues that had been raised. In an interview with the *Times-Dispatch*, he admitted that 1910 was disastrous and that several mistakes were made. He declared that he was committed to "getting a real team" for 1911. Commenting on the Eastern League situation, he noted that several northern teams were clamoring for the franchise and that the option was not there for him at this time. He declared, "The public don't want this any worse than I do." He promised fans he was constantly on the lookout for an opportunity to move Richmond into a faster league, with the most realistic hope being the Tri-State League, a league composed of many of the former Atlantic League cities. The press concluded that "this is the kind of talk that Richmond fans have been waiting for." There was renewed hope for the 1911 Virginia League season.[28]

The 1911 season would be another dismal one for the Colts and the Virginia League. Bradley had displayed high expectations for his club. James "Jeems" W. Sullivan was hired to manage the Colts. Bradley expressed so much confidence in Sullivan he vowed to "leave everything in his hands." The confidence was rewarded with a 2–0 victory over Danville on opening day. Unfortunately the opening day victory was not a harbinger for better days for the Colts. The club finished the season fourth in the league, mustering only 56 victories with 62 losses (.475). The victory total tied the club for fifth place with Lynchburg, but the winning percentage placed the club slightly ahead of the Hill City 56–65 record (.463). Richmond captured fourth place by a mere .012 percentage points. Two factors helped prevent a worse finish for the Colts. Late in the season, Bradley released Sullivan and named Steve Griffin as manager. Griffin had a strong reputation for his ability to mange ballplayers, and, to his credit, Richmond finished strongly. While Griffin's accomplishments helped the Colts earn a few victories down the stretch, the fourth place finish should be attributed to three canceled rainouts. As a result, the Richmond club played three fewer games than Lynchburg and finished ahead of Lynchburg in the standings because of three fewer losses.[29]

Despite the poor attendance at Colt games, baseball was not suffering from lack of interest in Richmond. In fact, the game's appeal was perhaps at the height of its popularity. The amateur games were generating so much attention from both spectators and participants that the existing teams formed the Richmond Amateur Baseball Association. This organization was designed to create several new leagues and oversee the construction of three ballparks specifically for these clubs.[30]

Professional ball at its highest level also captured the fascination of Richmonders. On October 10, 1911, Broad Street Park was the site for a game of Major League All-Stars playing against Connie Mack's World Series-bound Philadelphia Athletics. Leading the all-stars were Ty Cobb, Tris Speaker, Walter Johnston and former Richmond ballplayer Norman "Kid" Elberfeld. The all-stars defeated Mack's Athletics 13–8 before 9,000 ecstatic Richmond fans. A few days later, when the Athletics met the New York Giants in the World Series, several thousand Richmonders crowded outside the *Times-Dispatch* Main Street office to "see the game" on the electronic bulletin board that hung on the side of the building. The crowd was so large that Main Street had to be shut down to accommodate the spectators. As the series progressed, the crowds grew larger. The *Times-Dispatch* theorized that one would have to "delve deep into the archives of history…to learn of an event which has produced more interest locally than the present battle between the two champion baseball teams."[31]

The poor attendance at Colts' games was not due to Richmond's lack of interest in baseball. The problem was with the Colts themselves. Richmond fans demanded better players and a higher classification of play. Ownership was against a move to a league that would increase expenses and payroll. Gus Malbert, writing for the *Times-Dispatch*, argued that the ownership was comfortable with the profits realized with the minimal effort and expense needed in the Virginia League. He contended that if the ownership would consent to a stronger classification of baseball, the appeal of the game would create greater gate receipts that would not only cover the increased expenses but would also generate a greater profit. Malbert stated that Richmond "is in a state of baseball rebellion." The fans and the city deserved better baseball.[32]

Ernest C. Landgraf proposed to end Richmond's baseball frustration by securing franchise rights in the newly formed United States League. In December 1911, William Abbott Witman of Reading, Pennsylvania, and others organized the United States League of Professional Baseball Clubs. This league was designed to rival the American and National Leagues for major league status. The new league adopted all of the playing rules of organized baseball, but it refused to recognize the territorial rights established by the major league clubs and was, therefore, regarded as an "outlaw league." The United States League was organized with eight teams: Chicago, Cincinnati, Cleveland, New York, Pittsburgh, Washington D.C., Reading, and Richmond. While the new league planned clubs in cities with established baseball teams, the league prepared its schedule to prevent a duplication of home games and did not threaten direct daily competition.[33]

During the winter of 1911–12, the Richmond newspaper was brimming with baseball news. People were excited about the prospect of major league baseball and the United States League. With considerable attention being focused upon the invading outlaws, W.B. Bradley and Steve Griffin frequently wrote to the *Times-Dispatch* with news of the Colts with the hope that renewed enthusiasm for their club would decrease the attention given to Landgraf's proposed club. The *Sporting News* reported that most of the baseball world showed little interest in the USL, but Richmond and Reading had an "unusual enthusiasm" for the league. However, the article discounted this excitement since both of these cities were "very inferior" minor league towns.[34]

Richmond's eagerness to accept the United States League was based on more than mere baseball interests; the new league was viewed as a vehicle to promote the city. A major booster campaign had begun in the fall of 1911. As part of the campaign, a weeklong "Booster Tour," composed of over 100 business representatives, chartered a Seaboard Air Line train and traveled throughout Virginia and North Carolina to "advertise Richmond, its industrial and mercantile greatness, and its many advantages as a distributing center and as a business town in general." The United States League was seen as a way to continue the promotion of

Richmond. The *Times-Dispatch* wrote, "It will sound mighty good to read on the scoreboards: Richmond 4, New York 0; Richmond 5, Cincinnati 2. Richmond will be in the class it deserves."[35]

The city eagerly awaited the start of the 1912 season. With two teams, its fans were assured of a professional game nearly every day of the week. Landgraf's Richmond Rebels, as northern newspapers dubbed the team, called Lee Park their home field. The ballyard, located on North Boulevard at Moore Street was constructed in only 28 days. Bradley's Colts once again played at Broad Street Park. While staying within the framework of the Class C league's salary limit, Bradley and Griffin increased their efforts to field a competitive ball club. While he had considerably more leverage in signing ballplayers, Landgraf was hindered by the expectations to produce a major league caliber team despite the fact that most of the best ballplayers were already signed to American and National League contracts. The Rebels' only name players were former major leaguers Ralph Seybold and Bert Blue. Seybold, the former American League home run leader for the A's, had started his professional career in Richmond, but was forty-one years old and had not played league baseball since 1908. Blue had been a reserve catcher with the Athletics but had played in only seventeen major league games. During the 1911 season, he played in the Class D Ohio State League.[36]

The excitement created by the United States League also heightened the interest of Richmond fans in the beginning of the Virginia League season. The Virginia League opened its season two weeks before the United States League, and the Colts were greeted on opening day with the now-ritual parade through the streets. The procession was cheered by fans; however, darkening skies, hail, and lackluster play drove many of the spectators from the stands before Petersburg defeated the Colts 7–3. Large crowds continued to patronize Broad Street Park, and, in mid–May, the Colts drew more than 4,000 for a Saturday game. When the Rebels opened their season on May 1, it was reported that over 9,000 fans came to Lee Park to cheer the home team to victory over Washington 2–0.[37]

The *Times-Dispatch* reported regularly on both of the home teams. Updates of Colts' games and Virginia League standings were posted daily, although they were relegated to the bottom of the page or pushed to the second sports page. The United States League received top billing in the local paper. The standings of the United States League, American League, and National League were grouped together under the heading, "Results of the Three Big Leagues." Richmond was one of the few cities to recognize the league in the same class as the AL and NL. However, it did not take long for the *Times-Dispatch* to cease the comparison.[38]

While the United States League was well received in Richmond, it struggled elsewhere. By May 28, New York dropped out of the league after only fifty fans showed up for a game. It was reported that Richmond, with its strong attendance, and Pittsburgh, with perhaps the best press coverage, were the only teams making money. Reading, near bankruptcy (court papers were filed June 1), could not keep its players from signing contracts with teams in organized baseball. The team had to disband. Despite these troubles, the league owners met in Pittsburgh and voted to continue. This plan may have been optimistic. On June 24, the *Times-Dispatch* headline read, "Players Determined Not to Play Again Until They Are Paid." The United States League spent the next two weeks without an official schedule. Teams played each other in an attempt to keep busy and make some money, while the owners tried to reorganize the league. By June 24, 1912, the United States League was finished. The Rebs finished with a 22–13 record (.629) and were in second place behind Pittsburgh.[39]

The Virginia League also experienced difficulties in 1912. In efforts to revive the league, the circuit had added teams from Newport News and Portsmouth and expanded to an eight-club format for the season. The VL began to experience its financial failures about the same time that the United States League was falling apart. On June 5, the Danville club announced that it was losing money but would continue. Suffolk and Bluefield, West Virginia, entered bids for franchises in the league. However, magnates decided to drop Lynchburg along with Danville and continue as a six-club league.[40]

On the field, the Richmond Colts enjoyed a successful season in 1912. After losing their first game, the club had a break-even April, posting a 5–5 record by the time the USL started its season. The club was 21–17 when the USL first announced its troubles on June 4. As the season progressed, the Colts vaulted into first place on August 28 but then lost two games to Roanoke to drop out of the lead. When the season ended, the Colts were in third place behind Roanoke and Petersburg. The Colts' 77–56 (.579) record was a dramatic improvement over previous years.[41]

After years of frustration with the ball club's performance, the Richmond fans and press were beginning to look at W.B. Bradley with favor. The strong performance of the 1912 Colts eased some of the criticisms; however, other concerns still existed. The condition of Broad Street Park had deteriorated significantly since its opening in 1897. Bradley announced plans to build a new ballpark at the beginning of the 1912 season. However, dissension among Bradley and the other members of the ownership group prevented plans from progressing. When the United States League failed in June, Bradley put forth a bid to purchase Lee Park, but the owners of the Richmond Baseball Corporation and P.J. White and Son, the contractors, were engaged in a contract dispute over the final $600 payment for construction. The USL franchise board of directors charged that the contractor failed to complete the construction in a satisfactory manner and still had "much work" to complete. The legal battle over the park prevented its sale to Bradley and his partners.[42]

Before the 1913 season, Bradley was successful in securing land and constructed a new ballpark. Also known as Broad Street Park, the new facility was located several blocks west of the former field. Similar to the original Broad Street Park, this field was built upon land leased from the Richmond, Fredericksburg and Potomac Railroad. The land was located where Broad Street intersects with Addison Street. The *Times-Dispatch* described the "Bradleyized enclosure" as being "to the west of a certain shoe manufactory and to the north of a hop-pressing emporium whose shadows lure and sometimes lead." The lease with the RF&P was terminated after the season in 1916 when the railroad determined the location would be used to build a new rail passenger terminal. Broad Street Station, long abandoned as a train station, still exists and is the current home of the Science Museum of Virginia[43]

Richmond fans had high hopes for the Colts in 1913. Hopes were enhanced by the return of Steve Griffin as manager and the promise of strong play as was exhibited at the end of the 1912 season. The fans' hopes were rewarded as the Colts won the opener by defeating the Goobers of Petersburg 3–0 behind the strong pitching of Charley Stain. The club remained at the top of the Virginia League standings for most of the season. However, player injuries the last few weeks of the season caused the Colts to relinquish the leadership to champion Petersburg and runner-up Roanoke. Griffin's boys finished in third place with a 74–60 record (.552).[44]

Bradley decided the Colts needed new leadership in 1914, and Steve Griffin was released after the last game in 1913. Griffin acknowledged that the season had been disappointing but countered that it was not entirely his fault. Much of the demise was attributed to luck, or lack thereof. He realized that luck was against him when he reported for the first day of training and "fell through the incomplete clubhouse and cracked his ribs." Bradley selected Ray Ryan from Cincinnati to guide the Colts.

The first challenge faced by the Richmond club in 1914 did not occur on the field but in the boardroom of league magnates. League officials decided to formulate a new schedule for the 1914 season, a schedule which provided each team the same number of Saturday home games. This plan was vigorously opposed by the Richmond ownership, but it was approved by all of the other ball clubs. The modified schedule provided for the Colts to be away from their home park on weekends for the first time in the history of the Virginia League. In previous years, the schedule designers reasoned that since Richmond had the largest population and attracted the most fans per game, the entire league would receive financial benefit by having Richmond at home. However, owners now thought that if they altered the schedule to provide more games with local rivalries, Richmond/Petersburg and Norfolk/Portsmouth, the excitement generated by these games would create fan interest and boost attendance throughout the league. Gradually, the owners came to realize that the increased travel costs would outweigh the revenues derived from the new fan support. They also realized that by increasing the number of games a team would play against one opponent, they would likely reduce the competitiveness of the championship race. Without a pennant race, attendance was likely to decrease. The owners met two weeks before play started and drafted a calendar that presented a greater balance in the number of meetings between opponents. However, the new schedule did not make concessions to Richmond, and for the first time, the Colts played Saturday games on the road. The *Times-Dispatch* warned that this situation would spell financial ruin for the other teams in the league.[45]

As the season neared the summer midpoint, the league owners began to realize the folly of the schedule. Portsmouth had started the season miserably but began to win ball games. However, fan interest was lost along with the early season ball games. Without crowd support, the team struggled financially and was sold. The team's new owners projected that they would not be able to finish the season. Petersburg, although on a stronger financial base, was hopelessly in last place in the standings and was seeing fewer and fewer fans in attendance. On July 3, the magnates decided to create a split season. The winners of the two half-seasons would face each other in a playoff for the Virginia League pennant. The first half champion was crowned on August 1. The second season actually began with the games on July 2 and continued into September with the original schedule. The games played form July 2 through August 1 counted for both halves of the split schedule. The owners reasoned that this arrangement would increase attendance by crafting two pennant races.[46]

The split season produced some of the results desired by the owners. All of the teams completed the season, and the arrangement saved them from financial ruin. However, there was no playoff. Norfolk easily won both halves of the schedule and was crowned league champion. Richmond, under Ray Ryan, showed marked improvement over the previous seasons and finished second in each championship race. The Colts finished the season with a record of 78–56 (.582), while Norfolk posted a 93–48 (.660) record.[47]

On the field, one of Richmond's stars for the season was future Hall of Fame pitcher Burleigh Grimes. Grimes played only about six weeks for the Colts since he was on loan from the Birmingham Barons of the Southern League. He was recalled after his final Colt victory on September 12, 1914. In his major league career, which lasted from 1916 to 1934, Grimes was noted for his spitball. He was one of seventeen pitchers legally allowed to use the pitch after it was outlawed by organized baseball in 1920. When his career ended in 1934, he was the last of the spitball pitchers.[48]

It is ironic to note that Norfolk manager, Dr. Buck Pressley, had originally agreed to a contract to manage Richmond for the 1914 season. In 1913, Pressley managed Roanoke to second place in the Virginia League, while also maintaining a medical practice in the city. At the conclusion of the season, Pressley and W.B. Bradley agreed to terms to have the manager lead the Colts in 1914. Before he signed the contract, however, Pressley notified the Colts' owner that he was retiring from the game and planned to focus his attention on his medical career. A few months later, Roanoke's team president, H. C. Elliott, sold all but $100 of his interests in the club and then invested heavily in the Norfolk franchise. Mr. Elliott convinced Dr. Pressley to reconsider his baseball retirement and manage the Norfolk squad. Under Pressley's guidance, the Tars won the pennant with ease.[49]

During the 1914 season, the story that attracted the most attention from baseball fans in Richmond did not involve the Virginia League but instead focused upon two other leagues: the upstart outlaw Federal League and the Class AA International League. The Baltimore Terrapins of the Federal League created such a financial hardship for the city's International League franchise, the Orioles, that Oriole owner Jack Dunn sought to move his franchise. Richmond was his choice for relocation.[50]

The Federal League had its roots in the failed United States League of 1912. Although the USL was a financial disaster, the league sparked interest in the formation of another league outside of the framework of organized baseball. John T. Powers was the organizer of the Federal League. In 1913 the league was based in the Midwest with franchises in St. Louis, Detroit, Indianapolis, Pittsburgh, Chicago, Cleveland, and Covington, Kentucky, (in midseason this franchise moved to Kansas City). The league was determined to remain independent and took great caution in assembling rosters so as not to enter into direct confrontation with organized baseball.[51]

Encouraged by its success in 1913, the Federal League prepared ambitious plans for 1914. League owners selected James A. Gilmore as the new president and decided to expand into eastern cities. In the plans owners sought new modern stadiums and attempted to sign high caliber ballplayers. The goal was to establish their league as a third major league. The eight-team circuit dropped Cleveland from its roster and positioned new teams in Buffalo, Brooklyn, and Baltimore. The Federal League was able to sign high profile players to contracts and was able to create popular interest in its franchises. The league was now anxious to enter into direct competition with organized baseball. In Baltimore, the Federal League expansion team, the Baltimore Terrapins, built Terrapin Park directly across the street from the Orioles' American Park.[52]

Baltimore had a long and proud history in baseball, especially in the major leagues. In the 1890s, the National League Orioles won three consecutive championships. In 1900, the National League decided to reduce to eight teams and released the Baltimore club. The upstart American League welcomed Baltimore, but, in 1902, the franchise was relocated to New York. Baltimore owner Ned Hanlon attempted to bring another major league team to Baltimore but was unable to secure a franchise in either league. He then purchased the International League franchise from Montreal and moved it to Baltimore. Jack Dunn, a former National Leaguer, was hired as the player-manager of the club in 1907 and guided it to the IL pennant in 1908. Dunn purchased the club from Hanlon in 1909 and established a reputation for developing exceptional baseball prospects. His teams were often regarded as the strongest in the minor leagues.[53]

Ned Hanlon saw the Federal League as the opportunity to restore major league baseball to his beloved Baltimore. The city enthusiastically welcomed the outlaws. Although the Oriole club was widely regarded as having the better talent of the two Baltimore baseball teams, the fans were enchanted by the concept of a return to major league status. On opening day in 1914, a crowed of 28,000 saw the Terrapins, behind the pitching of Jack Quinn, defeat Buffalo 3–2. Scalpers were getting as much as $10 for tickets. The day was celebrated with a parade and the city mayor threw out the first ball. The same day, the Orioles hosted an exhibition game with the New York Giants and drew only 1,500 fans, most of them in attendance only because they could not get tickets for the game across the street.[54]

As the season progressed, the Terrapins routinely drew 20,000 or more. The team played well, remaining in contention for the league pennant until late in the season. The success of the Federal League caused the Orioles to suffer greatly. Attendance figures were measured in the hundreds despite the Orioles' hold on first place in the league. Dunn, facing financial ruin, sought to move his organization to Richmond. Richmond fans were anxious for a higher classification of baseball, and businessmen were eager to promote the city.[55]

In the summer of 1914, Alvin M. Smith, president of the Richmond Business Men's Club, declared an open meeting to discuss the possibility of bringing the Orioles to Richmond. Within three days, organizers were able to secure the support of W.B. Bradley, owner, and Thomas B. McAdams, president of the Virginia League Colts, and raised nearly $15,000 in subscriptions toward the $62,500 purchase price for stock in the club. In the purchase agreement, Dunn reserved fifty percent of the stock for himself and agreed to a twenty-percent cash payment with the balance being paid in installments.[56]

However, the public's enthusiasm for better ball in Richmond was soon crushed by the Virginia League. Despite having the support of the Richmond franchise, the other league magnates voted against the proposal to move the Richmond franchise to Lynchburg and allow the Orioles to relocate to Richmond. At the July 3, 1914, meeting that created the Virginia League split schedule, the directors determined that the city of Richmond was too important to the league's financial success. The move would only be allowed if $15,000 was paid to the league in exchange for the territorial rights to the city. That same day, the International League directors also voted to block the move.[57]

Without the approval of either league, the sale was cancelled. With the denial of the same, Richmond missed the opportunity to have Babe Ruth represent the hometown team on the diamond. Dunn, already having lost over $28,000 on the season, was forced to sell his star players. In a deal worth nearly $25,000, Ernie Shore, Ben Egan and Ruth were sent to the Boston Red Sox. In the end, Dunn sold a total of ten players to several clubs, including the New York Yankees (formerly the Baltimore Orioles; relocated to New York in 1902) and Cincinnati. The Orioles went from being the probable pennant winner to a disappointing fifth place finish.[58]

At the International League's winter meetings, the league owners decided to reverse their position on Dunn's proposal to move to Richmond. Dunn and the Richmond Exhibition Corporation, under the leadership of president Alvin M. Smith, vice-president Dr. William H. Parker and secretary/treasurer Ben W. Wilson were able to bring Dunn and the Orioles to Richmond. To make room for the International League franchise, the Virginia League accepted $12,500 for the territorial rights to the city. W.B. Bradley agreed to surrender his franchise to the city, including the players under reserve so that the Virginia League might relocate the team to a new city. Rocky Mount, North Carolina, was chosen as the expansion city, and the Virginia League extended beyond the borders of the Old Dominion for the first time.[59]

Although Broad Street Park had only been used for two seasons, extensive renovations were needed to meet International League standards. During the winter, the grandstand seating capacity was increased from 2,000 to 2,500, and a large and "more up to date clubhouse" was built with accommodations for the visiting teams. The first two rows of seats were removed and replaced with six rows of chairs, totaling 856. The admission cost for a reserved chair was 75 cents, the highest ticket at the ballpark. Grandstand seats were 50 cents, and general admission for bleachers was 25 cents. Dunn assumed that the local fans would begin to prefer the first-base bleachers more than they had previously, as that was the preferred seating side in northern cities. In addition to changes in seating capacity and comfort, Dunn's most significant improvement was to have turnstiles installed at the park; attendance would no longer have to be estimated or counted by hand.[60]

The city was exuberant in its welcome of the International League to Richmond. Mayor George Ainslie declared a half-day holiday for April 27, 1915, the team's opening day. In the proclamation, he encouraged businesses to close early so that their employees would be able to attend the game. The day was celebrated with an automobile parade followed by a brass band. Dignitaries in the parade included Mayor George Ainslie, Virginia governor Henry Carter Stuart and International League president Ed Barrow. The festive atmosphere drew 7,500 baseball and civic enthusiasts to the park. The excitement was so great that the gates had to be opened a full three hours before the game. The overflow crowd witnessed the home team defeat the visiting Toronto Leafs 11–8.[61]

When Dunn moved the Orioles to Richmond, the club was officially renamed the Virginians. In their opening day game, the team was forced to overcome a deficit four times before gaining the victory. The *Richmond Times-Dispatch* applauded a team "that has the spirit to fight an uphill battle. On all sides they were dubbed the Climbers, and Climbers they shall be called." As had been exhibited in the past, the newspaper took the lead in creating a nickname for the town's team and throughout the season referred to the team not as the Virginians but as the Climbers.[62]

Richmond's first year in the International League was disappointing to many fans. The club finished the season with a 59–81 record and placed seventh in league standings, one place from the cellar. Buffalo was the pennant winner at 85–50 (.632). The only club to finish behind Richmond was Jersey City, 52–85 (.380). Jersey City had been struggling financially for three years in a row and was the subject of constant relocation discussions. The only significant achievement for the Richmond team was turned in by Allen "Rubberarm" Russell. His 239 strikeouts earned him the league title and helped propel him to an eleven-year major league career with the Yankees, Red Sox and Senators. Despite its poor record on the field, the Climbers did attract people to the ballpark. The club's season attendance was second only to that of the league leader, Providence. While Richmond did not fare well in the International League, the relocated Colts, now playing in Rocky Mount, North Carolina, under the name Tarheels, went on to capture the Virginia League pennant.[63]

The month of December 1915 was a tumultuous time for the Richmond franchise. As the International League prepared for its winter meeting, there was speculation that several of the league owners were inclined to drop Richmond from the league. At the close of the season, it was apparent that the Federal League would not return for another season, and with the Federals out of Baltimore, several owners wanted to return the Monumental City to the International League. Jack Dunn stated that he was committed to Richmond unless there was opportunity to reclaim his rights to Baltimore. After a month of intense negotiations, Richmond was able to remain in the International League. The Richmond Exposition Company purchased Dunn's majority interest in the franchise. Dunn then purchased the floundering Jersey City franchise, took the best players from Richmond and relocated to Baltimore. The league also moved the bankrupt Harrisburg franchise to Newark, New Jersey.[64]

Dunn's departure left the Richmond Exposition Company with a baseball franchise but no manager and few players. William Andrew "Uncle Billy" Smith, previously with Atlanta, was chosen to manage the Climbers. He had managed teams for twenty-one seasons and won six minor league championships. Uncle Billy was also a notorious tobacco chewer. It was said that "the tighter the game, the more he chews. And the size of the chew is sometimes immense."[65]

Smith's team opened the season in surprising fashion. The team opened at home with the champion Buffalo Bisons and won 9–7. The Climbers defeated the Bisons in the next two games as well. The Climbers' winning ways continued into early June when they were leading the league. The Richmond boys, however, could not retain the lead throughout the season and found themselves sixth in the standings after splitting a doubleheader with Baltimore on the last day of the season. The final record of 64–75 (.460) was a mere three games ahead of seventh place Rochester. Dunn's Orioles finished third with a record of 74–66 (.529).[66]

In 1917, the Richmond Exposition Company was forced to find a new playing field for the Climbers. The Richmond, Fredericksburg and Potomac Railroad reclaimed the land that had been leased for Broad Street Park so that a new passenger terminal could be built. With assistance from City Council, the Exposition Company was able to purchase the abandoned Lee Park, last used by the United States League in 1912. A contract was awarded to R.M. Anderson & Company to erect a new grandstand. The new ballpark was called Boulevard Field. In its acquisition of the ballpark, the Richmond Exposition Company was re-chartered as the Boulevard Athletic Field Corporation. The leadership remained nearly identical to the original organization. Alvin M. Smith was president, Ben Wilson was secretary/treasurer and Grover C. Duis and William H. Parker were members of the board of directors. The *Times-Dispatch* noted that the ownership arrangement marked the first time in the history of professional baseball in Richmond that the club was the owner of the playing grounds.[67]

The 1917 baseball season opened amid a sense of uncertainty. On April 4, 1917, two weeks before opening day, Congress ratified President Woodrow Wilson's declaration of war. Europe had been engaged in war since 1914, but, for the most part, Americans had been able to continue with relatively normal lives. Now that the country was formally engaged in the war, normal life was sure to end. As the European conflict escalated, attendance at baseball games began to decline. In 1914, when combat started, there were forty-two minor leagues operating in the country; in 1917, only twenty leagues opened the season, and, of these, only twelve would finish the season.[68]

On April 17, 1917, opening day for Richmond in the International League, the usual parade and assembly of dignitaries took on a more patriotic posture than in previous years. The day began with the traditional baseball parade through the streets of the city, ending with the players taking the field before 7,000 fans. The ceremonial first ball was thrown out by Governor Henry Carter Stuart, and the Richmond and Rochester players began the game with Jesse Tannehill, who had played for Richmond in 1895–96, serving as one of the two umpires. The game was halted at the end of the sixth inning when a military parade entered the gates at Boulevard Field. In an effort to help recruit men to meet Virginia's quota of 800 men for the Navy, a parade of Bluejackets, Marines, and the fifty-eight piece Marine Band had marched through the city. As a scheduled part of the parade, the military men entered the stadium and performed drills for the crowd before continuing their march to Capitol Square.[69]

As the sixth inning ended, the sounds of the military bugle corps announced the arrival of the Marines and Bluejackets. At the head of the procession were Captain R.B. Sowell and the Richmond police, followed by a squad of bicycle officers. A man attired as Uncle Sam and riding a "Democratic donkey" was at the head of the column of men in military uniforms. The cheering crowd was brought to its feet as the band played "Dixie" during the entrance procession. After watching the Marines perform marching drills, the crowd was once again brought to its feet as the band played the "Star Spangled Banner." The game resumed after the procession left the field to continue to Capitol Square. In the game, Richmond fell behind three times but managed to rally and tie the score each time. However, the Rochester club emerged victorious in ten innings. [70]

The Climbers struggled in the early part of the season. On May 24, manager Billy Smith was released, and Otto Knabe was named manager. Knabe had formerly played for the Philadelphia Phillies and had managed the Baltimore Terrapins in the Federal League. In 1916, he started the season playing second base for Pittsburgh and ended with Chicago. Besides managing, Knabe also played second base, and it was hoped that he would serve as a mentor to a young local player named Eddie Mooers. [71]

Knabe could do little to help the Climbers as the club finished the season in last place, having a record of 53–94 (.361). The only consolation that Richmond's management and fans could take from the season was that on the last day the club prevented Jack Dunn from having an opportunity to capture the International League pennant. The Climbers were scheduled to play a doubleheader with the Orioles in Richmond. The weather forecast called for rain, and Dunn wanted to have the game switched to Baltimore. The Richmond management refused; the local officials were still upset that Dunn had conspired to return to Baltimore in 1916 with most of Richmond's good players. The final two games between Richmond and Baltimore were cancelled by bad weather. Toronto, under the guidance of player-manager Nap Lajoie, took the pennant by winning both games of a doubleheader with Rochester. [72]

The war had significant effects upon baseball—and especially the minor leagues. Attendance declined as the nation's call to join the armed services took fans from the seats. Others were engaged in labor for the war effort and did not have time for leisure or were afraid to be viewed as slackers by wasting time watching men play a game. Wartime travel restrictions and player military enlistments increased the burdens placed upon ball clubs. In its recap of the 1917 season, the *Times-Dispatch* correctly surmised that the ownership of the Climbers suffered heavy financial losses—the losses being so great that it was speculated the owners were contemplating not fielding a team if the war continued. The same sentiment was shared by many of the owners of International League franchises.[73]

In the spring of 1918, Provost Marshal General Enoch H. Crowder issued a "work or fight" order which mandated that all men of draft age not engaged in work essential to the war effort were subject to the draft. The draft rule cast doubt on the possibility of professional baseball for 1918. As a result, the International League owners voted to disband the league. However, later that day, the owners of the Baltimore, Toronto, Rochester, Buffalo and Newark franchises formed a new league called the New International League. The vote to disband had been a ruse to eliminate Richmond, Montreal and Providence. The owners of the five other clubs reasoned that the clubs on the geographic outskirts of the league strained the feasibility of operating the league within the travel restrictions imposed by the war effort. The new league added teams in Syracuse, Binghamton and Jersey City to complete its roster. With the scheme of five owners, Richmond was out of the International League.[74]

CHAPTER V

The Virginia League Again, 1918–1928, and the Eastern League, 1931–1932

The scheme to oust Richmond, Montreal and Providence from the International League is viewed as trickery only in historical hindsight. The *Richmond Times-Dispatch*'s report of the March 1918 league meeting expressed no shock or outrage at the vote to disband the league and immediately create a new International League. In fact, the paper was quick to fault the residents of Richmond with failure to provide enthusiasm and financial support for the team as the causes for Richmond's failure to remain in organized baseball's highest classification of the minor leagues.[1]

Before the International League owners scheduled the fateful day of meetings that ended the league and formed a new one, Richmond's ability to remain in the league was publicly questioned in the city. On Tuesday, March 26, 1918, an open meeting was held in the auditorium of John Marshall High School to discuss the team's financial past and possibilities for the future. The Sunday, March 24 *Times-Dispatch* printed an article encouraging baseball fans of "every description" to be present at this important meeting and to purchase a subscription for season passes to Virginians' games. The passes were available for $28 and included the war tax levied on amusements. Despite the endorsement of the paper, a mere

125 supporters attended the meeting. At the meeting, it was revealed that the club had averaged $10,000 in losses over the previous two seasons and would need $50,000 to run the ball club in the upcoming season. A minimum of 500 season passes would need to be sold. Ninety-eight subscriptions were sold that night with pledges for eighty-one more.[2]

However, the next day the International League directors voted 6–2 to disband the league. The formal vote was conducted by sealed ballot. In an article on March 29, 1918, it was surmised that the two votes to continue the league were from Jack Dunn of Baltimore and James McCaffrey of Toronto. Another article in the same day's edition of the *Times-Dispatch* reported that Ben Wilson, secretary of the Richmond club, sent a telegram to the paper indicating that the Virginians and the Newark club were the two teams that voted against the motion to disband. Regardless of the vote, the paper noted that the heavy financial losses and the public's failure to support the team made the vote to end the league a necessary action on the part of the organization. The contemporary accounts all pointed to finances as the cause of Richmond's failure to remain in the International League, not a conspiracy by the other owners as listed in most modern accounts of the incident.[3]

Even Alvin Smith, president of the club, had his memory affected by historical hindsight. In an article published in 1954 on the eve of Richmond's return to International League baseball, it was noted that his 1949 recollections of the 1918 events represented a different story than that printed in the 1918 newspapers. He claimed that he had been so taken back by the movement to disband that he hadn't had time to think of fighting it in court. He credited the maneuver by Dunn and the other owners as the only reason Richmond failed to remain in the league. In his support of the 1954 team, he went so far as to say that Richmond had supported play in the International League once before, and he surmised it would do so again. It seems the $10,000 loss and the limited season ticket subscriptions were no longer in his memory as the cause of the Richmond team's demise.[4]

Despite the war conditions and financial struggles of the International League franchise, Richmond did not spend the 1918 season without a professional baseball club. After the International League folded, W.B. Bradley and the Virginia League re-entered Richmond. Bradley, president of the Virginia League, was eager to have Richmond and its potentially large fan base as part of the Virginia League. In the same March 29, 1918, article that announced the vote to dissolve the International League, the *Times-Dispatch* indicated that Bradley and the Virginia League were interested in restoring a team to Richmond.[5]

Richmond's entry into the Virginia League was not accommodated immediately. Throughout the month of April, the Virginia League owners debated three questions: Should the league try to continue despite the war? Should the city of Richmond be admitted into the league despite its failure to support an International League team? If Richmond was admitted, which team would be asked to withdraw?[6]

It took over a month before all of the answers were discovered. Early season amateur games in Richmond drew a greater attendance than the 1917 season average for International League games in the city. Bradley noted that it was originally speculated that the general population and civic organizations "were opposed to amusements while America is at war and were opposed particularly to baseball. That doesn't seem to be the case at present. I think on the whole people want amusement, something to divert their minds from the war." The organizers of the Southern Association of Baseball Clubs shared his sentiments. When they announced their season schedule, team presidents Heineman of New Orleans and Frank of Atlanta speculated that the war year would be good for baseball. While the Virginia League and Southern Association held strong hopes for the 1918 season, few others did. Only nine minor leagues began the season, with none of them playing a complete schedule. Even the National and American Leagues ended their season after the games of Labor Day weekend.[7]

On April 8, 1918, league owners determined that the Virginia League would continue, and they also decided to accept Richmond back into the league. While Bradley had maintained a public interest in including the city, many of the league owners pointed to the March 26 meeting and the lack of popular support for a team in the minors highest classification as cause for concern that they would not support Virginia League ball. After witnessing great support for the amateur leagues in Richmond, the committee seemed comfortable that the Virginia League would be supported by the city. In fact, the league began to recognize that it needed Richmond. "It wants the city," announced Bradley on April 12, "because it has been found necessary in the past existence of the circuit to annex some well-populated and important locality in order to give some push to the baseball season." The only problem was how to fit Richmond into the schedule. All of the current franchises were interested in remaining in the league. Several plans were discussed, including expanding to an eight-club circuit. Prior to the opening of the season, the league owners decided that the Virginia League would feature only four teams in 1918, with the probability of expanding to six in 1919. The four for 1918 were Richmond, Norfolk, Newport News and Petersburg. They adopted a ninety game schedule, and play was to begin on May 23, 1918.[8]

Richmond's 1918 entry in the Virginia League went by the name "Colts" and was led by President Ben W. Wilson and Manager George Stinson. The Colts played their home games at Boulevard Park, which was owned by Wilson's corporation. The players were mostly young men with limited playing experience, consisting mostly of college baseball. On the recommendation of Richmond College baseball coach Frank Dobson, two players with experience on the "Spiders" baseball club were featured on the squad—Malcolm "Mac" Pitt at third base and Thomas "Tom" Miller in centerfield. Pitt, still a collegiate player, was on temporary contract with the club; Miller was given a professional contract with the Colts.[9]

After the turbulent winter, Richmond fans welcomed the first game of the Virginia League season in splendid fashion. Nearly 2,000 fans turned out for the opening day festivities. The day began with the annual parade through the city. The procession originated at the Richmond Hotel, and among those present were Governor Westmoreland Davis and Mayor George M. Ainslee. When the procession concluded at Boulevard Park, Governor Davis threw out the ceremonial first ball. The Colts did not disappoint the fans as they defeated the Petersburg Goobers 4–1. The highlight of the game was Tom Miller's sixth inning homerun over the left field fence.[10]

The season started well, but baseball came to an abrupt end on July 20, 1918. On July 19, Secretary of War Newton D. Baker upheld a lower board's ruling in the draft appeal by Washington catcher Eddie Ainsmith. Ainsmith had been called to military service under the "work or fight" order issued in the spring. In the appeal decision, Baker ruled that baseball was not an essential industry. He recognized that the game provided social value in relaxation and a reprieve from the "stress of intensive industry and occupation." However, in the trying times of war, "the demands of the army and the country are such that we all must make sacrifices, and non-productive employment of able bodied persons useful in the national defense, either as military men or in the industry or commerce of our country, cannot be justified."[11]

The evening of Secretary Baker's decision, Virginia League owners decided that the games of July 20 would be the last of the season. During the deliberations to end the season, it was proposed that the clubs should finish out the month of July, but the motion did not receive a second. The decision to end the next day was passed unanimously. One reason the owners closed the season quickly was declining attendance, especially in Richmond. The poor attendance was not necessarily attributed to low interest by the fans, but rather the draft. Many of the typical spectators were engaged in military service.

The Colts entered the final day of the season in second place, behind Newport News. Both ball clubs had twenty-eight victories, but the Shipbuilders had only lost twenty games, compared to Richmond's twenty-one defeats. By chance, the two teams were scheduled to face each other at Boulevard Field on July 20 and provided the league with a championship match-up. The Colts took advantage of the opportunity and won the game 5–2 and captured the pennant with 29 victories (.586) compared to 28 (.571) for Newport News. Both teams had 21 losses.[12]

When the Armistice was signed ending the war at 6:00 a.m. on November 11, 1918, there was immediate hope that baseball would return in 1919. Return it did. Baseball saw a resurgence that was similar to the boom experienced after the Civil War and the Spanish-American War. Attendance at major league games doubled in 1919 and hit nine million in 1920. The Virginia League took advantage of the renewed interest in the game. For 1919, the league expanded to six clubs, adding Suffolk and Portsmouth. They adopted a split season, with the first half ending on July 5 and the second on Labor Day. The league also sought higher status, petitioning for Class B protection in organized baseball. With the higher rank, an improved caliber of players was sought and the salary limit was set at $1,600 with a restriction of no more than thirteen players to a team.[13]

During the off-season, the Colt management agreed to hire Frank Dobson, coach of the Richmond College Spiders, to manage the team. His tenure with the club began with a 9–6 loss to the Petersburg Goobers on opening day. The next day, the Colts lost the second game of the year to the Goobers 5–1. Dobson's Colts continued to suffer, amassing a 3–8 (.273) record by May 26 when it was announced that the club was seeking a new manager.[14]

B.W. Wilson was able to sign Charles Albert "Chief" Bender as the new player-manager. Bender, a native of the Chippewa tribe through the maternal side of the family tree, gained the nickname "Chief" as a result of his mother's heritage. He earned fame as a pitcher on Connie Mack's champion Philadelphia Athletics, playing for the club from 1903 to 1914. With the Athletics, Bender was part of five pennant teams, and he became the first pitcher to earn six World Series victories. In 1915, Bender played in Baltimore with the Federal League. His major league career ended in 1917 with the Philadelphia Phillies. He was elected to the Hall of Fame in 1953. When Ben Wilson signed Bender to join the Colts as player-manager, the Chief was trying to revive his major league career and was in negotiations with Pat Moran, manager of the Cincinnati Reds. Bender, however, was more impressed with Wilson's offer and took over the Colts on May 29, 1919.[15]

Bender took control of a team with a 4–10 record and began to turn things around immediately. In the first game, the Colts won 8–4. By the end of the first half of the season, the club had moved out of last place and had a 20–31 (.392) record. Petersburg claimed the first half title with a 33–18 (.647) record. In the second half, Bender's Tribe (or Indians, as the Richmond team was affectionately referred to by this time) easily captured the pennant with a 40–19 (.678) record. Norfolk finished in a distant second at 33–27 (.550). In appreciation of his efforts, the Richmond fans, under the guidance of Norman Johnson, created a fund drive to raise $2,000 to purchase an automobile for Bender. This fund, plus a contribution by owner Wilson, was sufficient to present Bender a new automobile at the end of the season.[16]

The Indians' second half pennant should have set the stage for a seven-game Virginia League Championship Series between Richmond and Petersburg. However, a dispute over rules and financial arrangements prevented the two teams from determining a season champion. The rules dispute was between the owners of the ball clubs. Ben Wilson contended that the games should be played at alternate locations, with Petersburg, the first half winner, hosting the first game and Richmond the second. His plan would have the Saturday game in Richmond. Mr. Kidd, owner of the Petersburg team, contended that the National Agreement rules provided that the first two games be played at the home park of the first season champ. Wilson wanted the home team to retain the grandstand receipts while dividing the daily revenue with the players in a 50–50 share. Kidd contended that Wilson was attempting to over-commercialize the series and retain more profit for himself, especially by conniving to have the Saturday game played in Richmond. To complicate matters, the Petersburg players threatened to strike on grounds that the owners were attempting to take money away from the players. Their contention was that the National Agreement provided that the gate receipts from the first four games of the series were to be divided amongst the players of both teams with the owners earning the profits from any of the remaining games. This plan ensured that players would earn a minimum of two-thirds of the post-season gate receipts compared to Wilson's fifty-percent plan. As a result of the disputes, the series was cancelled.[17]

In 1920, the Virginia League expanded to eight clubs, adding two North Carolina teams—Rocky Mount and Wilson. The league again decided to employ the split season. This year the championship series did not have the dispute as occurred in 1919. The Colts, behind a new manager Lee Gooch, easily captured the first half by winning 43 and losing only 14 games. Their outstanding record gave them an eleven and a half game margin over second place Portsmouth (33–27, .550). At the mid-point in the season, the 1920 ball club brought about comparisons to Perry Lipe's 1908 Richmond team. The *Times-Dispatch* noted that the remarkable aspect of the 1920 club was that there were no "stars" on the team. The Colts exhibited solid ability at all positions. At the end of the season, several of the Richmond players were sought by major league teams. Pitcher Mike Kircher was sold to the St Louis Cardinals, and the Chicago White Sox drafted first baseman Jimmy Poole and pitcher Guy McWhorter. The Sox also expressed interest in shortstop Luke Stuart and second baseman Jesse Baker. After the season, the third baseman, "Bing" Arragon, returned home to Cuba to play on a Cuban all-star team in a barnstorming tour with a team of major league all-stars made up of many members of the New York Giants and Yankee's star Babe Ruth.[18]

The Colts' early success was not duplicated in the second half of the season. They finished 33–25 in third place behind first place Portsmouth (39–19, .672) and second finisher Petersburg (39–22, .639). The league championship series featured Richmond and Portsmouth, with the opening game being hosted by Portsmouth with an alternating home and away rotation. The league made certain that disputes over the location would not cancel the series as it did the year before. But, despite the league's efforts, there was a minor controversy before the series started. A few days before the pennant series, the Truckers sold their shortstop, Pie Traynor, to the Pittsburgh Pirates for $10,000. The club then petitioned the Colts to allow them to play Rocky Mount's star shortstop, a man named Champlin. Ben Wilson refused on the grounds that the club was already playing a utility man named Winston who was acquired after the league date for roster changes. The league rules mandated that a player had to be with the club thirty days previous to the post-season series. Wilson's contention was that the series was to be played by the Colts and Truckers, not by a collection of all-stars. Wilson gave in when he realized that he did not have the backing of league president Bradley, "as he did not want to cheat his boys out of the series."[19]

The contest proved exciting. The opening game, a 5–5 tie before a crowd of 7,000, was called on account of darkness. The clubs then traded at-home victories—the Colts winning 2–1 at Boulevard Park and the Truckers winning 8–3 in Portsmouth. The Colts took control of the series by winning the next two games, 3–0 in Richmond and 6–2 in Portsmouth. The Truckers rebounded 7–4 before 5,000 fans on Saturday afternoon at Boulevard Park and then evened the series on Monday with a 5–2 victory. The Truckers then captured the Virginia League pennant with a 10–9 thriller in the deciding game.[20]

A few days after the close of the 1920 season, Ben Wilson announced that his mercantile business was requiring more time and that he was relinquishing active ownership of the Richmond baseball club. He stated that he would retain his controlling interest in the club but that he was employing Ken E. Finlay to serve as president of the Richmond club. Finlay, owner of the Broadway Theater in Richmond, was the former owner of the pennant-winning London Baseball Club of the Canadian League. A native Canadian, he had been a college star in both ice hockey and lacrosse.[21]

In addition to bringing championship experience to the Richmond club, Finlay was able to establish a working relationship with lower minor league circuits. One of his theatrical associates was the owner of the Danville club of the Piedmont League. He and Wilson intended to utilize this relationship to have the Class D Danville club serve as a "training ground" for future Colts. Finlay's plan to develop the Danville club as a farm team was built upon a concept started by Robert Hedges in 1913 and popularized by Branch Rickey throughout the 1920s. Rickey's St. Louis Cardinals farm system began in 1920 with part ownership of the Houston Buffaloes in the Texas League. By 1928, the cardinals owned, in whole or in-part, seven minor league franchises and controlled thirty-two franchises by 1940. Rickey's use of the farm system played a pivotal role in the development of the St. Louis Cardinals World Champion Gashouse Gang of the 1930s. Finlay's relationship with the Danville club insured the Colts would have a steady supply of ballplayers in the upcoming season and beyond. With Finlay as club president, exciting times were expected for the Colts. Most expectations were for action on the field, but during the Virginia League winter meetings the Colts were once again at the center of a controversy that threatened to destroy the league.[22]

At the winter meetings, the league magnates agreed to follow the lead of the major leagues and prohibit the spitball and "other freak deliveries." The salary limit for players was established at $2,800, with a committee of three created to enforce the rule. All Virginia League members supported both decisions. The controversy once again centered on Saturday games, and club owners voted that no team would host more than two-thirds of the Saturday contests. These games generated the greatest attendance and were the most profitable. Wilson hoped to utilize the strengths of having one of the strongest ball clubs in the circuit and his location in the city with the greatest attendance to persuade the committee to commit a home game to the capital city each week. The two-thirds rule was not acceptable to Wilson. He stated, "Unless Richmond is given 100 percent Saturday games, you can consider me out. My franchise will be disposed of and the league can make other plans." He initially conceded that he would be willing to rent his ballpark to "some person acceptable to him should a change in ownership of the Colts" be necessary. A week later he modified the statement, clarifying that if the league refused to grant Richmond home games every Saturday and a new franchise was sought for the city, they would have to erect their own playing grounds. Wilson owned two-fifths of the stock of the Boulevard Field Corporation and had the support of the other stockholders.[23]

To support the position that Saturday games were vital to Richmond, Wilson released figures that revealed that all league members benefited from Saturday games played in the capital city. Under league rules, a portion of the gate receipts were shared by the home and visiting team. On holiday games, the total league attendance was pooled and shared evenly by all eight clubs. In 1920, Richmond paid out $10,570.70 to the visitors and received $7,657.91 for its road games. The club received $2,912.79 less than they paid out. In the holiday pool, Richmond contributed a league high of $5,728.87. Norfolk was second with $4,602.86, and Newport News contributed the least at $1,171.03. Each team received $2,808.35 in pooled funds. Ben Wilson contended that "under no other conditions can we operate without a loss and we must have all Saturday contests."[24]

After the dispute of the October meeting, the league owners reconvened on Saturday, November 6, 1920, to determine the 1921 schedule. To enter a team in the Virginia League, each owner needed to furnish a bond of $2,000 to the league treasury. Wilson refused to attend the meeting or post the guarantee unless he was assured of at least twenty home Saturdays. The other moguls denied this request, and, by failing to submit the fee, Wilson, in effect, surrendered the franchise. The seven other owners unanimously voted to declare Wilson's stake forfeited. The league decided to explore its options: scale back to a six-club circuit (if a current member was willing to withdraw); accept an offer from one of the several interested parties in Richmond for the franchise rights; or seek a new city for the eighth Virginia League franchise.[25]

The Virginia League franchise committee headed by C. Moran Barry, owner of the Norfolk club, spent several months determining the fate of the Virginia League. The committee agreed that it was important for the league to have a team in Richmond. Of the several interested parties, the committee selected Jake Wells as the new franchise owner. Wells had not been active in baseball since he sold his Richmond franchise to W.B. Bradley so that he could devote his time to his movie and vaudeville theater business. Wells was the principal owner and president of the new organization. Ray Ryan was brought in to manage the club and serve as secretary of the Richmond Baseball Club when the team became a registered corporation. Included in the list of associates were H.C. Ebel, Ware B. Gray and Virginia League president William B. Bradley as business manager.[26]

While the league was still deciding upon proper title of the Richmond franchise, the new ownership group was preparing plans for the construction of a new ballpark. By the end of December 1920, it was announced that surveyors and engineers deemed Mayo Island an acceptable site for construction of a modern facility that would be suitable for both baseball and football. Mayo Island had not been used for baseball since the failure of the original Virginia League. The construction contracts with H. Carl Messerschmidt, architect, and E.L. Bass and Brothers, builders, were signed on February 11, 1921. The *Times-Dispatch* reported that the organization filed the application for a building permit the next day.[27]

The permit called for the park and its facilities to be on east side of the twenty-acre island. Island Park, as the facility was named, was situated between the 14th Street Bridge and the Seaboard AirLine Railway bridge and was adjacent to the Virginia Boat Club. The permit described the overall dimensions of the park as 400 by 500 feet, with a "frontage of 200 by 60 feet." The playing field measured 294 feet down the left field line, 400 feet to centerfield and 356 feet down the right field side of the grounds. A few feet beyond the left field fence was the James River. A wall was constructed on the left field playing area to help prevent stray baseballs. Spectators would sit in boats in hopes of gathering in a water-soaked homerun ball. The original plan estimated the construction costs to be $12,000. A year later, it was reported that the total cost amounted to $66,333, inclusive of the purchase of the lot and construction of the park.[28]

Despite the construction of Island Park, Boulevard Park was not to remain idle in the summer of 1921. Ben Wilson sought to create a baseball war in the city. Wilson and the Amateur Baseball Commission of Richmond came to an agreement that had the various amateur leagues playing doubleheaders every Saturday and presented the option for two or three weekday contests. With the opportunity for a first-class baseball field, the Amateur Association saw its ranks increase to thirty-four teams playing in eight different leagues.[29]

Despite the fact that Boulevard Field was not controlled by a club that subscribed to the National Agreement, Wilson was also able to secure a major league exhibition game between the Brooklyn Dodgers and New York Yankees for April 7, 1921. Ed Barrow, business manager for the

Yankees, wrote that he was satisfied with the arrangements and assured that the game would be played. The Yankees ball club featured two former Richmond players—Jack Quinn who had played for the Colts in 1908 and "Chick" Fewster who played third base when Jack Dunn brought his International League franchise to Richmond. However, the main attraction for Richmond fans was the opportunity to watch Babe Ruth play baseball.[30]

Wilson's version of a baseball war against the Virginia League was not limited to the amateur season and major league exhibition games at his park. He filed suit in the City Circuit Court against the Virginia League and the owners of the seven franchises that forfeited his team. In his court case, Wilson claimed that the expulsion of his team was illegal, and he sought $50,000 damages, that total being his estimated value of the franchise, the value of the eight reserved ballplayers claimed by the league, and his percentage of the league treasury. The players represented the largest portion of the total at $30,000. The league responded that it had acted within the bounds of the rules of Organized Baseball. The case marked the first time that the validity of these rules/laws were challenged in court. At the end of the trial, a jury awarded Wilson $6,500. In the league's appeal of the verdict, Judge R. Carter Scott upheld the amount of restitution. Bradley, as league president, and the other six organizations and their owners were ruled liable for the $6,500 damages.[31]

Despite Wilson's lawsuit, the Virginia League forged ahead with plans for the 1921 season. The league once again featured eight cities, with two in North Carolina. The split schedule was adopted with the two winners meeting in a championship series. During the series, sixty percent of the gate receipts of the first four games was pooled for players. The winning team earned sixty percent of the pool, and the remainder went to the second place finishers. The season schedule was lengthened to provide each team with 138 games, sixty-nine at home and sixty-nine on the road. The increased number of games pushed the end of the season to September 24, the latest baseball had been played in the Virginia League. The Richmond club was awarded home games on sixteen of the season's twenty-two Saturdays. League admission prices were fixed at 40 cents for general admission with grandstand seating prices left to the discretion of the home team. At Island Park, the grandstand seats cost patrons an additional 20 cents. Admission for ladies was 25 cents, and boys were admitted for only 20 cents. The admission prices included the war tax on entertainment that began being levied while the United States was engaged in the World War I.[32]

The 1921 season began in Richmond with the traditional fanfare of parades, political dignitaries, and a crowd of 7,000 on hand to witness the Colts' 6–5 loss to the Petersburg team. After losing the second game of the season 14–3 to Petersburg on their home field, the Colts won the third game 7–5. This up and down momentum continued for the Colts throughout the season. On May 14, the Colts climbed atop the league standings but held the lead for only one week. The club finished the first half of the season with a 30–30 (.500) record and in fourth place. Rocky Mount and Wilson finished at the top with 38–25 (.603) records. Portsmouth finished third at 34–38 (.472). The first half pennant was awarded to Rocky Mount on July 18, when the Wilson Broncos and Richmond Colts played the last three innings of a game that had been abbreviated earlier in the season. Richmond won the game 10–4 and improved its first half record to 31–30.[33]

The second half of the season was riddled with controversy. Poor play led to decreased popular support and financial troubles in Petersburg. When the grandstand was destroyed by fire, the club could not afford to rebuild, so the league was forced to move the team. The franchise was awarded to the ownership group in Tarboro, North Carolina. At the time of the move, the club had amassed a paltry 4–22 (.154) record and was in last place. However, the franchise shift was the least of the league's troubles. Violations of the league salary limit by the strongest clubs instigated a series of protests that once again threatened the stability of the league.[34]

As the season neared the midway point, protests were raised against Rocky Mount and Wilson over abuses of the salary limit. Since the clubs finished at the top of the league standings in July, the first half pennant championship and a berth in the league playoff was in question. Although the league had awarded the pennant to Rocky Mount, the Portsmouth and Newport News clubs appealed to Judge Kenesaw Mountain Landis, the commissioner of Organized Baseball, in hopes of having the league decision overruled. In a decision delivered on September 10, Judge Landis determined that the Carolina teams were in violation of the limit and awarded the pennant to the Portsmouth Truckers. At the time of the ruling, the Wilson Bugs had a commanding lead in the second half race. President Bradley utilized the Landis ruling to nullify all of Wilson's games previous to July 23, the date that the club's salary level was reduced to meet the league limit. As a result of the ruling, the Bugs went from first to fourth and Norfolk, at 46–28 (.622), was able to claim the second half pennant. Portsmouth, the first half winner, finished second at 44–28 (.611), and Richmond was third at 44–29 (.603). Norfolk and Portsmouth squared off for the season flag.[35]

While Norfolk and Portsmouth met in the official Virginia League title series, the Carolina teams paired up for their own championship series. They contended that most of the other clubs in the league were also in violation of the salary limit. Therefore, the season titles should be restored to Rocky Mount and Wilson. As the winners of each half of the season, their owners felt that the clubs should be contending for the league flag. In hopes that Judge Landis would rule in their favor, the clubs staged their own league championship series. Rocky Mount defeated the Bugs in four of the five games to claim the unofficial pennant.[36]

In the league-sanctioned series, controversy continued. After five games, Portsmouth had a 3–2 game edge over Norfolk. However, the series was never finished. The Norfolk players were in disagreement with the management over the players' share of the post-season gate receipts. In reaction to management, the players established a plan to "laydown" the series to Portsmouth. Some players even purchased rail tickets to take them home after the sixth game of the series, proving that they had no intention of trying to win and extend the series to a seventh and deciding game. At the request of Mr. Barry, the Norfolk team owner, the Virginia League began an investigation of the allegations against the Norfolk players. In the end, Portsmouth was awarded the league championship.[37]

As in the previous seasons, the fate of the Virginia League was in doubt during the winter. Two teams were placing claim on the league pennant. The Petersburg team folded in August, and the replacement Tarboro, North Carolina franchise was not entirely stable. The Suffolk team nearly folded as the season ended, and that city was unlikely to continue to support a baseball franchises. Many of the owners were dissatisfied with the league in 1921 as a result of the disputes and a sense of disunion defined by state boundaries was being formed. To add further to the league's troubles, W.B. Bradley, citing conflicts of interest in his dual role as a member of the management for the Richmond Colts and as league president, announced his resignation from the presidency on February 2, 1922.[38]

The selection process for a new president only increased the tension among the Virginia League ball clubs. In the early discussions, Rocky Mount and Wilson supported the election of W.G. Branham, president of the Piedmont League and a resident of Durham, North Carolina. The Virginia clubs were split in their support of Frank Lawrence of Petersburg and Edward R. Willcox of Norfolk. After two months of heated debate, the league moguls finally elected William S. Moye of the Rocky Mount club as Bradley's successor.[39]

Under the new leadership, the Virginia League embarked on the 1922 season with only six teams; Suffolk and Tarboro (transferred from Petersburg) opted not to field ball clubs. In a departure from tradition, the Colts did not open the season at home, nor was the rival Petersburg Goobers the inaugural opponent. The Richmond club traveled to Newport News to play the Shipbuilders on opening day. Although the Colts were not playing at home, Governor E. Lee Trinkle, accompanied by Hiram Smith, his chief of staff, and several Newport News city officials were on hand for the opening day ceremonies. The festivities included the governor throwing out the first ball, although his toss was about six feet short of the plate. Unfortunately, the Colts' effort in the game came up just as short as the governor's; the Shipbuilders won 9–2.[40]

The opening day loss was indicative of the early part of the season for the Colts. The Colts returned home and won only once in their first six games. After this dismal week, Ray Ryan resigned as manager of the Richmond club and returned to Welch, West Virginia, where he owned an automobile business. Left fielder John B. Keller served as interim manager until club officials named Ruben "Rube" Oldring as manager on May 30. In the month that Keller was the leader of the Colts, the club improved slightly. However, it was still in last place in the Virginia League with a 12–20 (.375) record.[41]

Oldring had gained notoriety while he was a teammate of Chief Bender on Connie Mack's championship Athletics. Richmond baseball fans became familiar with Oldring during the 1919 season when he was the player/manager of the Suffolk team. In his first few weeks at the helm of the Colts, Oldring made several personnel changes with the hopes of strengthening the ball club. In his efforts to secure talent, Oldring established a player loan arrangement with "Chief" Bender who was the manager of the baseball club in Reading, Pennsylvania. Oldring, however, was unable to change the fortunes of the club; Richmond ended the season in the league cellar with a record of 49–68 (.419). Wilson won the season title with a 68–52 (.567) showing. [42]

At the close of the 1922 season, prospects for the continuation of the Virginia League were questionable. The 1922 season was a financial disaster for all teams, with only Richmond and Norfolk reported as being able to break even. The other clubs were not as fortunate. In May of 1922, poor attendance in Rocky Mount prompted the owners to offer their team to Lynchburg. The Hill City, citing the "shaky" financial condition of the existing clubs, declined the offer. Rocky Mount was able to stay in the league when the circuit's directors voted to have gate receipts shared by the visiting and home clubs rather than going solely to the home team.[43]

The Richmond club was not immune to financial trouble. In mid–

July, the club stockholders met to discuss the team's "state of affairs." According to the schedule, the Colts were about to embark on a four-week period (July 15–August 17) in which they would have only three home games. Attendance had been declining, and, with a prolonged absence, it was likely to continue. After the other league owners refused Richmond's plea to alter the schedule, the local owners questioned the value of continuing their investment in baseball. Since the present owners took control of the club in 1921, the stockholders had invested over $74,000, including land and construction of a ballpark, and had yet to see a positive return on their investment. However, the owners reasoned that since a $2,000 bond had been pledged to the league, it would be wise to play out the season.[44]

About two weeks after the owners' decision to continue the 1922 season, it was announced that the ownership of the Richmond club had been sold. The present structure had the Richmond Baseball Club with Jake Wells, president; McGinnis Hatfield, vice-president; H.C. Ebel, treasurer; and W.B. Bradley, secretary and business manager. The team owned both Mayo Island Park and the Virginia League baseball franchise rights in Richmond. In the new structure, the corporation sold the franchise rights and players of the Richmond team but retained ownership of Island Park. The president of the new franchise owners was James E. Crass. Crass had been a substantial shareholder in the previous ownership group and had been one of the investors that purchased the Richmond Climbers of the International league from Jack Dunn in 1916. In the new ownership structure, Rube Oldring expanded his role with the Colts. He was one of the new shareholders, but he continued as field manager and also assumed the role of business manager of the club.[45]

In the months before the 1923 season was to start, the Virginia League once again faced threats to its existence. Although all six clubs made a commitment to the continuation of the league, threats by other leagues seeking to add Richmond and Norfolk and the troubled sale of Newport News made the 1923 season seem unlikely. Being the only financially stable clubs in the circuit and the largest centers of population in Virginia made the cities of Richmond and Norfolk attractive to circuits seeking southern expansion. Earnest C. Landgraf proposed one such league. Landgraf's first involvement with baseball in Richmond occurred during the failed outlaw United States League's lone season in 1912. He had been the owner of the Richmond Rebels franchise. After the league folded, he had returned to the northeastern states and remained active in various leagues and cities in organized baseball. In 1922, he presented a plan for a "North and South" League (also referred to as the "Atlantic

League") that would potentially feature several teams in eastern Pennsylvania, such as Allentown, Harrisburg, York, Lancaster or Easton, Trenton in New Jersey, Wilmington in Delaware, and Richmond, Norfolk and possibly Portsmouth in Virginia. The newspapers in the three Virginia cities were all anxious for a higher classification of baseball. Despite the encouragement of the press to abandon the Virginia League, the owners of the three teams pledged that they were committed to the idea of the Virginia League. They stated that they would only seek other league affiliation if H.P. Dawson could not sell his Newport News franchise and the Virginia League could not exist as a six-club circuit.[46]

Dawson was having difficulty finding a buyer for the franchise rights. He announced his intention to sell the rights in July when the Richmond stockholders were contemplating quitting the season. At the time, he expressed a desire to purchase the Richmond franchise if he could sell the Newport News club. League officials hoped that Petersburg would be encouraged to acquire the rights to the vacant franchise. However, baseball men in that city passed on the opportunity. Dawson and the league then turned their attention to Wilmington, North Carolina. It seemed as if interests in that city would accept the franchise, but the offer was declined. Kinston, North Carolina, inquired about the franchise, but league moguls questioned that city's ability to support Class B baseball. After nearly six months of attempting to move the franchise, Petersburg finally accepted the Virginia League on January 13, 1923, and the Goobers were once again part of the circuit.[47]

With the sale of the Newport News club, James E. Crass and H. P. Dawson were able to announce the sale of the Richmond club to Dawson. The *Richmond Times-Dispatch* reported in November 1922 that a sale agreement had been reached but that it was contingent upon the Newport News sale. Dawson's first action as owner of the Richmond Colts was to announce that David Robertson was signed to manage the club. Robertson had played with the New York Giants and had a busy sporting goods store and insurance business in Norfolk. Dawson also announced that he was leaving his position with the Seaboard Airlines Railroad in Portsmouth and was accepting another position with the company that would allow him to live in Richmond and focus on the ball club in the spring and summer months.[48]

Under Robertson's leadership, the first year of Dawson's ownership of the Colts was a very successful one. The club finished with nine victories in the last ten games, including a 17–5 walloping of the Rocky Mount Broncos in the last game. The fantastic finish left the Colts in a frustrating situation—only .001 behind the Wilson Bugs. The Colts had

71 wins and 53 losses (.573), while Wilson won 70 games but lost only 52 (.574). The Colts were not ready to concede the pennant and appealed to Virginia League President Moye that Wilson and Rocky Mount should be compelled to play the rain-cancelled game from the last week of the season. His ruling, with the backing of Mike Sexton, President of the National Association of Baseball Clubs, was that Wilson, as the home team, had the prerogative to decide if the game should be replayed. G.T. Fulgham, owner of the Wilson club chose not to play, recognizing that a victory meant little but a loss would cost him the pennant.

Dawson then made a second appeal, this time in an attempt to have one of Richmond's losses discounted. In reviewing the schedule, it was discovered that the Colts and the Petersburg Trunkmakers had played each other one game more than they were scheduled. The extra game was the result of a rain-delayed game being played while Mr. Pleasants, the official scorekeeper for the Petersburg club, had been ill. During one of the Richmond and Petersburg series in August, the game was played, but Pleasants did not receive a copy of the score report. When the clubs then met in the first week of September, he advised the Petersburg ownership that the two clubs had a postponed game to play. Dawson contended that the "extra" game, a Richmond loss on September 4, should not count in the standings. Moye ruled against the Colts, and the Bugs captured the 1923 Virginia League championship.[49]

In September, President Moye announced that he would not seek re-election at the league's winter meetings. His principal reason for resigning his position was the lack of cooperation among league owners. He declared, "Not for ten times the salary now paid would I again consent to serve." Dave Robertson had a similar impression of the Virginia League and announced his retirement as Colts' manager. He cited poor handling of league affairs as his reasons for not wanting to remain affiliated with the league. Richmond owner H.P. Dawson was also outraged at the management of league affairs and threatened to sue the Wilson club and President Moye.[50]

When the league's winter meeting was held in January, the attitudes of all three men had changed. W.S. Moye cited his two years of experience which placed him in a better position to run the league than any other candidate. He was selected for a third term as league president. Dave Robertson indicated his desire to return to the Colts, but the club released him on December 13, 1923. He was later hired to manage his hometown Norfolk Tars. H.P. Dawson had filed an injunction against the Wilson Bugs to prevent them from receiving the gate receipts from the championship series that pitted the Virginia League pennant winners against the South Atlantic League champion. When the Virginia League Board of Directors voted Wilson as the rightful titleholder, Dawson dropped his claim to the title.[51]

With the pennant controversy and league presidency decided, the league members were able to concentrate on preparation for the 1924 season. In February, Dawson announced that Jack Onslow, a former big league catcher for the New York Giants and Detroit Tigers, would serve as player-manager for the 1924 edition of the Richmond Colts. The Colts also featured two players from Cuba. Angel "Bing" Arragon was with Richmond briefly when the club was in the International League. He then was with the New York Yankees before returning to the minor leagues in Toledo. He came back to Richmond in 1920 and became a fan favorite as the Colts' third baseman. In the off-seasons, Arragon continued to play on Cuban all-star teams that participated in barnstorming tours with major league all-stars. The other Cuban player on the Colts' roster was Jose Ramos, an outfielder. Ramos also proved popular with the fans and enjoyed a career with the Colts that lasted through the 1925 season. Other members of the 1924 squad included Hal Weafer at first base and Guy Lacy at second. Joining Ramos in the outfield were Al Malonee and mid-season acquisition Stanley Stack. In addition to Onslow, Tommy Abbott served as backup catcher. The pitching stars were Frank Dodson, Joe Maley and Benson Brillhart.[52]

This combination of players secured the 1924 pennant for Richmond as the Colts compiled a record of 76–59, edging out runner-up Portsmouth (75–60). Similar to the controversy that tainted Wilson's claim to the 1923 pennant, Richmond's championship was marred by games not played on account of rain. As the Virginia League entered the last week of play, the Colts held onto a one-and-a-half game lead over Portsmouth. The Richmond club was scheduled to play three games at Portsmouth and then finish with three games at home against Wilson. The Truckers finished the season with three games against Rocky Mount and one postponed game against Norfolk. Rain, however, canceled all three games between Richmond and Portsmouth. Richmond was only able to manage a single victory in the three games against Wilson. Portsmouth won the first two games but lost both of its games on the final day. Richmond earned the pennant by a two-game margin. Frank Lawrence, Portsmouth owner, appealed to H.P. Dawson to play a three-game series to decide the pennant. Dawson refused, stating, "If I had been given consideration in the past, I would be disposed to accept the challenge." Lawrence, recognizing that league rules took the pennant from Richmond the previous season, now supported the Colts' claim to the flag and conceded the title to

Richmond without continued protest. Lawrence said, "The fates were against me. Congratulations."[53]

For the first time since the Virginia League was founded, the league appeared stable going into the off-season. The Petersburg franchise was once again for sale, but this time there were several cities including Danville, Lynchburg, and Kinston vying for the rights to the vacant franchise. After Kinston, North Carolina, was accepted as the league's sixth city, the board of directors considered expanding the league to encompass eight ball clubs. However, bids from groups in Petersburg and Danville were rejected as "too vague." In December, William G. Bramham, president of both the South Atlantic League and the Piedmont League, was unanimously selected to succeed William S. Moye as president of the Virginia League. He then served as president for all three leagues. The directors of the Virginia League were excited for the future of the league in 1925.[54]

During the off-season, Dawson did little to disrupt the Colts 1924 pennant-winning lineup, as many of that squad's members returned for the 1925 season. The most significant change occurred in the field management of the club. Jack Onslow left Richmond after the 1924 season to become a coach with the Pittsburgh Pirates, where he helped guide the team to the World Series. Dawson was unable to find a suitable manager and decided to open the season running the club himself. However, after a few weeks, he turned the managing duties over to field captain and second baseman Guy Lacy. After three weeks, Lacy relinquished the managing duties so that he could concentrate on his playing. Dawson resumed management for a brief period when Lacy was once again placed at the helm. Under Lacy's guidance, the club broke out of a pack of four teams that were grouped within five points of each other on August 22 and claimed the league flag for the second consecutive season. The Colts push to the front was keyed by a sixteen-game winning streak that ended when Portsmouth pitcher Joe Poetz no-hit the Colts for a 5–1 victory. The Colts finished the year at 79–54 (.594), and Portsmouth was the runner-up with a 74–59 (.536) record.[55]

The Colts' 1925 championship season was earned by outstanding individual performances. Otis Carter set a Virginia League record by hitting forty-one homeruns during the season. He then belted three more in the championship series with South Atlantic League champ Spartanburg. Hal Weafer won the league season batting title with a .398 average. Strong performances sent four players to a higher classification. Carter and Manager Lacy were sold to the New York Giants; the Yankees recalled pitcher Ben Shields; and Jose Ramos moved up to a Class A ball club.

Also during the season, Richmond fans were pleased to see the return of Richmond native and middle infielder Eddie Mooers. Mooers had first played with the Colts in 1917. He then played with Newark and Baltimore in the International League for several seasons. In 1923, he bought out his contract, retired from professional baseball and returned to Richmond. He remained active in the local amateur leagues and came out of retirement in the summer of 1925.[56]

The Colts' consecutive claims to the Virginia League pennant continued in 1926. The team earned the Virginia League pennant by finishing the season with a 83–68 record. Troy Agnew replaced Lacy as the player-manager for 1926. However, on July 19, health problems forced him to resign, and his replacement was former manager Rube Oldring. Oldring managed the team to the pennant. As in the previous season, outstanding performances helped the ball club. Stanley Stack eclipsed Otis Carter's Virginia League homerun record by hitting forty-four round trippers, and six Colts finished with batting averages above .309; four pitchers finished the season with at least seventeen victories. Two local men played significant roles on the club: pitcher Taylor "Deacon" Joliff, a graduate of the University of Richmond, won four games in the last eight days of the season and Eddie Mooers became recognized as a team leader. Many of the other managers in the league regarded Mooers as the keystone of the Colts' success.[57]

In addition to seeing winning baseball, the Richmond fans enjoyed a new grandstand on Mayo Island. The original grandstand and bleachers were destroyed by fire in June 1923 when a fan carelessly dropped a cigarette on a "waste heap under the stands." Within two weeks of the incident, a new grandstand was erected; however, the new facility provided limited seating. It was not until the winter of 1926 that a new steel grandstand was constructed. The new facility increased seating capacity to 6,000 and featured "opera-style" seats. The club utilized the occasion of the new construction to honor Edward Christopher "Pop" Tate, one of Richmond's first baseball heroes, by renaming Island Park as Tate Field. Tate, a Richmond native, was part of the first professional team to play in Richmond. He enjoyed a major league career with Boston and Baltimore in the late 1880s and 1890s. After his tenure in the major leagues, Tate continued his baseball career by playing, managing, and umpiring in the minor leagues. When his baseball days were over, Tate joined the Richmond police department and delighted baseball fans with appearances on the policeman's amateur team.[58]

Despite winning the pennant and having a new ballpark, the 1926 season was not a complete success for the Colts. Although the team won their third consecutive pennant, the club witnessed a decline in attendance. The ticket prices remained stable with grandstand tickets at 75 cents, covered bleacher seats at 65 cents, general admission 50 cents, colored bleachers 35 cents, and boys were admitted for a dime, but fans came to the park in decreasing numbers. Part of the decline was explained as a result of the increased popularity of golf as a recreational activity. However, Dawson reasoned that the main reason for the decline was the location of the ballpark and believed poor seating and limited parking accommodations were to blame. Despite construction of the new grandstand, Dawson wanted to move the club into a ballpark located in the west end of Richmond, even if he had to build it himself.[59]

Dawson reasoned that a ballpark under his ownership would increase attendance and also allow him to increase his operating revenue. In a park under his ownership, he would have control of concessions and fence and scorecard advertising, something he did not have at Tate Field. Operating expenses would also be reduced in terms of baseball cost—the new park would not lose balls to the river, as the one on the island was prone to do. To help reduce his financial risk, Dawson sold half interest in the Richmond club to George S. Barnes. Barnes' career had been in hardware and building, but he had also been active as a local baseball executive. The two partners announced plans to buy the Raleigh, North Carolina franchise in the Piedmont League. Both men owned equal shares in each franchise, with Barnes serving as the principal operator of the Richmond franchise and Dawson running the Raleigh club. Shortly thereafter, these men unveiled plans to build a 10,000 seat steel beam and wooden plank park on Richmond, Fredericksburg and Potomac Railroad land near the corner of Roseneath Road and Broad Street under a ten-year lease arrangement. Allen Saville was awarded a contract to grade the land, but the construction of the grandstand was never started. Dawson and Barnes needed the city council to approve the closing of "C" Street, a small and little used street in the area. Closing of the street would allow for a park with field lines of 325 feet down the right field line, 400 feet to center, and 350 down the left field line. Without the closing of this street the area proposed for the ballpark was too small. By late January, the council had not closed the street, leaving little time to build a park for the upcoming season.[60]

Another impediment to building a new ballpark was concern regarding the stability of certain Virginia League franchises. While finding a site was the primary concern, Dawson and Barnes did not want to invest money in construction until they were certain that the field would actually be used. On December 17, 1926, the *Richmond Times-Dispatch* printed an article which stated that four of the six Virginia League franchises were "undecided" about the prospects for baseball in 1927. While finances of their own clubs worried them, many of the league moguls were also concerned that Richmond, the largest city in the league, was struggling to attract a popular following. Through the winter months, Wilson, Kinston, Petersburg, and Portsmouth all threatened to give up on the Virginia League. Near the end of January, Kinston threatened to quit the league and Wilson, not wanting to be the only North Carolina-based franchise, began making overtures to join the Carolina-based Piedmont League. Virginia League officials began looking into the prospect of a league composed of only Virginia cities and proposed plans that varied from continuing as a four-club circuit to expanding the Virginia League into Roanoke, Lynchburg or Danville. After negotiations continued with the Virginia cities for several weeks, Kinston sought reinstatement of its franchise. By March, the owners had restored the Carolina franchises, and the Virginia League continued with the same six teams as in the previous season. These men even expressed their belief that the turmoil of the off-season had increased popular interest in the league and attendance figures were expected to be high. With the league's franchises in place, Barnes charged W.L. Cherry, the Colts' team secretary, with negotiation with W.B. Bradley and the other owners of Tate Field for lease arrangements. Those negotiations were delayed by the suicide of Jake Wells, the principal owner of the ballpark corporation. His brother Otto Wells assumed control of much of Jake's business interests, including Island Park.[61]

The Colts' management hired Eddie Mooers as player-manager for the 1927 season. Mooers' promotion to manager marked the first time that a native Richmonder managed the local franchise. Returning players included Al Malonee, Stanley Stack, Hal Weafer, Jose Ramos and Taylor Joliff. With these returning stars and the selection of Mooers as manager, many people expected the Colts to capture their fourth straight league pennant. In the season opener, the Colts and Petersburg Broncos battled to a 3–3 tie in an eleven-inning game that was halted by darkness. The outcome was indicative of the season to come. In June, Mooers resigned his role as manager and was replaced by Lewis McCarthy, formerly a catcher with the New York Giants. Mooers claimed that the strain of running his auto dealership, which he started with his brother a few years earlier, and managing was too much. He continued as a player for the Colts. When McCarthy took over, the club was fourth in the league with a 32–35 record. The Colts finished with a 65–65 record with an even .500 winning percentage. The final record qualified the club for third place in the circuit. The Portsmouth Truckers secured the pennant on September 3, with over a week left in the season and finished at 76–52. Petersburg finished second at 72–61 (.541).[62]

Immediately after the Virginia League season came to a close on September 10, 1927, the prospects for the league's operating in 1928 were in doubt. When George Barnes was questioned about the league's status, he remarked that he could not comment, as several moves that "might change the entire league status, particularly affecting the fortunes of the Richmond club" were being contemplated. Within a month, it was apparent that the Virginia League would not return. Barnes announced that the Richmond club was scaling back on payroll, would not retain some of its veteran players and, along with the Norfolk club, would seek to join the Class C Piedmont League. The suggestion that these two Virginia clubs join the six North Carolina clubs would allow the circuit to move up to B Class. However, the plans fell apart over monetary issues. The Carolina franchises wanted the Virginia teams to shoulder the majority of the transportation costs for travel into the Virginia cities. In response, the Virginia franchises entertained offers from northern baseball men, led by Earnest C. Landgraf, for inclusion in a league that planned to feature teams in eastern Pennsylvania and New Jersey. The Carolina reaction was to vote against expansion of the Piedmont League into Virginia's largest cities. In the end, the new league with the Pennsylvania and New Jersey cities did not materialize. Richmond, Norfolk, Petersburg, and Portsmouth resurrected the Virginia League and opened play as a four-team circuit on April 19, 1928.[63]

On the eve of opening day in 1928, Robert Harper, sports editor of the *Times-Dispatch* commented that the 1928 season of the Virginia League was a "test year for professional baseball" in Richmond and the other regional cities. If the teams were successful in terms of attendance and gate receipts, the league would be able to continue and maybe expand to other cities in the state, or perhaps Richmond and Norfolk would be able to finally join a league with other teams on the Atlantic seaboard. Failure, he speculated, would likely end baseball for several seasons in the capital city. He noted that many fans felt that, in order to revive interest in the professional game in Richmond, the city should be without a team for a season. Harper hoped that this scenario would not become a reality. He expressed the hope that the league could continue, but, to his chagrin, the Virginia League failed to complete even half the season and was disbanded on June 5, 1928.[64]

The Virginia League had meager chance for success in 1928. Inclement weather forced the cancellation of many early season games, and poor play discouraged fans from attending games. Low attendance created serious financial problems in Petersburg, Portsmouth and Norfolk and prompted rumors that these franchises would seek to move elsewhere. In an effort to revive interest in the Colts, Barnes released manager Olin Perritt and signed former Colt skipper and future Hall of Famer Albert "Chief" Bender. Bender's previous appearance with the Colts was in 1919 when he guided them during the second half of the season. Bender joined the team on June 4, after he had completed the season as manager of the U.S. Naval Academy nine. It was hoped that his presence in a Richmond uniform would revive baseball interest not only in Richmond but throughout the Virginia League. League moguls even agreed to rearrange the schedule to better accommodate Richmond's signing of Bender. However, Richmond and the Virginia League did not get the opportunity to see what the impact of this former major league star would have on the league. On June 2, Portsmouth and Petersburg announced that they were dropping out of the league. Richmond and Norfolk planned two weeks of games with each other while an alternate league could be found. The Piedmont League refused to accept the two clubs and William Bramham informed the clubs that after the Virginia League had disbanded, their contracts with the players were no longer valid. The series between Richmond and Norfolk ended after just two games.[65]

During the brief season, the Colts amassed a 15–27 (.357) record and were tied with Petersburg at the bottom of the league standings. Norfolk had the best record at 26–13 (.667) and was one game ahead of Portsmouth at 25–14 (.641). In the two exhibition games with Norfolk, the Colts won the first game 4–2 in Bender's managerial debut in Richmond. The next day, the Norfolk Tars evened the series with a 7–6 victory in a game that described the teams as "battling as if the championship of the world were at stake." The failure of the Virginia League ended Richmond's longest succession of consecutive seasons with professional baseball, and the city would now be without a professional team until 1931.[66]

In 1931, Richmond became a member of the Eastern League. William B. Bradley was mainly responsible for this arrangement, whereby Richmond joined Albany, Allentown, Bridgeport, Hartford, New Haven, Springfield and Norfolk in the Eastern League. The year 1931, however, was one of the most turbulent in the city's baseball history. This was attributed to ownership disputes that forced the ball club to change ownership several times. These disputes necessitated several changes in field management and even forced a change in the location of home games. In efforts to keep fans interested, gimmickry was utilized to bring spectators to the ballpark. During the season, lights were introduced, and the first night game was played in the city. On another occasion, a female nine provided opposition for the Colts.[67]

Bradley had employed the former Colt manager Ray Ryan as his business manager. Early in the season, Ryan managed to oust Bradley, and he re-organized the Richmond Baseball Corporation with Charles A. Somma as president; Ryan continued as business manager.[68] However, shortly thereafter other difficulties arose. Somma resigned from the corporation, leaving Ryan in control of the club.

Although Richmond was a member of the Eastern League in 1931, the club was in financial difficulties, and, on Memorial Day, the Richmond Hotels Corporation and the Investment Holding Corporation of Norfolk acquired warrants to secure gate receipts and much of the team property, including uniforms and equipment. The team was forced to play the games in the ensuing week in borrowed uniforms. Ryan and Bradley also entered into a bitter dispute over the concessions revenues at Tate Field. The disagreement led to court filings and forced the executive director of the league, Fred J. Voos, Jr. to ask Ryan to relinquish the club to league control in early June.[69]

The league directors, in association with Henry Staples and William H. Parker, members of the Richmond City Chamber of Commerce Recreation Committee, sought a local buyer for the team. If one could not be found, the league would sell the franchise to an interested party in Portland, Maine. The Chamber of Commerce was able to raise subscriptions for most of the necessary $10,000 to maintain the franchise in Richmond but still needed the $5,000 league deposit. Charles Somma re-entered the picture and posted the $5,000 guarantee, thus regaining the rights as principal owner of the club. He cited "civic duty" as the guiding force for his action. Immediately after acquiring the club, he announced that he had entered into an agreement with Colonel John A. Cutchins of the City Stadium Corporation to play the remainder of the home games at the newly constructed West End stadium. He then replaced Fred Williams, the manager, with Bob Murray, the club's second baseman. At the time Murray took over, the club was in last place in the league with a 13–29 record.[70]

The Richmond baseball club proceeded to the last week of June before more difficulty emerged. On June 26, it was reported that Somma was in a "receptive mood" to sell the club. Ray Ryan and a group in Providence, Rhode Island, expressed an interest in the club, but Somma wanted the club to remain in Richmond. On July 4, the Chamber of Commerce, with league approval, once again acquired control of the club. The club was incorporated as Richmond Colts, Inc., with William H. Parker as president; Henry Staples as vice-president; Luke Fairbank as treasurer; C.C. Michie as secretary; John Fairbank as counsel; and Murray as team manager.[71]

While the early part of the season was marred by ownership disputes, the last-place club suffered from an unusual identity crisis. When the club was re-organized as the Richmond Baseball Corporation, Somma and Ryan had not presented a nickname for the franchise. The city's two newspapers each ran contests to determine a name. The *Times-Dispatch* selected "Byrds" from its fan contest, while the *News Leader* chose "Rebels." After several weeks, the club ownership prevailed upon the press to drop both names and restore the name "Colts," which they agreed to do.[72]

On the field, the Colts' performance was horrible. They ended the first half of the season in the cellar with a 24–39 record. The second half of the season they wound up one place from the cellar with a 31–38 record. Low attendance and rainouts hampered the Colts' financial situation. In efforts to increase attendance, the owners resorted to gimmicky exhibition games. On September 1, after their regular game with Hartford, the Colts played a second game with the traveling House of David club. This club traveled with a portable lighting system. The lights were situated atop fifty-four foot retractable poles, and the entire system could be erected in about two hours. The game was the first night game held in Richmond. The House of David team was known for its talented players and their bushy beards. The Colts won this first night game in the city 8–4 before a crowd of 5,000 spectators. A week later, the Colts played a game against the Hollywood Girl Stars. This team of women was coached by Irish Muesel, a former player with the New York Giants. In a fifteen-week barnstorming tour, the Hollywood Girls won 39 of 91 games against male baseball clubs, one of which was the Richmond Colts.[73]

The turbulent year of 1931 prompted the Richmond Colts to announce that they were dropping the franchise after unsuccessfully attempting to establish a working relationship with a major league club. Fred Voos once again intervened to insure that the Eastern League franchise remained in Richmond. On December 30, 1931, he regained control of the franchise. However, the league could not escape financial ruin. On July 18, 1932, the league directors announced that the league was disbanding at the close of that day's games.[74]

CHAPTER VI

The Richmond Colts and the Piedmont League, 1933–1953

By the time that the Eastern League disbanded, Edwin "Eddie" Hale Mooers had acquired ownership of the Colts. Mooers, a former Colt infielder, was currently a prominent Richmond businessman. He was the owner of Mooers Motor Company, a Packard franchise, and he was in financial position to purchase the club. He acquired the Colts, assumed the club's debts, and, in the winter of 1932–33, sought membership in the Piedmont League. On February 27, 1933, at a meeting of Piedmont League directors in Wilmington, North Carolina, Mooers was granted the Piedmont League franchise for Richmond. For the next twenty years, professional baseball in Richmond was intimately associated with the life and career of Eddie Mooers.[1]

In 1933, the Piedmont League, a Class B organization, consisted of Richmond and five North Carolina franchises: Greensboro, Charlotte, Durham, Wilmington, and Winston-Salem.[2] For the next twenty years, Richmond would be a member of the Piedmont League. However, the Richmond franchise of Eddie Mooers was different from the other clubs. Throughout these years, the Colts would remain an independent club, owned and operated by Mooers, without an affiliation with any major league club. All of the other clubs were farm teams of major league clubs, among them the Brooklyn Dodgers, Red Sox, Yankees, Cardinals, and

Cubs. This meant that although the Colts were independent, Mooers had to seek players wherever he could obtain them. For a while, he had a "working agreement" with the Giants and Senators whereby they might option a player to him for a period of time. A short while after their February meeting, the directors of the Piedmont League announced a 140 game schedule for the 1933 season, opening on April 21 and closing on September 6. Each team would have seventy home games and an equal number on the road. The league would play a split season but have no playoffs in September. The 140 game schedule would be standard for the league for the next twenty years.

The Colts home park was Tate Field, located on Mayo Island. Although Tate Field had been the home of a minor league baseball club for several years, it was not a modern ballpark. It did not have lights, and only day games could be played there. In 1933, ballparks in all Piedmont League cities had lights and featured night games. Mooers' aim was to bring Tate Field into conformity with the other parks in the league, and, during the first half of the 1933, season lights were installed on Mayo Island. The first night game there was on July 24 against the Durham Bulls. Prior to this date, afternoon games were usually scheduled for 3:30 p.m. After the lights were installed, Colt game time was 8:00 p.m. Prior to the start of the season Mooers announced that general admission to games would be 40 cents; grandstand seats, which were covered, would be 55 cents; and admission for boys would be 25 cents.[3]

On March 1, 1933, Mooers announced that the manager for the Colts would be Jack Onslow. Onslow was well known in Richmond because in the 1920s he had served as Colt manager when the team was a member of the Virginia League. Onslow and the Colts began spring training on Mayo Island on April 3, three weeks prior to the opening date of the season. During this period, the Colts played exhibition games with several local semi-pro clubs and others from Norfolk and Lynchburg. An exception was a game with the Baltimore Orioles on April 8, which the Colts lost 8–4. The Colts opening game of the 1933 season was on April 24 against Winston-Salem. This contest was played before 2,500 fans. Jim Trexler, a local semi-pro pitcher who had been impressive in a tryout with the Colts and had been signed by Mooers, pitched Richmond to an 8–4 victory over the North Carolina contingent.[4]

The Colts played slightly better than .500 ball during their first season in the Piedmont League, averaging .521. Overall they won 73 games and lost 67. Their performance during the first half of the season was 39–31 and they placed second to league-leading Greensboro. During the second half of the season, they were 34 and 36 and placed fifth in the

Mayo Island Park/Tate Field in flood (courtesy of Dementi Studio in Richmond, Virginia).

league, only one place from the cellar-dwelling Winston-Salem nine. The leading hitter for the Colts was their right fielder Charles Wade who hit .323, which was thirty-seven points below the league leader John Mize of Greensboro. Wade's twenty-four homeruns were second in the league. The Colts had one twenty game winner: Herman Holshauser compiled a 24–10 record and John Marena was 16–10. Jim Texler, who won the season's opener against Winston-Salem, wound up the season with an unimpressive 9 and 11 record. Both Holshauser and Wade were chosen by fans in a poll conducted by the *Charlotte Observer* for membership on the Piedmont League All-Star Team.[5]

Spring training for the Colts in 1934 was interrupted by the James River flooding that encased Tate Field in mud and debris. Mooers, however, was permitted by the University of Richmond to train on the University's Millhiser Field. Flooding on Mayo Island would be a problem for the Colts throughout the 1930s. Other floods occurred in 1935, 1936 and 1937.[6] After each flood, there was a costly rehabilitation since often a portion of the park facilities were carried downstream or had to be rebuilt. In addition to periodic floods, in the off-season of 1941 there was a fire on the island, which destroyed all playing facilities. This disaster prompted Mooers to purchase land and construct a new ballpark at Norfolk and Roseneath Roads in the western portion of the city of Richmond.

The Colts had a new manager for 1934 since Jack Onslow was not rehired by Mooers. Throughout the two decades that Richmond was a member of the Piedmont League, it was the general practice of Mooers to change managers practically every season. From 1933 through 1953, only three managers, Lance Richbourg (1938–39), Eddie Phillips (1940–41), and Vincent Smith (1949–50), served as Colt manager for as many as two seasons; a new manager was appointed for each one of the remaining fifteen seasons. The manager for 1934, as announced ten days before spring training began, was Edward Hendee. Hendee had played first base for the Colts the previous season and was popular with the Richmond fans.

Prior to the opening of the Piedmont League season on April 23, the Colts played exhibition games against several International and Major League clubs. In a game with the Philadelphia Athletics, which drew more than 2,000 fans, they witnessed a massive home run by the Athletics' first baseman, Jimmie Foxx. Foxx's hit cleared the left field fence, traveled out of the park, off the island, and landed in the James River.[7] Two weeks later, the Colts, sporting new uniforms (white with blue trimmings), lost their home opener to Norfolk, 5–4 in ten innings. League directors had decided to maintain the split season format but with the winner of the first half playing the winner of the second half for the league championship.

During the 1934 season, there was one development which prompted a slight modification in the league schedule. This concerned Sunday baseball. When the Colts entered the Piedmont League in 1933, baseball games on Sunday were permitted in all of the North Carolina cities. However, there was a blue law in Virginia which prohibited professional baseball being played on Sunday. This law, which was enacted in 1877, stated, "If a person, on a Sabbath day, be found laboring at any trade or calling, or employ his apprentices or servants in labor or other business except in household or other work of necessity or charity, he shall be deemed guilty of a misdemeanor and punished by a fine of not less than five dollars."[8] Earlier there had been some agitation in Richmond for the lifting of this law, claiming that baseball was a recreational activity and was a public benefit. One of those who voiced support for Sunday baseball was Frank Dobson, the baseball coach at the University of Richmond. In a speech before the Richmond Chamber of Commerce, he advocated the repeal of the Sunday blue law prohibiting the playing of professional baseball on Sunday. Despite the efforts of baseball enthusiasts, there was no change in the law during 1933.

The advocates of Sunday baseball were encouraged in the spring of 1934 that the courts might render the 1877 law obsolete. In April, theaters in Richmond and other Virginia localities, which had been closed on Sunday because of the blue law, were allowed to open and operate on Sunday.[9] Also in the spring of 1934, there was a testing of the law in Richmond and in Norfolk. On Sunday, April 29, Norfolk played Wilmington before 4,500 fans. And although eighteen players and three umpires were arrested, local authorities permitted the game to be played. Three weeks later, Eddie Mooers announced that the Colts would play a charity game with the Wilmington club on Sunday, May 18. This game was for the benefit of the Crippled Children's Hospital in Richmond.[10] Although Manager Ed Hendee and a number of the Colt players were arrested, the game was allowed to be played. In the meantime, the Corporation Court in Norfolk acquitted a Norfolk player and the police court cases against the other players were dismissed. The Norfolk court held that "baseball had a beneficial moral and physical effect on the community and that, therefore, it constituted a necessity and could not be construed as in violation of the fifty year old blue law statute."[11] The decision of the Norfolk court influenced other areas of the state and from the mid-spring of 1934, Sunday baseball was played without interference in Virginia. Starting Sunday, June 10, baseball games on Sunday would be common in Richmond and throughout the Piedmont League.

The Colts opened the 1934 season with a ten-inning 5–4 loss to Norfolk before 2,000 fans at Tate Field. During the season, the Colts often played before crowds numbering from 1,000 to 3,000, and it was during this season that the Colts instituted the observance of Ladies Day. Ladies Day at the ballpark, which had been inaugurated in the major leagues in the mid-twenties, had been adopted by numerous minor league clubs. On at least two occasions—in mid–June and on July 19—the Colts observed Ladies and Boys Night. On these occasions, female fans and boys age sixteen and under were admitted to the game without charge. Ladies Night/Day would be an occasional feature observed several times a season at Colt games throughout the team's tenure in the Piedmont League. Although the Colts played before enthusiastic fans, their overall record was not quite as good as it had been in 1933. For the first half of the "split season," the Colts won 29 and lost 41, which placed them fifth in a six-team league. During the second half of the season, they compiled a 31–37 record and finished in fourth place. The team's leading hitter was Bill Andros who finished the season with an average of .309. The Colts did not have a twenty-game winner since their leading pitcher, John Pezzullo, ended the season with a record of 16 wins and 4 losses; the Colts ace of 1933, Herman Holshouser, had a record of 11–11.[12]

Throughout 1934, the Piedmont League remained a six-team league. However, two of the 1933 members, Durham and Winston-Salem, had dropped out of the league and were replaced by Columbia, South Carolina, and Norfolk. During the season, there was another change when the Red Sox shifted their operations from Columbia to Asheville. Prior to the beginning of the season, league directors decided that there would be a championship playoff series at the end of the season. The playoffs would pit the winner of the first half of the season against the winner of the second half. Charlotte was in first place during the first half of the season, and Norfolk captured first place in the second half of the season. In the championship playoff following the close of the season, Norfolk defeated Charlotte in four straight games for the championship of the Piedmont League.[13]

In January 1935, floods inundated Mayo Island with ten feet of water and left a deposit of mud and debris on Tate Field. However, Mooers engaged workmen to renovate the area and have it ready for spring practice which began on March 25. This year the Piedmont League continued to feature six teams; however, Greensboro had dropped from the league, and Portsmouth had been admitted. By March 21, the Colt's new manager, Eddie Rommell, arrived in Richmond to supervise practice and the exhibition season before the league opened on April 25.[14] Rommell was one of the first knuckle-ball pitchers in major league baseball, and he had a twelve-year career with the Philadelphia Athletics (1920–32) and was a member of the Athletics' championship teams of 1929–31. Later, after a brief managing career, he served as an American League umpire for twenty-two years.[15]

Prior to the season opening game, the Colts engaged in intra-squad practice games and played exhibition contests with several local semi-pro outfits, as well as Toronto of the International League and the Red Sox and Athletics of the American League. During these weeks, Rommell was optimistic, saying that he thought the Colts were "a good ball club," and he was "pleased with the spirit of the men."[16] Richmond's season opener on April 25 was an away game at Asheville, and the Tourists defeated the Colts 16–6 before a crowd of 3,723. The Colts' opening home game was on April 29 against Norfolk before a crowd of 2,200. The Tars "swamped the Colts" 19-4.[17] These opening games were a preview of the disastrous performance by the Colts during the first half of the 1935 season. At the end of the first half of the season, the Colts occupied the cellar position with 30 wins and 41 losses. The Colts, however, with player help from the Orioles, Giants and Athletics, were able to turn the season around during the second half. When the season ended on September 12, the Colts led the league with a record of 40 wins and 25 losses, with a seasonal record of 70 and 66.

In August, a flood again inundated Tate Field, and the Colts had to play several games at the Richmond City Stadium. However, the field was cleared and ready for play when the championship series began. The playoffs were between Richmond, and the league's first half winner, Asheville. The Colts won this series four games to two to claim their first Piedmont League championship.[18] Eddie Mooers was so pleased with his team and Manager Rommell that prior to the last game with Asheville, he presented Rommell "a big, shiny, brand new automobile."[19] Rommell, who pitched occasionally and had a record of 6–2 was greatly assisted by outfielder George Ferrell, the older brother of major leaguers Wes and Rick, who batted .377, had twenty-five homeruns and was voted the most valuable player in the Piedmont League. Two other Colt regulars, Jim Galvin and Ernie Horne, also hit over 300. The Colt's leading pitchers for 1935 were Charles Foreman (15–5) and Tom Carey (13–10). In a poll conducted at the end of the season by the *Times-Dispatch*, which included the votes of the different managers in the league, two Colts, Ferrell and Foreman, were named to the Piedmont League All-Star Team.[20]

In addition to the observance of Ladies Night on several occasions in 1935, the Colts sponsored the first Mens Night in the history of professional baseball on August 8. On that evening every man who was accompanied by an admission-paying lady was admitted to the game free of charge. On this night, it was reported that 2,500 fans were at Tate Field and saw the Colts defeat the Asheville club 4–1.[21] It seems that Mens Night was a one-time experiment, and it did not become a customary observance at the ballpark. Despite winning the Piedmont League championship, Mooers declared at the end of the season that he had lost money each year the team had been in the league. Expenses involved installing lights at Tate Field and the periodic cleaning of Tate Field and rebuilding of fences and grandstands following the many floods accounted for much of the loss. However, Mooers never indicated he was giving up on professional baseball in Richmond.[22] Following the playoffs, the Colts disbanded and most of the players headed home for the winter. It was noted, however, that several Colts, including pitchers Jim Trexler and Charles Foreman, would spend the winter in Richmond.[23]

Prior to the beginning of spring training in 1936, Eddie Mooers announced that the manager of the Colts for the coming season would be the popular outfielder and league-leading hitter, George Ferrell. Before the Colts could begin practice, Mooers had to make arrangements with University of Richmond officials for permission to practice on the University's Millhiser Field because a recent flood had inundated Mayo Island, and it would require several weeks to get Tate Field in playing condition. Also, Mooers had to make arrangements with city authorities for permission to play exhibition games at city stadium. By April 1, all necessary arrangements had been completed, and Manager Ferrell and the Colts began practice at the University of Richmond.[24] Prior to the opening game of the Piedmont League season on April 23, the Colts played exhibition games with Albany, Montreal, and the Red Sox. The Colts' home opener against Asheville was also played at city stadium before 4,000 who saw the Tourists spoil the occasion with a 4–3 win. When the Colts returned from their first road trip on May 4, the renovations and clean-up at Tate Field had been completed, and they were allowed to play the first game of the season in their home park. They lost to Rocky Mount 11–8.[25]

In 1936, the Piedmont League continued to be a six-team league, but the membership was not the same as it had been in 1935. Rocky Mount and Durham had replaced Wilmington and Charlotte; these two cities together with Norfolk, Portsmouth, Richmond, and Asheville comprised the league's membership. Prior to the beginning of the season, league directors modified the system for determining the league championship. They abandoned the split season practice and adopted the Shaughnessy playoff system. This system had been devised several years earlier by Frank Shaughnessy. He had been a manager of International League clubs and, in 1938, would be elected president of that league, a position he would hold for the next twenty-four years.[26] This system provided that at the close of the baseball season the top four teams would engage in a series of games to determine the league champion. The first-place team would play the third-place winner, and the second-place team would play the fourth-place occupant. The winners of the best three-of-five game series would then play each other for the league championship. The playoffs provided a monetary incentive for the players involved. Each player of the winning team in a playoff received an increment of $1500; the players of the losing team received $750 each.[27] The Shaughnessy system was adopted in 1936 and would be used by the Piedmont League thereafter, although after several years the best-of-five game series was changed to the best-of-seven game series.

George Ferrell opened the season as the manager of the Colts and also the team's right fielder. However, after a disastrous opening month in which the Colts won eight and lost twenty games, Ferrell informed Mooers that he was resigning as manager but would remain with the Colts as a player. This was acceptable to the owner, and Mooers then assumed the role of field manager himself—a role he filled for the remainder of the season and also for the 1937 season.[28] Mooers was able to obtain some player assistance from the Athletics and Giants, and, as the 1936 season progressed, the Colt's record improved. When the season ended on September 9, the Colts were in third place in the league standings with a record of 76 wins and 66 losses. George Ferrell led the Colt hitters with a batting average of .335. One other Colt, third baseman Ernie Horne, was the only other Colt to hit .300 with an average of .325. The team's leading pitcher was Bill Jeffcoat who compiled a 15–10 record. Three other hurlers, John Leonardo, Jim Trexler and John Pezzullo, also had winning seasons, each with ten or more victories.[29] In the Shaughnessy playoffs, the Colts lost in the first round to Norfolk, and Durham won over Rocky Mount. In the finals, Norfolk defeated the Durham Bulls to win the league championship.[30]

During the 1936 season, Colts' owner Eddie Mooers announced on May 19 that every Monday night would be Ladies Night at Tate Field. Ladies would be admitted for a fee of 25 cents, and there was no mention that they would have to be accompanied by a gentleman escort.[31] Another one-time innovation at Tate Field occurred on the night of June 18. At this time, the Colts were to play the Norfolk Tars, but this was the evening of the much ballyhooed heavyweight fight between the American phenomenon Joe Louis and the German heavyweight and former world champion Max Schmeling. The fight was to be broadcast, and Mooers knew this would keep many fans from the ballpark. Thus, Mooers announced to the press that he had arranged for the broadcast of the fight to be relayed to amplifiers at Tate Field and that fans could watch the game and simultaneously listen to the fight. Approximately 2,000 attended the game; they saw the Colts defeat Norfolk 4–0 and listened to the fight, which ended in the twelfth round when Schmeling knocked out the young Louis for the American's first loss of his career.[32]

In the off-season of 1936–37, Piedmont League directors announced a 143-game schedule for the coming season, which would open on April 22 and close on September 8. In 1937, the league was expanded to eight teams, with the new members being Charlotte and Winston-Salem. Colt owner Eddie Mooers would serve as field manager once again for his team. Prior to the opening of the season, he expressed the belief that the Colts would "be better than they were last season" and noted that he had been promised help by Connie Mack of the Athletics and Bill Terry of the New York Giants. The Colts began spring practice on April 1 at Tate Field and, prior to the opening of the season, played exhibition games with Jersey City, Montreal, Buffalo, and the Philadelphia Phillies.[33] The Colts won their home opener against Portsmouth 13–4 before 2,700 fans and, a couple days later, departed on their first road trip. While the team was out of town, the James River flooded Tate Field. However, this was not a severe flood and workmen were able to have the field ready when the Colts returned a week later.[34] It was during the opening weeks of the 1937 season that the local press began referring to the Colts as the "Mustangs." The press did not cease using the term Colts but often used the terms Colts and Mustangs interchangeably.

It appears that trying to perform the duties of field manager, handling the responsibilities of ownership, and overseeing the front office business of the Colts created a strain on the personality of Eddie Mooers. This was reflected in his on-field behavior and his relations with the umpires. For example, in a game at Asheville on May 31, which the Colts lost 20–3, Mooers had an altercation with one of the umpires. His vigorous protest of a decision in the game led to his being banished and fined $100, the heaviest fine in the history of the Piedmont League.[35] Although league president Dan Hill modified the fine after reviewing the situation, this was only the first of a number of run-ins Mooers had with officials during the season. In mid–July, in a game at Tate Field, Mooers was ejected from the game by umpire Walter Barbare over his prolonged argument with the umpire as to whether a Portsmouth outfielder caught or trapped a line drive from a Colt batter. When Mooers left the field, Colt fans expressed their opinion of the umpire by showering the field with soft drink bottles. A final encounter of Mooers with umpires came a month later in Portsmouth—also with umpire Barbare. Mooers' insistence that the Portsmouth pitcher was not placing both feet on the rubber prior to throwing the ball prompted a heated altercation with the umpire that resulted in Mooers being escorted from the park by police. By this time, Mooers was beginning to realize that the tensions/problems associated with being owner and manager were more than he had assumed. In August, he revealed to the press that this was his last year as field manager, and that next season he would limit himself to "front office affairs" of the club.[36]

Despite the frustrations/problems of owner-manager Eddie Mooers, the Colts ended the 1937 season in fourth place and qualified for the playoffs. The Colt hitters were led by third baseman Ernie Horne who hit .337. Other .300 hitters were Norman "Babe" Young, Colt first baseman at .332, and George Ferrell, who hit .321. The Colts had a twenty-game winner in Tom Ferrick, who compiled a record of 20 and 12. John Leonardo, Clem Driesenwerd and Bill Renne were winners of ten or more games each. In a poll conducted by the sports writers of the Piedmont League cities, three Colts were placed on the league's all-star Team. They were third baseman Ernie Horne, first baseman "Babe" Young, and left fielder George Ferrell. In the Shaughnessy playoffs, the Colts lost in the first round to the Norfolk Tars. The other first round winner was Portsmouth, which defeated Asheville. In the finals, Norfolk defeated Portsmouth and was proclaimed champion of the Piedmont League for 1937.[37]

Eddie Mooers maintained his resolve to cease activity as field manager of the Colts, and, prior to the 1938 season, he hired Lance Richbourg to manage the Colts for the coming season. Richbourg was an outfielder who had formerly played for the Boston Braves. He arrived in Richmond early in March, ready to supervise spring practice which began on April 1. Before the Colts opened the season at Durham, they played exhibition games with Jersey City, Montreal, and the Philadelphia Phillies. On April 24, they opened their home season against Portsmouth before 4,371 fans, the largest opening day crowd since Mooers acquired the franchise. The crowd was not disappointed as the Colts won 6–5.[38] The 1938 season was not a good one for the Colts; they won 66 games and lost 72 and wound up in fifth place in the league standings. They did not qualify for the playoffs. The principal weakness of the team this season was pitching and their leading hurler, John Leonardo, who was 16–13. The team featured five .300 hitters, led by "Babe" Young with an average of .356; manager and outfielder Lance Richbourg hit .317. For the Piedmont League All-Star Team, selected by the sports writers in league cities, Young was the only Colt chosen.[39]

During the 1938 season, there were several "specials" designed to boost attendance. On July 16, there was a ceremony to present gifts to George Ferrell and catcher Clarence Anderson. These men had won Bulova watches because they had hit homeruns over the Bulova sign in left centerfield during the season. In August, the Men's Bible Class of Bainbridge Street Baptist Church sponsored a "Richbourg Night" to honor the Colt manager. The Bible Class presented him a gift of $10 and a new leather wallet. Special collections for the popular manager were also taken on this occasion which resulted in a gift to Richbourg of $80. The special occasion, which drew the largest crowd of the 1938 season, was on August 24 when Jesse Owens made an appearance at Tate Field. Owens was the American sprinter who had captured several gold medals at the 1936 Olympic Games held in Berlin. On this occasion, Owens gave a demonstration of his speed, which was witnessed by more than 5,000 fans, among whom the press reported more than 1,200 Negroes. The final of the "specials" at Tate Field was the presentation of gifts to the "most popular Colts." In a poll conducted by the local press, pitcher Jim Trexler received 6,415 votes, 2,000 more than the runner-up catcher Steve Kuk. On the evening of August 26, various Richmond merchants presented the following gifts to Trexler: a leather traveling bag, an RCA radio, a watch, and a ham. The latter was presented to him by the Grace Street Meat Market.[40]

Although the 1938 Colts were not very impressive as a baseball team, the 1938 season was a memorable one in Colt history because this year their games, for the first time, were broadcast to the public by radio station WRTD, an NBC blue network affiliate in Richmond.[41] Radio broadcasts of games came late to Richmond. Many minor league teams had featured radio broadcast of games since the early mid-twenties, and most of the major league clubs were broadcasting their games prior to 1938. From mid-season 1938 through the 1940 season, Colt games were aired by radio station WRTD. In 1941 and 1942, station WRNL in Richmond featured the broadcast of Colt games. During the years 1943, '44, '45, and '46, Colt games were off the air. In 1947, broadcast of Colt games was resumed, this time by station WLEE. WLEE would continue to broadcast Colt games throughout the 1953 season, the Colts' last in the Piedmont League.

For the first time since he acquired the Colts, owner Mooers appointed the same person to manage the Colts for two successive seasons. Lance Richbourg, who led the Colts in 1938, was asked to continue as manager for 1939. However, because of illness, Richbourg did not arrive in Richmond until several days after spring practice began at Tate Field on March 23. Until his arrival, Mooers directed the Colts' workouts. Mooers also announced that this would be the last season that the Colts would conduct spring practice at Tate Field. He informed the press that beginning in 1940 the Colts would have spring practice away from home.[42] After his arrival, Richbourg assumed direction of spring drills and prepared the Colts for a series of exhibition games before the Piedmont League opened on April 20. Richbourg expressed his belief that the Colts would "do better in 1939 than they did last season." The Colts opened their season at Winston-Salem and were defeated 11–4. Two days later in their home opening game, the Colts won from Portsmouth 8–3. Throughout the season, however, the Colts struggled to play .500 ball, and, as the season wore on, there was criticism from the press and fans of the popular Richbourg. In addition to the observance of several Ladies Nights at Tate Field, there were several other happenings during the season. One was a visit and performance of Al Schacht, the "Clown Prince of Baseball" on May 11. Before a game with Winston-Salem, he entertained a crowd of 1,200 fans with his forty-five minute comedy routine. Later in the season, there was a ceremony at Tate Field honoring George Ferrell. In a poll conducted by the local press to determine the "most valuable Colt," the overwhelming choice was the veteran George Ferrell. In a program on August 12, he was presented a silver trophy provided by the Richmond jeweler Fred Kohler, inscribed with his name and the title "Most Valuable Colt, 1939."[43] Tate Field was also the scene of an ugly and frightening event on July 24. During a doubleheader, which the Colts lost to Rocky Mount 6–1 and 5–4, there was an attack on an umpire, witnessed by more than 1,200 fans. During the second game, an unidentified spectator threw a "pop bottle" which hit umpire Jim Calleran in the head and knocked him unconscious. He was rushed by ambulance to Stuart Circle Hospital where x-rays revealed that although he suffered a concussion there was no skull fracture. The press deplored this incident, and both Richbourg and Mooers visited the umpire in the hospital. They gave him their condolences and presented him a vase of flowers which the Colts sent him. This incident prompted the league president, Ralph Daughton, to offer a $50 reward leading to the arrest and conviction of any person guilty of throwing a bottle, rock, or brick at an official during a game.[44] The guilty party who beaned umpire Calleran at Tate Field was never apprehended.

At the close of the 1939 season on September 8, the Colts had a record of 70 wins and 71 losses, slightly below .500 but good enough in the league for fourth place and participation in the playoffs. George Ferrell was the Colts' leading hitter with a .344 average, and Jim Trexler led the pitching staff with a 19 and 9 record. In the first round of the playoffs, the Colts were eliminated by the Asheville Tourists, and Rocky Mount ousted the Durham Bulls. In the championship finals, Asheville defeated Rocky Mount to claim the league championship. Four days after the close of the season, Lance Richbourg resigned as manager and player and informed Mooers that he and his family were departing for his cattle ranch near Fort Pierce, Florida.[45] This meant that for the 1940 season the Colts would have a new manager, and Owner Mooers was given ample time to find the "right man."

About three weeks before the Colts were scheduled to depart to

Wilson, North Carolina, for spring training, Eddie Mooers announced that the manager for the coming season was Eddie Phillips. Phillips was a catcher with seventeen years experience in major and minor league baseball, and the previous year he had managed Wilkes-Barre of the Eastern League. Phillips informed the press that he would be a playing manager and expected to catch 100 of the scheduled 142 games. Phillips and twenty-one Colts departed Richmond via bus for Wilson on March 31. They would train there for ten days and then return home for exhibition games with Jersey City and Toronto before the opening of the Piedmont League season on April 17. At the time the team departed for training, Phillips told a reporter that the Colts needed help—specifically a couple of pitchers, an outfielder, and an infielder.[46] Mooers was aware of the Colts' need for help, and he had a promise from Bill Terry that the Giants would try to assist him in obtaining a pitcher or two. One week before the season opened, a Cuban rookie outfielder, Luis Olmo, arrived in Richmond.

The Colts opened the 1940 season at home against Rocky Mount and defeated the visitors 7–3. This was the beginning of what was to be one of the finest seasons in Colt history. Throughout the season, they contested Asheville and Rocky Mount for the league leadership, and when the season ended in September the Colts were in first place—one and one-half games ahead of the Asheville Tourists. This was the first Piedmont League pennant the Colts had won. Colt hitters were led by left fielder Jim "Buster" Maynard, who compiled an average of .337, hit thirty homeruns, and was voted the league's most valuable player. Third baseman Eddie Horne hit .336, and first baseman Bill Prout and shortstop Larry Kinzer hit .331 and .306, respectively. Veteran George Ferrell hit .290 and rookie Olmo hit .271. The Colts also featured two twenty game winners in pitchers Lynn Watkins (20–11) and Harry Banzer (20–13). Jim Bivins, who won 13 and lost 12, pitched the only no-hitter of the season when the Colts defeated the Durham Bulls 1–0 on June 19.[47] The Colts ended the season with 77 victories and 59 losses. However, in the playoffs they were defeated in the first round by the Bulls, four games to three. In the other first round series, Rocky Mount eliminated Asheville. In the championship series, Durham defeated Rocky Mount and was proclaimed Piedmont League champion for 1940. Despite the fact that the Colts lost in the playoffs, Mooers announced that he had already chosen the team's manager for 1941—it would be Eddie Phillips.[48]

Although the Colts had a winning season in 1940, Manager Philips was the victim of misfortune on two occasions. On May 18, when he was hitting .358, a foul tip broke the little finger on his right hand. This rendered him out of action for several weeks during which time the catching duties were assumed by Harry "Moose" Krause. Again, a couple of months later in a game at Durham, Phillips suffered another broken finger. These injuries sidelined him for much of the season, and his hitting average slumped about 100 points from what it was before his injuries.[49]

During the 1940 season, Mooers and the Colts promoted a number of special events designed to attract fans. On June 4, Al Schacht, the "Clown Prince of Baseball," returned to Tate Field and performed his forty-five minute comedy act prior to the game. A week later, it was announced that on June 14 the Colts would observe Hillbilly Night, with hillbilly bands from the city and other areas performing and competing for a prize. These festivities, the press noted, would precede the game. In July, the Colts observed their first Father/Son Night. At this time, all boys aged fifteen and under were admitted free if accompanied by their father. During this same month, the Colts observed a modified form of Ladies Night. One night, all ladies were admitted to the game for 10 cents each and were given ticket stubs. During a period between innings, a drawing was held and lucky ticket holders were awarded gifts. This gimmick helped to attract over 3,500 fans to Tate Field. In August, the Colt management designated a special day to honor Eddie Horne, Colt veteran third baseman. Horne had suffered an injury and was in the hospital. On this occasion, a special collection was taken for him at the game, and he received a gift of $101. Earlier in the season, there had also been a day to honor the veteran outfielder George Ferrell. Both occasions attracted a large number of fans.[50]

About a week before the Colts were to begin spring practice in Greenville, North Carolina, manager Eddie Phillips arrived in Richmond. Upon his arrival, he was informed that twenty-six Colts had returned contracts and that there were sixteen rookies who would be trying out with the Colts. Before departing Richmond on April 1, 1941, he informed a reporter that this season Richmond would have a "hustling ball club" and that some of the rookies "looked good on paper." The Colts were in Greenville from April 1 to 12. They then returned home for several exhibition games before the Piedmont League opened on April 24. The league would be slightly different this season but would still be composed of eight teams. During the off season, the Red Sox moved their operations from Rocky Mount to Greensboro. Upon their return home, the Colts played exhibition games with Newport News of the Virginia League, the Philadelphia Phillies, Montreal, and Springfield and Hartford of the Eastern League. Rain canceled the Colts' season opening game at Tate Field, but the following evening the Colts defeated the Durham Bulls before 1,200 fans.[51]

With the season less than a month old, the Colts lost their ballpark. In mid–May, the grandstands, concession areas, and dugouts were destroyed by fire. Mooers then negotiated with city authorities to play home games at city stadium until the Tate Field area could be rehabilitated. The city added seats to the stadium area and installed lights, and, during the months of June and July, Colt games were played at that facility. For use of the stadium, Mooers paid $70 rent for each game. By the end of July, Tate Field was restored, and Colt home games were played there for the remainder of the season.[52]

The fire at Tate Field was the last straw in a long line of incidents that prompted Mooers to take action on a new facility. The almost annual flooding on Mayo Island—sometimes more than once a season—and the expense of cleaning up and repairing the field had caused Mooers concern for some time. In February 1938, he had tried to negotiate with city authorities for a new park on the north portion of the Fair Grounds. The concept was for the city to build a park seating 3,500 people, and Mooers would lease it each year from March 1 through September 20. These negotiations failed to materialize, and Mooers was left with Tate Field, a facility which he leased each year from its owner, Mose Nunnally. The lease obligated Mooers to clean up after flooding, which by 1938 had cost the Colt owner more than $15,000.[53] Mooers was disappointed that negotiations for a new park in 1938 were not successful, but he continued to hope that some arrangement could be made for the Colts to leave Mayo Island. In a 1940 conversation with a *Times-Dispatch* reporter, he declared there was a "dire need in Richmond for a new ball park" and termed Tate Field an "eyesore." The fire at Tate Field in the spring of 1941 convinced Mooers that the only way his team was to have a new park was for him to build it. In the summer of 1941, about two months after the fire, the press announced that Mooers had acquired nine and one-half acres of land at Roseneath and Norfolk Streets, near the 3400 block of West Broad Street, and that construction would soon begin on a new ballpark.[54] The announcement noted that the new facility would be of steel and concrete construction and when completed would seat more than 5,000 persons. The announcement concluded that work on the facility would begin the next week but that the park would not be ready until the 1942 season.[55]

Throughout the 1941 season, the Colts struggled to make the playoffs but they did not have the players who had led them in 1940. Buster Maynard was sold to the Giants in the fall of 1940, twenty-game winner Hank Banzer had been drafted into the army, and third baseman Eddie Horne and George Ferrell had retired.[56] The Colts ended the season with 67 victories and 71 losses for fifth place in league standings and out of the playoffs. For the season, the Colts had one .300 hitter, Luis Olmo, who hit .310 and one twenty-game winner—Jim Bivins compiled a record of 20–14. These two Colts were selected by a poll of league managers for the Piedmont League All-Star team.[57]

Ladies Night was observed by the Colts during the 1941 season, and there was a ceremony late in August honoring the "most popular," and the "most valuable" Colt. Shortstop Larry Kinzer was designated "most popular" and Luis Olmo was honored as "most valuable" Colt. On another occasion, a raffle was conducted at the park with ticket stub winners being awarded a booklet of ten pairs of tickets to Colt games.[58] During the second week of August, the local press noted a historic event of sorts, which occurred on Sunday night, August 10. On this date, 1,541 fans were at the restored Tate Field to see the Colts defeat Asheville 15–8. It was noted that this was the first Sunday night baseball game in Piedmont League history. Mooers changed the time from afternoon to evening because of the hot weather. Earlier police chief E.H. Organ had informed Mooers that "he could see no objection to playing on Sunday night."[59] An unusual affair for a ballpark was held at Tate Field on the evening of August 31. It took place between the end of the first game and the start of the second in a doubleheader with the Durham Bulls. There was a wedding between Colt pitcher Dewey Wilkins and Helen Sheffield with the Reverend R.B. Watkins, pastor of Raleigh Forbes Baptist Church, officiating. The affair had been publicized and more than 3,300 fans were at the park to witness and celebrate the wedding. The Colts, evidently inspired by this affair, won both ends of the doubleheader from the Bulls.[60]

The Piedmont League playoffs in 1941, which did not include the Colts, involved Norfolk, Portsmouth, Durham, and Greensboro. Norfolk was defeated by Durham in the first round and Greensboro eliminated Portsmouth. In the finals for the league championship, Durham won from Greensboro in four straight games.[61]

Following the close of the 1941 season, Mooers and manager Eddie Phillips conferred about prospects for the 1942 Colts. Mooers was pleased with Phillips and wanted him to continue as playing manager. However, following his injuries of the past season, Phillips told Mooers that he liked managing but that his playing days were over. Mooers then gave Phillips his release. Later, when Phillips was hired as manager of the Greenville, South Carolina entry in the Class B South Atlantic League, Mooers told a reporter that he was pleased to know that Phillips was "still in baseball."[62] In December 1941, Mooers signed the former major league outfielder Ben Chapman to serve as playing manger of the Colts for 1942. During the season, Chapman would fill a utility player role for the Colts.

Mooers field (courtesy of *Richmond Times-Dispatch*).

In the course of the season, he played a variety of positions including centerfield, third base, first base, left field and pitcher. He also pinch-hit on a number of occasions. For the season, he hit .324, and as a pitcher his record was 6–3. Chapman seems to have been a popular player with everyone except the umpires. In mid–August, he was honored at a "Ben Chapman Night." On this occasion, nearly 4,000 fans were at the game, and Chapman was presented a number of gifts, including a traveling bag, a watch, a pen and pencil set, and $400 in cash. His rapport with Piedmont League umpires was quite a contrast to that with the fans. Once, when he protested the decision of umpire Bud Newman, he was banished from the game. The reaction of some fans to this incident was to run onto the field and accost the umpire, who was rescued by the police. During the first round of the playoffs at the end of the season between Richmond and Portsmouth, an altercation occurred between Chapman and umpire I.H. Chase. In this encounter, Chapman struck the umpire. For this outburst, Chapman was banished from baseball for one year and fined $100.[63]

The 1942 campaign for the Colts and Chapman began on April 1, with two weeks of spring training at Wilson, North Carolina. Spring

Eddie Mooers and Ben Chapman (courtesy of *Richmond Times-Dispatch*).

training began as workmen were "rushing" to have the new park ready for the home opening game on April 25. Construction on the new ballpark, which would be called Mooers Field, had been underway since the previous summer and although it was not "quite complete" when the Colts returned from Wilson on April 17, the facilities were available for playing. The new park cost in excess of $100,000 and had grandstand seating for approximately 5,000 persons. It was a modern facility and not, as Mooers had said of Tate Field, an "eye sore." The first games at Mooers Field were exhibitions with Lancaster of the Eastern League, and the Colts won both contests.[64] The Colts opened the season at Durham on April 23 but returned home to face the Bulls in the Colts' home opener at Mooers Field on April 25. On this occasion, 2,638 fans were on hand and Virginia's governor, Colgate W. Darden, threw out the first pitch. The game was not an auspicious start for the Colts as they lost to the Bulls 14–4.[65]

During the first season at the new ballpark, there were a number of promotional events designed to attract fans to Mooers Field. The first of these took place about three weeks into the season. On May 14, there was a game between the Colts and the Norfolk Naval Training Station for the benefit of the Navy Relief Fund. On this occasion, the Naval Station was victorious 3–2. Their pitcher was Fred Hutchinson of the Detroit Tigers.[66] One of the most popular features of the season took place on Friday night, June 11. This program, prior to the game, featured vocalist Sunshine Sue and her group. Sunshine Sue was a popular figure on radio station WRVA's Old Dominion Barn Dance program. This program was a weekly Saturday night feature on the station, and some considered it a Richmond version of Nashville's Grand Old Opry. The press estimated that approximately 2,900 fans attended this program and the game which followed. The evening of July 9 was "War Bond Night" at Mooers Field. On this evening, five $25 bonds were awarded to lucky ticket holders—one to a lady fan, one to a man, one to a "bleacherite," one to a boy and one to a Negro fan. Later that same month, the Colt management promoted a running and throwing contest between Colt and Portsmouth players as a prelude to the evening game. This exhibition included a seventy-yard dash, base circling, and an accurate throwing contest.[67] On another occasion and prior to his departure for service in the Marines, there was an appreciation night for pitcher Jim Bivin. At this time, he was given a gift of $114.68 collected from fans at the game. One of the highlights of the season for baseball fans in Richmond was the appearance of Bob Feller and the Norfolk Naval Training team on July 20. In this game, witnessed by 1,665 fans, Feller struck out fourteen Colt batters, and he also hit a homerun as the Naval team defeated the Colts 6–4. The final of the season "specials" was held on August 2 when there was a pre-game program featuring "Happy" Frank McKeown, who was promoted as "an armless baseball comedian." The press reported that more than 4,600 persons were at Mooers Field for this program and the doubleheader with Greensboro. Interspersed with these events were the observance of various Ladies Nights.[68]

There was one observance during the 1942 season which was not a "special;" it was ordered by the Federal Government. On the night of June 17, reflecting wartime conditions, there was an experimental blackout in the state of Virginia. This was ordered by the National Office of Civilian Defense and was to test the effectiveness of the blackout and enforcement personnel before an emergency situation might arise. The blackout was from "dusk to dawn," and, on this night, there were no baseball games played in any Virginia city.[69]

When the Piedmont League concluded on September 7, the Colts were in third place behind Greensboro and Portsmouth; Charlotte ended the season in fourth place. The Colts' Louis Olmo led the league in hitting with an average of .337. He was also the triple crown winner in the league as well as its most valuable player. The team's only other .300 hitter was manager Ben Chapman with a .324 average. Curt Johnson led Colt pitchers with an 18–7 record. Only two other pitchers won as many as ten games: Guy Fletcher was 13 and 9, and, before Jim Bivin departed for the Marines, he also had a 13–9 record. When the Piedmont League All-Star Team, selected by managers of the different clubs, was announced in mid–August, it included three Colts—Olmo, Johnson and Chapman. Chapman was chosen for his versatility as all-star utility player. In the first round of the Shaughnessy playoffs, Richmond lost to Portsmouth, and Greensboro eliminated Charlotte. In the playoff finals for the league championship, Greensboro defeated Portsmouth and was declared league champion for 1942.[70]

With Chapman banished from baseball for a year, Mooers had to seek a new pilot for the 1943 Colts. As it turned out, Mooers did not have to look far since he appointed the Colt veteran shortstop Larry Kinzer. Kinzer hit .306 for the Colts in 1940, and the previous season he hit .263. Kinzer and the Colts began spring practice on Mooers Field on April 10 to prepare for the season opener at Durham on May 4. This season, due to players going into military service and limitation on travel, the Piedmont League was reduced to 130 games and league membership to six teams: Richmond, Norfolk, Portsmouth, Lynchburg, Roanoke, and Durham. When Kinzer began drills on April 10, only six Colts were present. However, a week later, seventeen were working out at Mooers Field and Kinzer expressed satisfaction with their progress. One of the rookies in camp was a Cuban pitcher Julio Acosta.[71] Some former and potential players had given up baseball for the duration of the war and had gone to work in the shipyards and various other war industries. For such work, the pay was better than the $200 monthly average salary in the Piedmont League, and it might also prevent them from being drafted. The Colts' leading hitter and the league's most valuable player for 1942, Luis Olmo, had been acquired by the Brooklyn Dodgers.[72]

After one month of training and intra-squad play, the Colts departed Richmond on May 3 for a three-game series with the Durham Bulls. They won three straight at Durham, and the teams then returned to Richmond for the Colts' home opener on the night of May 7. The Colts defeated Durham 8–7 before 2,756 fans. The 1943 season would be a successful one for the Colts. When the season ended, they had a record of 72 victories and 57 losses, good enough for second place in the league standings and one place behind the Norfolk Tars. Although the Colts featured only one .300 hitter, second baseman Tony Castano, who hit .333, was the batting champion of the Piedmont League. The Colts pitching staff was led by the Cuban rookie Acosta, who posted a 17–8 record. One of these wins was a no-hit 8–0 victory over Portsmouth on June 5. Two other pitchers, Curtis Johnson and Al Sima, won 14 and 10 games respectively.[73] In the first round of the playoffs, the Colts were eliminated by Norfolk in four games and Portsmouth defeated Roanoke. The Tars then won over Portsmouth to claim the championship of the Piedmont League. At the close of the season, Acosta was sold to the Milwaukee Brewers of the American Association League for a reported $7,500.[74]

During the 1943 season, the game time at Norfolk and Portsmouth was modified to conform with the Office of Civilian Defense directive that no night baseball would be permitted in cities along the Atlantic coast. Most games in these cities were afternoon or twilight games. The ban on night baseball would be lifted for the 1944 season.[75]

In addition to a few observances of Ladies Night, there was only one special event at Mooers Field during the 1943 season. On August 22, the fans and team held an appreciation day for Larry Kinzer. At this time, he was presented a watch, cufflinks and tie pin, a floral tribute from a devout Negro woman fan of many years (Nannie Powell), and a gift of $275 contributed by the fans. On this same occasion, Julio Acosta was recognized as the team's "Most Popular Player," the result of a poll conducted by the local press, and he was given a traveling bag. On the evening of July 28 before the start of the seventh inning, the Colts and fans observed a period of silence in "respect of John Smith." Smith was the veteran groundskeeper who kept the playing field in "top condition." The previous day, while working on the field, he dropped dead.[76]

Since 1938 there had been radio broadcasts of Colts games. The home games were live and the away games were "aired or recreated through wire reports." On April 4, prior to the opening of the season, Mooers informed the press and the public that WRNL, which had broadcast the games for the past two years, did not renew their contract for 1943. Mooers noted that since no other station was interested in carrying the games, there would be no broadcasts in 1943. Actually, as noted previously, the broadcast of Colt games would not resume until 1947.[77]

When the Piedmont League opened on April 27, 1944, it was an all–Virginia circuit for the first time in its history. During the off season, the Durham Bulls departed and were replaced by Newport News. Norfolk, Newport News, Portsmouth, Richmond, Lynchburg, and Roanoke now comprised the Piedmont League, and this alignment would remain stable for the next nine years. Declining attendance in the North Carolina cities, problems associated with securing competent players in the wartime shortage of personnel, and government restrictions on travel exacerbated the problems of league members and helped to prompt a realignment of the league.

In the meantime, in February 1944, the Colt manager and shortstop, Larry Kinzer, who was currently on the staff of the lower school at Fork Union Military Academy, was reclassified by his draft board and was subject to possible early induction into the army. This prompted Mooers to seek Ben Chapman and try to have him as manager for the Colts in 1944. Chapman, whose suspension from baseball ended in the fall of 1943, was available, and, prior to the beginning of spring training, was signed by Mooers for a salary of $1500 a month.[78] Chapman arrived in Richmond several days before training began on April 3. When the Colts began practice, he informed a reporter covering the team that this season he promised to "have no more run-ins with umpires." During the first week of April, Chapman and twenty-two Colts began spring drills at Mooers Field. The Giants had promised owner Eddie Mooers that they would try to send him some help before the season opened. Prior to the opening game, the Colts played exhibition contests with military contingents from Fort Lee, Camp Pickett, and a team from the 324th Fighter Squadron. All of these military nines were from encampments located in the greater Richmond area.[79]

The Colts home opener with Newport News on April 27 was postponed because of rain and was played the following day before 2,000 fans. The Colts were victorious 13–6. The next day, with manager Chapman pitching a one-hitter, the Colts won 11–0. As the season progressed, the Colts' position in the standings fluctuated from third to fifth place. At the close of the season on September 10, they occupied fourth place, sufficient to assure them a position in the playoffs.[80] Although the season was not as turbulent for Chapman as the 1942 one, his promise to have no contests with umpires was soon cast aside. Less than one month into the season, he was banished from a game because of his vigorous and prolonged dispute with the decision of an umpire. Within less than a week, in another altercation with an umpire, Chapman was forced to leave the game, and he was fined $50 for his conduct. Chapman's final run-in with an official occurred two months later when he was ejected from a game because of his objection to the call of the home plate umpire.[81] Chapman's problems with Piedmont League umpires ended on August 1 when he was purchased by the Brooklyn Dodgers for a reported $10,000. At that time, Chapman possessed one of the best pitching records in the league—13–3. The wartime Dodgers felt that he would be a good addition to their staff.[82]

When Chapman went to Brooklyn, Mooers named his first baseman, Taylor Sanford, as interim manager of the Colts. Sanford had been
a popular player at the University of Richmond and was currently baseball coach and athletic director at Randolph-Macon College in Ashland,
Virginia. A month later, the Colts ended the season in fourth place, behind
Lynchburg, Portsmouth and Norfolk. In the first round of the playoffs,
the Colts were eliminated by the Lynchburg Cardinals, and Portsmouth
won over the Norfolk Tars. In the championship series, Lynchburg
defeated the Portsmouth Cubs four games to three. At the close of the
season, the Colts' seventeen-year-old shortstop Granville Hamner, a .283
hitter, was purchased from Mooers by the Philadelphia Phillies. Hamner
thus joined several other Colts and Piedmont alumni in the majors.[83]

For the 1944 season, the Colts did not have a single .300 hitter.
Interim manager Taylor Sanford led Colt hitters with an average of .294.
When Chapman left the Colts on August 1, his 13–3 record was the best
of any Colt pitcher. At the end of the season, the Colts' winningest pitcher
was Bucky Jacobs who was 12–6. Carmine DeRenzzo was the only other
hurler to win as many as ten games.[84] Except for the observance of several Ladies Nights, there were few innovations at Mooers Field in 1944.
However, the Colt management did make concessions to men in military
service, as organized baseball did throughout the country. In May, it was
announced that "fifty soldiers who have seen foreign service and are now
recuperating at the Army Air Base in the city attended the game as guests
of owner Eddie Mooers." A short while later, the press reported that Mooers had arranged for the local USO (United Service Organization) to dis-
tribute fifty free tickets to service men and women for each remaining
home game of the Colts' current season. Although Colts games were not
broadcast in 1944, Mooers arranged, through the local chapter of the
American Legion, for station WRNL to provide special broadcasts of
Colt home games to the veterans at McGuire Hospital.[85]

Perhaps the most popular or special feature of the Colts' 1944 season was the exhibition game that the Colts had with the Washington
Senators on July 11. Much publicity was given to the visit of this major
league club, and special admission prices for the contest were announced.
The weather was clear and mild on the evening of July 11, and a crowd
of 5,740 persons crowded into Mooers Field. The local press reported
that this was the "largest baseball crowd ever recorded in Richmond."
Manager Ben Chapman pitched for the Colts, but the Senators prevailed
7–1. Another popular feature which was held at the close of the season
was an appreciation night for interim manager Taylor Sanford. On this
occasion on September 8, 1,560 fans were at Mooers Field to honor

Sanford and see the Colts play the Norfolk Tars. Testimonials from players and officials and a gift of $250 contributed by fans were the highlights of the evening.[86]

In the winter of 1944–45, Mooers offered the managership of the Colts for the 1945 season to Taylor Sanford, who had served as interim manager when Chapman went to the Dodgers the past August. Sanford declined Mooers' offer because of duties at Randolph-Macon College. However, he agreed to remain a member of the Colts and to play first base.[87] Mooers then appointed Frank Rodgers as manager for the coming season. Rodgers had been an outfielder for the Colts in the early thirties and later managed teams in the Coastal Plains and the Bi-State Leagues. Rodgers arrived in Richmond, and Colt spring drills began at Mooers Field on April 2. The opening game of the season was scheduled for April 26. After two weeks of spring practice and intra-squad games, the Colts played several exhibition contests. In the ten day period prior to the league's opening date, the Colts played a semi-pro team from Staunton, a military nine from Camp Patrick Henry, and another army club from Fort Story. The opening game of a 140-game schedule for the Colts was an away contest with the Newport News Dodgers on April 26. It was an inauspicious beginning for the local nine as the Dodgers won 7–6. Two days later, playing the same team at Mooers Field, the Colts were victorious 3–0.[88]

Throughout most of the 1945 season, the Colts were challenging the Norfolk Tars for the league lead. However, the Tars, with help from the parent New York Yankees pulled ahead late in the season and won the pennant by five games. The Colts closed the season in second place with a record of 76 victories and 60 losses. Newport News and Portsmouth were third and fourth, and these four teams were involved in the playoffs for the league championship. In a remarkable difference from a year ago, the Colts in 1945 boasted four .300 hitters. Bill West, a left fielder, led the league in hitting with an average of .376, and he was also voted the league's most valuable player. Taylor Sanford hit .347, shortstop Courtney Driscoll had a .343 average, and third baseman Earl Pugh hit .314. Centerfielder Calvin Green was one percentage below .300 as he hit .299. Although the Colts did not have a twenty game winner, pitcher Mario Picone was the league's top winner with a record of 19–6 and he led the league in strikeouts with 202. Bucky Jacobs had an earned run average of 1.78 and a record of 16–6. Two other Colt hurlers, John Windzigl and Tom Faulkner, won eleven and twelve games respectively.[89] During this last season of the war years, there was only one special event at Mooers Field. This was an "Appreciation Day for Frank Rodgers," and it was held on the evening of

August 26. At this time, Rodgers was presented "a war bond, two traveling bags and a gift of $385.00 in cash."[90]

In the Shaughnessy playoffs, the Colts defeated Newport News in four straight games to advance to the finals. In the other first round, the Portsmouth Cubs surprised many baseball fans by defeating the league-leading Tars four games to three. In the championship finals, the Cubs defeated the Colts in four straight games and were declared Piedmont League champions for 1945.[91]

During the off-season, 1945–46, Frank Rodgers decided to leave Richmond. Later he signed to manage the Kinston, North Carolina team in the Coastal Plains League.[92] Probably upon the recommendation of Bill Terry of the New York Giants, Mooers then signed Ray Berres to manage the Colts. Berres was a thirty-seven-year-old catcher with sixteen years experience in professional baseball and was recently released by the Giants. When signed by Mooers, he announced that he expected to be a playing manager and would catch, maybe, 100 games during the season.[93] The new manager and thirty-seven candidates were on hand when spring training began on March 25. Because of some repair and maintenance work at Mooers Field, the first week of drills was held at Millhiser Field at the University of Richmond. On April 5, Mooers Field was ready and the Colts played the first of an eight-game exhibition schedule. In contests with International League clubs Toronto and Syracuse, the Colts suffered defeats. However, in contests with Eastern League clubs from Wilkes-Barre and Scranton the Colts were victorious.[94]

The Colts opened the 1946 season away from home at Newport News and lost to the Dodgers 13–11. After returning to Richmond, the Colts won their home opener, a doubleheader against Norfolk 4–1 and 5–1. These games were witnessed by 3,511 fans. The season was less than two weeks old when a modification in the time of weekend games was announced. Complying with the State Corporation Commission's directive to conserve energy, the Colts announced that from now on all weekend doubleheaders would begin at 2:30 p.m. Also, for a time, night games would become twi-night ones, beginning at 5:30 p.m. This same modification also applied to Norfolk, Newport News and Portsmouth.[95]

The 1946 season could be described as a disaster for the Colts. For most of the season, they were in either fifth or sixth place, and as the Colts floundered Barres became the object of fan and press criticism. His response to the Colts' plight was to resign and turn management over to someone else. On August 11, he left the hapless Colts and Eddie Mooers appointed the team's first baseman Mike Schemer as interim manger. At this time, the Colts were struggling to keep out of the league cellar.[96] A month later, the season ended with the Colts in fifth place, one spot from the cellar. Their record for the season was 60 victories and 80 losses. They had one .300 hitter, centerfielder Calvin Green, and no twenty game winners. Their leading pitcher was Chico Diaz, a native of Cuba, who posted a record of 13 and 8. No Colt was named to the league's all star nine. The Colts failed to make the playoffs, which included Roanoke, Portsmouth, Newport News and Norfolk. The eventual champion was the Newport News Dodgers.[97]

On March 1, 1947, the *Times-Dispatch* sports section featured two items about the Colts. One was that Eddie Mooers had appointed Robert "Bob" Lotshaw as manager of the Colts for the 1947 season; the other was that Mooers had sent out contracts to thirty-six prospective Colts. Lotshaw was a first baseman with many years in professional baseball, and it was correctly assumed that he would play first base. In March, prior to the opening of spring training at Mooers Field, Lotshaw and Mooers made a trip to Florida to talk with members of the Giants, Senators and Tigers organization about possible help during the coming campaign.[98] After ten days in Florida, the Colt duo returned to get ready for spring drills which began on April 1. After two weeks of conditioning prior to the season's opening game on April 24, the Colts played exhibition games at Mooers Field with Decatur, Iowa, of the Three-I-League and Utica and Allentown of the Eastern League.[99]

The Piedmont League schedule for 1947 was very much like previous ones. It provided for 140 games with each team having seventy home dates and seventy away games. The season opened on April 24, and the last game was scheduled for September 7. The Colts opened the season with an away game at Newport News. Although the Colts won this game 11–3, manager Bob Lotshaw was ejected from the game by the plate umpire because of Lotshaw's vigorous and persistent arguing over called strikes. This was the first of a number of run-ins Lotshaw had with game officials during the season. In this respect, he was much like Ben Chapman. Later, in a contest at Mooers Field, Lotshaw and the Colt second baseman, Emil Cabrera, were banished from the game for disputing an umpire's decision on a play at third base. Two weeks later at a game in Norfolk, Lotshaw was ejected from the game for protesting decisions and for cursing plate umpire Frank Murray. Lotshaw's prolonged arguing and his refusal to leave the field until the umpires threatened to forfeit the game to the Tars led to a threatened suspension and an unannounced fine for the Colts manager. By mid–July, the local press noted that Lotshaw "had been kicked out of five games" and that owner Mooers was not pleased with his manager's conduct. Mooers was quoted as saying, "In

Class B baseball a team can't afford to lose players because of arguments with the umpire. ... It can't afford to lose its manager."[100] Evidently Lotshaw "got the message" as there were no reports of altercations with umpires throughout the latter portion of the Piedmont League season.

The 1947 Colts enjoyed the best attendance of any team in Colt history. The attendance figure for the seventy home games was approximately 170,000—for an average attendance of more than 2,400 a game. The largest crowd at Mooers Field was the opening game against Roanoke on May 4. On this occasion, 6,079 fans were present, and on July 4 an estimated 5,500 witnessed the Colts split a doubleheader with Newport News. At another time, a Ladies Night crowd of 4,000 saw the Colts lose to Roanoke 6–4.[101] Perhaps the increased attendance was associated with the additional publicity the team received via the radio broadcast of its games. After a four-year hiatus, the Colts were back on the air. Local radio station WLEE, a Mutual Network affiliate, resumed broadcast of Colt games in 1947. This station would continue such broadcasts as long as the Colts were members of the Piedmont League (through the 1953 season).

The Colts ended their 1947 campaign in fourth place, behind Roanoke, Norfolk, and Portsmouth and qualified for a spot in the playoffs. For the 1947 season, the Colts had two .300 hitters; left fielder Len Morrison was the team's leading hitter with a .315 average. Morrison also tied with Portsmouth's Vern Shetler for the league's homerun title with twenty round-trippers. The Colts' winningest pitcher was John Michael who compiled a 14–13 record. Four other hurlers won ten or more games: Bill Waldt, Walt Sumey, Jim Trexler, and Chico Diaz. One Colt, shortstop Bud Hardin (.271) was chosen by the league managers as a member of the Piedmont League's All-Star Team.[102]

In the post-season playoffs, the Colts were eliminated in the first round by Roanoke. The Colts won the first game in this series, but the Roanoke contingent swept the next four. In the other first round, Norfolk eliminated Portsmouth four games to nothing. In the championship series, Roanoke won from Norfolk four games to three and was declared champion of the Piedmont League for 1947.[103]

Mooers did not renew the contract of the Colts' 1947 contentious manager Bob Lotshaw. During the off-season Mooers sought advice form colleagues in baseball and, in February 1948, announced that the new manager for the 1948 edition of the Colts would be Charlie "Greek" George. George was a catcher and had compiled many years in professional ball. However, this would be his first experience as manager. The Colts would not only have a new manager but also a new and improved method of transportation for the 1948 campaign. On March 12, the local press noted that Mooers had purchased a "super deluxe bus" to replace the old "school bus looking bus" the Colts had been using—a vehicle which "rode something like an ox-cart." The new bus was described as having capacity for twenty-nine. It had reclining seats, rubber seat cushions, and reading lights.[104]

When spring practice began at Mooers Field on March 29, George promised that the Colts would be a hard-working and "hustling" team and that he planned to catch 100 or more of the 140 games scheduled for the season. George, however, was disappointed in his plans to be a playing manager. In one of the early games (May 2), he was in a collision at home plate with a Lynchburg base runner and suffered a "dislocated left knee." This injury required him "to be out of every day action for the rest of the season," and he was relegated to managing from the bench.[105] Following spring drills and exhibition games with Petersburg of the Virginia League, Jersey City of the International league and Albany and Wilkes Barre of the Eastern League, the Colts opened the 1948 season at home with a 10–3 victory over Newport News. This contest was witnessed by 5,246 fans.[106]

The 1948 season was a disastrous one for the Colts. They ended the season on September 7 in the league's cellar with a record of 64 wins and 75 losses. By mid-season, fans and the press were criticizing the managing skills of George. Although he did not experience troubles with umpires as some Colt managers, the press reported dissension between George and various Colt players over what was termed "his meat-axe approach in dealing with players." One of his confrontations with players involved the team's leading hitter, Lewis Davis. The press noted that George offered Mooers his resignation in mid-season but was persuaded by the owner to complete the season. When the season ended, the Colts had only one regular who hit .300, right fielder Lewis Davis with a .312 average. The Colts' leading pitcher, Red Ennis, posted a 16–12 record, and Mike Rossi was 15–9.[107] In the league playoffs, which included Newport News, Portsmouth, Lynchburg and Roanoke, the Newport News Dodgers were victorious and were Piedmont League champions for 1948.

During the oftimes contentious and disappointing season, there was one solemn occasion observed at Mooers Field. On the evening of August 17, in a game with the Norfolk Tars, the game was halted at the middle of the fourth inning and a period of silence was observed "in honor of the memory of Babe Ruth who died yesterday of cancer."[108]

With the resignation of "Greek" George at the end of the season, Mooers began to focus attention on who he would have to manage the Colts in 1949. Mooers did not have to search long or far since he appointed the popular 1948 Colt second baseman, Vincent "Vinnie" Smith, to manage the Colts for the coming season. Smith arrived in Richmond early in March to meet the Colts and prepare for the trip to Sebring, Florida, where Mooers had made arrangements for spring training. The Florida facility was owned by a group of Sebring citizens, and it was the spring training center for the Newark Bears from 1936 to 1941 and also for two years after the war.[109] The Colts were scheduled to depart Richmond on March 18 and return to Mooers Field on April 7 to engage in exhibition games prior to the opening of the Piedmont League season on April 22.

On March 18, Smith and eighteen Colts left Richmond via bus and twenty-four hours later arrived at their training base in Florida. This journey to and from Florida was broken by an overnight stop in Waterboro, South Carolina. Before leaving home, Smith told the players that he hoped there would be "none of the dissension which the team experienced last season."[110] At a later date, Smith spoke before the Sportsmans Club of Richmond, and it was reported that he had "kind words for all members of the team." He also told his audience that he did not believe the Colts would end the current season in the league's cellar.[111] After two weeks in the Sunshine State, the Colts returned to Mooers Field and in the following days played exhibition games with Petersburg, Albany, Buffalo and the Boston Braves. The latter game drew 9,382 fans, and Mooers declared that this was "the largest turnout for baseball in Richmond's history." The Braves, the previous season's pennant winners in the National League, defeated the Colts 12–7.[112]

The Colts opened their 1949 season at Newport News and lost to the Dodgers 7–5. Two days later, the same two teams opened the season in Richmond, and the Colts were victorious 6–5. The 1949 season witnessed a remarkable turn-around for the Colts. When the season ended in September, the Colts were in third place with a record of 71 wins and 68 losses; they were joined in the playoffs by Portsmouth, Lynchburg and Roanoke.[113] The Colts' right fielder, Ralph Davis, was the team's only .300 hitter with an average of .308; Manager Smith hit .249. The Colts' top pitcher was Jim Frederico who posted a 16–11 record. Two other hurlers, Mike Rossi and the veteran George Sumey, had 14–12 and 13–9 records respectively. The Colts were eliminated in the first round of the playoffs by Portsmouth, and Lynchburg ousted Roanoke. In the championship finals, the Lynchburg Cardinals were victorious over the Portsmouth nine by four games to two.[114]

Neither Smith nor any of the other Colts seemed to have had many

Opposite: **Vincent Smith (courtesy of Richmond Times-Dispatch).**

differences with game officials in 1949. Perhaps the new league rule that any one ejected from a game by an umpire was subject to an automatic fine of $10 prompted a greater degree of calmness on the ball field.[115] The 1949 Colts played host to one prominent baseball visitor during the season. On June 19, there was a ceremony at Mooers Field just prior to the start of the game when the "baseball immortal Cy Young was introduced." Young made a brief speech which was audible to the crowd through the field's public address system.[116]

Mooers and Colt fans were pleased with the team's showing and with the style and work of manager Vinnie Smith. And early in September, prior to the final game of the season, Mooers announced that Smith had agreed to return and would manage the Colts in 1950. Smith spent the off-season at his home in Pittsburgh and returned to Richmond during the first week of March 1950. He wished to confer with Mooers about the possibility of securing help for the Colts in two areas—pitching and the outfield. He also wanted to meet the returning Colts and make preparations for the spring training trip to Florida. The Colts would train for two weeks at the facility in Sebring, which was owned by the Sebring Firemens Association. Mooers liked this facility, and, during the spring drills, he signed a contract with the Firemens Association to use it as a spring training facility through the spring of 1953.[117] On March 18, Smith and thirty players departed Richmond for Florida. Several of the contingents were former college players, and some were players whose experience had been in Class C or D baseball. The Colts' Florida training ended on April 7 when they departed and headed for home to play their exhibition schedule prior to the opening of the Piedmont League season on April 26. The Colts played exhibition games with the Baltimore Orioles and Syracuse Chiefs of the International League, Petersburg of the Virginia League, Danville of the Carolina League, Albany of the Eastern League, Harrisburg of the Interstate League, and the Boston Red Sox.[118]

The Colts opened the 1950 Piedmont League's 140-game schedule on April 26 in a contest with Portsmouth. This was a home opener and was played before 3,173 fans who witnessed the defeat of the Colts 7–6.[119] The 1950 season was a struggle for the Colts, with pitching being a major problem. However, during the last week of the season, they succeeded in clinching fourth place in the league standings and thereby qualified for the playoffs. The Colts compiled an unspectacular record of 63 wins and 76 losses. Their leading and only .300 hitter was centerfielder Ralph Davis who hit .316; three other players hit .280 or better. The leading Colt pitcher was Mike Rossi who compiled a 15–15 record; Red Ennis and Carroll Sweiger had records of 12–11 and 10–16 respectively. In the playoffs, the Colts were eliminated in four straight games by the Portsmouth club. In the other first round, Roanoke ousted Lynchburg. In the championship finals, Roanoke was victorious over Portsmouth by four games to three.[120]

One innovation in the Piedmont League during the 1950 season was the holding of an all-star game. All-star players were chosen by the sport writers in league team cities and by the managers of the different clubs. The players chosen were designated Eastern and Western All-Stars. The Eastern All-Stars were chosen to represent Norfolk, Newport News, and Portsmouth; selections from Richmond, Lynchburg and Roanoke were designated as Western All-Stars. The all-star game was played at Mooers Field on the evening of July 13 before 3,942 fans. There were four Colts chosen as members of the western contingent: third baseman Roy Allen, centerfielder Ralph Davis, shortstop Dick Klaus, and Vinnie Smith. The western representatives were victorious in this extra inning (10 innings) contest 4–3.[121]

One schedule change introduced by Eddie Mooers during the 1950 season concerned the starting time for Sunday games at Mooers Field. Sunday games were usually played in the afternoon, beginning at 2:30. However, on August 1, Mooers announced to the press that the remaining Sunday home games would be played at night. He explained that the change was made because of the intense summer heat; fans, he declared, would be more comfortable and enjoy the game more after the sun went down.[122]

Two days after the Colts were eliminated in the playoffs manager Vincent Smith decided to call it quits and gave his resignation to Mooers. Smith was one of Mooers' favorite people, and he did not blame him for the Colts' 1950 record. Undoubtedly, he would have retained Smith for the 1951 season. However, Smith was disappointed with the Colts and with the team's lack of ability to get sufficient help from the Giants, Senators and others. He possibly saw the Colts' 80,000 drop in attendance from the 1949 season as a reflection of his ability to lead a winning team. Also, by the end of the season, Smith had been contacted by Chicago White Sox officials and invited to try out with them in 1951. It was agreed that if he did not make the White Sox team that he would be offered a minor league managership in the White Sox organization. When Smith resigned, Mooers remarked to a sports writer that he should have time to find a competent manager for the next season and stated that he wished to have a playing manager.[123]

During the winter, Mooers changed his mind about acquiring a playing manager when he had the opportunity to sign Billy Herman to manage the Colts. Herman had many years experience in major league ball, having played with the Dodgers and Cubs, and, in 1947, having served as manager of the Pittsburgh Pirates. Herman arrived in Richmond in mid–March to meet with Colt players and prepare to leave for spring training in Sebring, Florida. On March 26, Herman and twenty players departed Richmond, but, prior to leaving, he and Mooers had agreed that the Colts needed help. While in Florida, Herman was to talk with officials of the Washington Senators, Boston Braves, and others about having them option some players to the Colts.[124] The Colts were in training for two weeks and, during this time, also played two exhibition contests with the Tampa club of the Florida International League. The team returned to Richmond on April 11. Prior to their home opening game, the team played exhibition games with Buffalo, Albany, and the Philadelphia Phillies.[125]

The Colts' 1951 home opener was with Newport News. Before a crowd of 2,059, the Colts lost 4–3. In early July, after a ten-game losing streak and with the Colts in fourth place in league standings with a record of 41 wins and 45 losses, Herman resigned as manager. In an interview with a *Times-Dispatch* writer, he declared that he resigned "because he had a poor team and because he could see no hope of improving it." He noted that Mooers had promised to obtain players but had not been successful, that the Colts were weak in pitching, that two outfielders were needed, and that the team was weak at several other positions. Mooers' response was that he was disappointed and that he had tried to persuade Herman to remain until the end of the season. With Herman's departure, Mooers appointed third baseman Roy Allen as interim manager. In the meantime, Billy Herman was signed as a coach by the Brooklyn Dodgers.[126]

During the second half of the season under the guidance of Allen, the Colts experienced a remarkable turnaround. And when the season ended on September 3, the Colts were in second place in Piedmont League standings, second to Norfolk. The Colts' season record was 77 wins and 63 losses. Centerfielder Ray Poole led Colt batters and was the team's only .300 hitter with an average of .305. Four Colt hurlers won twelve games or more. Jim Frederico posted a 17–11 record; Dewey Wilkins was 16–9; Wade Browning was 16–12; and Red Ennis' was 13–11. The Shaughnessy playoffs involved Norfolk, Portsmouth, Newport News, and Richmond. In the first round, the Colts eliminated Newport News, and Norfolk defeated Portsmouth. The championship finals between Norfolk and Richmond was won by the Tars four games to two.[127]

During the 1951 season, there was one modification associated with Ladies Night, a feature at Mooers Field for many years. The press noted that on Ladies Night, fans would be required to pay the federal and state taxes which were levied on all adult tickets.[128] The practice of the Piedmont League sponsoring an all-star game between eastern and western clubs was continued in 1951. Among the all-stars selected by sport writers and league managers were two Colts—Ralph Davis, right fielder, and Bill Cox, first baseman. This second all-star contest was held in Lynchburg on the evening of July 23 and the Eastern All-Stars representing Norfolk, Portsmouth and Newport News easily won by a score of 8–0 before a crowd of 1,823.[129] A month prior to the all-star contest, the Colts played a special charity benefit game at Mooers Field. On June 3, the game with Roanoke, before 2,019 fans, was for the benefit of the Virginia Cerebral Palsy Fund. Another benefit game for this same charity would be played on May 22, 1952.[130]

Despite the Colts' impressive second half finish in 1951 under the interim manager Roy Allen, Mooers did not choose him to manage the Colts in 1952. After the close of the season, Allen left Richmond, and in February 1952 Mooers signed Tom McConnell to manager the Colts for the coming season. McConnell was no newcomer to the Piedmont League; he was with Charlotte in 1950 and during the 1951 season was a utility infielder with the Colts, playing mostly at shortstop. He had served in the U.S. Air Corps between 1943 and 1946 and had been in professional baseball since his return from service in 1946. For several years, he played for different teams in the Phillies' organization.[131] On March 22, O'Connell and a contingent of Colts left Richmond for two weeks of spring training in Sebring, Florida. Before their departure, he expressed to a sports writer that he was pleased to be with the Colts, and he expected a "good season." After spring practice, the Colts returned to Mooers Field on April 9 to prepare for the opening of the Piedmont League season on April 28. However, before the opening date, the Colts played exhibition games with Syracuse, Toronto and Schenectady.[132] The Colts' opponent for the season opener was Newport News, and, before 2,925 fans at Mooers Field, the Colts were victorious by a score of 6–1. The Colts not only won their opening game but went on a six-game winning streak during the first week and a half of the season.[133]

During the first month of the season, the Norfolk Tars dominated the league and began "running away from" the rest of the clubs. By June 20, the Tars had a twelve-game lead, and, with attendance lagging, the directors of the league decided to play a "split season." They hoped that this would spur interest in the league and boost attendance. Therefore, on June 26, the second portion of play in this, the first Piedmont League split season since 1936, began.[134] Little changed in the league as a result of the split season, and the Norfolk Tars continued to dominate the league and won the pennant by a margin of twenty-one games. One of these games, played at Mooers Field on July 12, featured Wilson Parson, a nineteen-year-old pitcher for the Tars. On this occasion, before a partisan crowd of approximately 2,000, he pitched a no-hitter against the Colts as Norfolk won 1–0.[135] The split season did not affect the Shaughnessy playoffs, which were based on the entire season record of a club. Others who were in the playoffs were Portsmouth, Richmond, and Lynchburg. The Colts had a third place record of 69 wins and 66 losses. The Colts had one .300 hitter, third baseman John Sivinski with a batting average of .317; manager O'Connell hit only .227. Their leading pitcher was Dewey Wilkins who won 18 and lost 10. Three other hurlers won ten or more games: George Sumey (12–11), Alton Brown (11–10) and Red Ennis (10–13).[136]

In 1952, there was a modification in the Piedmont League summer all-star game. Instead of it being a contest between Eastern and Western All-Stars, the 1952 All-Star game featured a contest between a team of all-stars selected by league managers and the league-leading Tars. Two Colts were chosen as all-stars—center fielder Joe Montiero and pitcher Red Ennis. This game was played at Norfolk on July 10 before 6,503 fans and the Tars defeated the All Stars 7–6.[137] In the first round of the post season playoffs, the Colts surprised the Norfolk Tars, and perhaps themselves, by eliminating the Tars four games to three. In the other first round, Portsmouth ousted Lynchburg. In the championship finals, the Colts lost the first game to Portsmouth and then won four straight. The last two games of this series were played at Mooers Field, and each was witnessed by an average of 3.500 fans.[138]

Despite the Colts having one of their most successful seasons in 1952, Eddie Mooers chose not to employ Tom O'Connell for a second season as manager for his team. When asked about his decision by a news reporter, Mooers replied that he refused to reappoint O'Connell for the same reason that he had not made Roy Allen manager earlier—he was displeased with the "failure of both men to maintain discipline on the club."[139] Mooers first offered the managership to his second baseman Garvin Hamner. Hamner declined the offer, and Mooers appointed Charles Letchas. Letchas was a veteran of seventeen years in professional baseball, ten of them in the Southern Association; and, during the war, he was with the Philadelphia Phillies. He was a utility infielder with the Chattanooga Lookouts in 1952, and he hit .288.[140] Letchas arrived in Richmond in mid–March, talked with Mooers about the Colt prospects, met team members as they arrived, and made preparations for spring training, which would begin at Sebring, Florida, on March 30. On

March 29, Letchas and thirteen Colts departed Richmond via bus, and Mooers assured him that other players would join them in Florida. Mooers also departed about this time for Florida; he was to visit the training camps of the Senators, Red, and Tigers to see if any players might be optioned to the Colts.[141] The Colts' schedule included ten days of drills. They would then return to Mooers Field to prepare for the opening game of the new season on April 23.

The 1953 season was quite different from the previous ones in several respects. For one thing, two new members had been admitted to the league. During the off season, the franchises of the Hagerstown, Maryland and York, Pennsylvania were admitted to the Piedmont League, making it once again an eight-team league.[142] The 1953 season was also the first season that a black player performed in the league. Six years after Branch Rickey and Jackie Robinson erased the color line in major league baseball, the Piedmont League had its first Negro players. During this season, three clubs—the Colts, Newport News, and York—all had Negro players on their rosters. The first black player signed by the Colts was Whit Graves, a right-handed pitcher. Graves was a native of Richmond and a graduate of Maggie Walker High School. For several years, he was a member of the Richmond Giants, a black semi-pro club. In 1950, he joined the Indianapolis Clowns, and, in the winter of 1952, played for a team in the Dominican Republic. Following conversations between Graves and Mooers, Graves was signed to a Colt contract in March 1953.[143] Also in the spring of 1953, Mooers welcomed three other black players for tryouts with the Colts. Garnett Blair had been a pitcher for the Homestead Grays in the early 1940s and also for several years after the war. For the previous two years, he had been coaching baseball at Virginia Union University in Richmond. The other two black players given tryouts were recent graduates of Armstrong High School—Louis Knight and Raymond Cherry. Of the four black players given tryouts by the Colts in 1953, only one was signed and was with the Colts for the season. Whit Graves was a pitcher for the Colts, and, at the end of the 1953 season, he had a record of 6 wins and 12 losses.[144]

The 1953 Piedmont League season opener for the Colts was on April 23 at Newport News, and the Colts won this game 10–5. Two days later in the opening home game at Mooers Field, with Graves pitching, the Colts defeated Norfolk 10–9.[145] The first week of the season might very well have been the high point of the season for the Colts. One month later, the team was in the league cellar, the same position they occupied when the season ended on September 8. By the first of June, reflecting the disintegrating morale on the team, three players quit and left the city.

One of these men had quarreled with manager Letchas, and the others left to "seek employment other than baseball." Mooers was shocked by the players leaving and said he was made "speechless" by their actions and declared it was "most unfortunate."[146] A losing team, low player morale, a bit of dissension and collapsing attendance prompted Mooers to try various gimmicks to attract fans to the games. One attempt was to promote a Bargain Day at the park. On June 6, it was announced that, on bargain day, admission prices would be cut for both adults and children. This device resulted in 1,069 fans attending a game in which York defeated Richmond 16–7. The press reported that this was the first time in a month that the attendance at Mooers Field had reached 1,000.[147]

A popular gimmick instituted by Mooers at Colt home games late in June involved a contest between certain fans and "Iron Mike." Iron Mike was an automatic pitching machine used by the Colts for the first time in spring drills in 1953. Manager Letchas thought the use of the machine was a fine idea, and it was brought to Mooers Field. The first game to feature Iron Mike was on June 25 when ten fans "chosen at random" were selected to attempt to hit pitches thrown by Iron Mike. The rules of the hitting contest declared that if a batter hit a pitch, which was scored a "base hit," he would be rewarded with a "book of tickets" to Colt games. A triple was worth $30, and, if one's hit was declared a homerun by umpiring officials, one received $50. On the first Iron Mike night, three fans won ten-game ticket books, but no one won any money. Iron Mike would be a regular feature at one game for each of the remaining home series of the Colts.[148]

Although the Piedmont League expanded to eight teams for 1953, prior to the close of the season, it became a seven-team league. In mid–July, after suffering financial losses in excess of $18,000 the Roanoke Red Sox closed shop and dropped out of the league.[149] This required a slight modification of the remaining schedule and emphasized some of the problems the league was experiencing. The increasing expansion of television was blamed for affecting baseball attendance. Whether this was a valid criticism or not, Piedmont League attendance was down in all cities, and, for the Colts' final game, only 220 were in attendance at Mooers Field.[150]

The Colts ended the 1953 season in the Piedmont League cellar with a record of 45 wins and 86 losses. Norfolk won the pennant, and the playoffs involved the Tars, Newport News, Portsmouth, and Hagerstown.

Opposite: **Eddie Mooers and Whit Graves (courtesy of** *Richmond Times-Dispatch*).

The league championship was won by Norfolk, defeating Newport News in the finals.[151] The Colts' lone .300 hitter in 1953 was centerfielder Joe Montiero who compiled an average of .311. The Colts winningest pitcher was Red Ennis at 12–12. A week before the close of the Colts' disappointing season, manager Charlie Letchas announced to the press that he was resigning at the end of the season and would not return for the 1954 season.[152]

During the Colts' twenty-one year tenure in the Piedmont League, they qualified for the post season playoffs on twelve different occasions. They won the league pennant once and the league championship playoff series twice. During the off-season of 1953–54, changes in the structure of major league baseball resulted in Richmond's becoming a member of the Triple A International League.

CHAPTER VII

Richmond and
the International League,
1954–2000

Shortly after the close of the major league baseball season in 1953, the St. Louis Browns franchise was moved to Baltimore. At that time, Mayor Edward E. Haddock, with the support of several businessmen, sought to have the Baltimore franchise of the International league transferred to Richmond. During the fall of 1953, there was considerable discussion in Richmond between Frank Shaughnessy, president of the International League, Mayor Haddock, Eddie Mooers, Piedmont League officials, and Harry Seibold. Seibold was a business executive who wished to acquire the International League franchise for Richmond. On December 17, 1953, it was announced that Mooers had sold his Richmond franchise to Seibold for $25,000 and that the International League was willing to reimburse the Piedmont League $25,000 for its loss of the Richmond territory. It was noted that all was conditional upon Richmond providing a suitable park for Triple A baseball. International League officials had declared that Mooers Field was not adequate for AAA baseball.[1]

On a visit to Richmond, President Shaughnessy had expressed the opinion that Parker Field might be renovated to serve as a baseball park for the city's AAA team. Parker Field was the site of the old fair grounds and was used by local high schools as a football playing ground. Parker Field was named in honor of William H. Parker, a long-time supporter of amateur sports in Richmond. Through the efforts of Mayor Haddock, the Richmond City Council approved the leasing of Parker Field, and the mayor announced that a corporation was being formed to sell $300,000 in bonds to provide funds to renovate the field and have it ready for the opening of the 1954 baseball season.[2]

On January 12, 1954, Richmond was formally accepted into the International League, replacing Baltimore. Eddie Mooers moved his Colts to the Petersburg-Colonial Heights area and was granted membership in the Piedmont League. At the same time that Parker Field was being renovated, Harry Seibold was busy trying to assemble his team. The International League sought to help him, and he acquired several former Oriole players. Other teams in the International League offered to make players available, and there was hope in Richmond that some major league clubs would also assist the new AAA entry. Most of the players Seibold acquired were older men and "past their prime." A few young players, with limited experience, were signed, and Seibold sought to form a "working agreement" with several major league clubs.[3]

At the same time that Seibold was seeking players, he hired Luke Appling to manage the team for the 1954 season. Appling had played twenty-one seasons at shortstop for the Chicago White Sox. He had previously managed the White Sox AA farm club at Memphis where he won the Dixie Series in 1952 and the pennant in 1953. Fans and local sport writers agreed that Appling seemed to be an excellent choice for the Richmond club. Seibold also signed Johnny Mize as a part-time coach for spring training and the exhibition season. He had hoped to sign Mize as a full-time players-coach, but the ex–Yankee star had agreed to work for a New York radio station during the regular season.[4]

Richmond opened its spring training season on March 7, 1954, in Sanford, Florida, with twenty-six players on its roster. Seibold was confident and optimistic about the team's chances for the upcoming season. He acknowledged that there would likely be holes in the pitching and middle infield positions, but he had contacted several major league clubs about their optioning players to Richmond.[5] In Richmond, Mayor Haddock, who led the cause of bringing Triple A Baseball to the city, had suggested that the team be named the "Confederates." Seibold agreed, citing the name's rich local significance, and it was formally announced that the new team would be the Richmond Confederates. Although the name was not expected or intended to offend anyone, Richmond's black community took offense to the team's name. Seeking to avoid any controversy that might alienate fans, Seibold agreed to change the team's name to Virginians, the name of Richmond's earlier entry in the Inter-

Edward Haddock (courtesy of Richmond Times-Dispatch).

national League from 1915–17. Richmond sport writers shortened the name to "Vees," which seemed to be popular with all concerned.[6]

By the end of the first week in April, the construction and renovations at Parker Field were completed. On April 8, 1954, the Virginians played an exhibition game with the New York Yankees before 12,000 fans. The Vees' first home game of the International League season was on April 21, a game in which the Rochester Red Wings were victorious. This might have been an omen of the type of season the Vees were to have. Two months into the season, the Vees occupied the cellar position in the league. Their season record of 60–94 placed them one position from the bottom of the league. Although the Vees did not win many games, 223,961 fans came to see them play. This was the third best attendance in the International League, and the fourth best in all of Triple A Baseball for the 1954 season.[7]

The 1954 season was a disappointment for owner Harry Seibold. Prior to the close of the season, he gave the local press a statement saying that, because of his large payroll and other expenses, he was considering moving the team to Tampa. And despite several rumors in the

off-season that the team was going to be moved, Seibold rehired manager Luke Appling and prepared for the 1955 season. The 1955 season was a disaster for the Virginians; their record of 58–95 placed them in the International League cellar. Attendance dropped by almost 100,000 as only 126,605 came to see the Vees play.[8]

The Vees' problems in the off-season overshadowed their problems on the playing field. Citing an unsettled tax claim of $79,717.68, the Federal Tax Collector seized the assets of the Richmond Virginians. The team's franchise, player contracts, and equipment were all seized to be sold to the highest bidder at public auction. Parker Field was not taken because it was owned by the city and leased to Seibold and the Virginians. Seibold owed admission taxes from the 1954 season and payroll taxes for both 1954 and 1955, and he owed the city back rent for the use of Parker Field.[9] Several days later Edward Haddock announced that a syndicate of six local businessmen was prepared to purchase the team at auction and continue its membership in the International League. Haddock revealed that the syndicate included Richard Reynolds, Jr., Lewis Markel, Dan Friedman, Jack Bernstein, E. Claiborne Robins, and Fritz Sitterding.[10]

On November 14, 1955, the auction was held at Parker Field, and the local syndicate bought the Virginians with a bid of $20,000, the only bid offered to the Internal Revenue Service for the team. The syndicate received the club's franchise, players contracts, and equipment. It also assumed responsibility for all back taxes owed and for rent due to the city of Richmond. Shortly thereafter, the syndicate reached a limited working agreement with the New York Yankees. Herman Krattenmaker was named general manager and former Yankee pitching great Eddie Lopat was named player-manager. With a new front office, new ownership and a major league working agreement, the Virginians began to prepare for the 1956 season.[11]

Although the Vees of 1956 were an improvement over the previous years, their record of 74–79 placed them in fifth place and out of the league playoffs. The team's season attendance of 214,533 was an increase of 90,000 over the previous year. The New York Yankees were pleased with the Vees' progress, and, at the close of the season, entered into a full working agreement with them. The Yankees also kept their agreement with Denver of the American Association. It was announced that the Yankees concluded they had enough talent for two Triple A teams.

Opposite: **Harry Seibold and Luke Appling (courtesy of** *Richmond Times-Dispatch***).**

Denver and Richmond would be on equal distribution of talent from the Yankees.[12]

The 1957 season was the best one for the Virginians since they became a member of the International League. Their record of 81–73 was good enough for third place—behind Toronto and Buffalo. Also during the season, the Vees drew a record attendance of 258,861. Although the Vees were eliminated by Buffalo in the first round of the playoffs, expectations were high for the Vees and manager Lopat for the upcoming 1958 season.[13]

The enthusiasm and success of the 1957 season did not carry over into 1958. The Virginians struggled all season and finished in the league's second division, nineteen games behind the pennant-winning Montreal and out of the playoffs. The 1958 Vees attracted 90,000 fewer fans than the previous season. But all hope was not lost. In the off-season, the Yankees announced that they would purchase the Virginians from the syndicate and operate the team as their number one Triple A farm club. Prior to the opening of the 1959 season, the Yankees replaced Eddie Lopat, who became their organizational pitching coach; Steve Souchock, who had managed the Yankee Double A affiliate at Binghamton the previous year, was named manager of the Vees.[14]

Richmond fans were excited about the 1959 season, and the 220,198 who came to Parker Field were not disappointed. The team closed the season with a 75–78 record and a fourth place finish, good enough to place them in the playoffs for the second time since they entered the league. The Virginians defeated pennant-winning Buffalo in the first round of the playoffs but lost in the finals four games to two to Havana.[15]

The 1960 Vees finished in second place in final league standings with a record of 82–70; however, they were eliminated in the first round of the playoffs. And despite the team's winning record, attendance at home games dropped by 30,000 from the previous season high. From 1960 on, it was mostly downhill for the Vees. The Yankees were not able to provide the team with the talent to succeed. In 1961, the team finished in sixth place; in 1962, the team experienced its worst record, with only 50 wins and 95 losses and ended the season one place from the cellar. Their 1962 attendance was the lowest ever as only 101,853 fans came to see Manager Warren "Sheriff" Robinson's hapless Vees.[16]

At the minor league baseball annual winter meeting in December 1962, the Yankees sold the team to its fourth owner, Romeo Champagne. Champagne was a millionaire New Englander who had made his fortune in the supermarket business. He would continue the working agreement with the Yankees, but named his friend Leo Cloutier, sports editor of the

Manchester Union Leader (New Hampshire), as the general manager for the team. A short while after the change in ownership, there were rumors that the new owner was planning to move the team to Miami or Tampa— rumors which Champagne denied.[17]

In 1963, the Virginians began their tenth season in the International League under new ownership and with a new manager, Preston Gomez. The changes did little to help the Virginians. They struggled all season and finished with a record of 66–81, one place from the league cellar. The 1964 season was equally disastrous for the Vees as they once again wound up one place from the cellar. The one star of the Virginians this year was pitcher Mel Stottlemyre who posted a record of thirteen wins and one loss; he would go on to greater success with the New York Yankees.[18]

Ever since he acquired the Virginians, there were intermittent rumors that owner Romeo Champagne was going to sell the team or move it to another location. Although Champagne denied such rumors, in the fall of 1964, during the winter meeting of the minor leagues, he accepted an offer from a group of Toledo businessmen operating under the name Lucas County Recreation Commission. It was reported that he accepted an offer of $80,000 for the Vees. The International League gave the new owners permission to move the team to Toledo where the team was renamed the Mud Hens. On Saturday, December 19, 1964, IL President Tommy Richardson officially announced that the Toledo franchise was accepted into the eight-team circuit. The Toledo group was able to continue the working agreement with the New York Yankees.[19]

Baseball fans and sports writers for the Richmond press were shocked and angry over the sale of the Virginians. The sports editor of the *Times-Dispatch* declared that the sale of the Vees was proof that "baseball is run by a bunch of idiotic hustlers." The editor's colleague called the sale "preposterous" and charged that Champagne knew nothing about baseball. The press placed most of the blame for the loss of the team upon the New York Yankees, who it was claimed never provided adequate assistance for the club.[20]

With the departure of the Virginians, it appeared that 1965 would be the first season since 1905 in which Richmond did not have a professional baseball team. However, events surrounding the impending move by the National League Milwaukee Braves to Atlanta, Georgia, gave Richmonders hope for another International League franchise for 1965. In November, the Braves, citing poor attendance in Milwaukee, entered into a twenty-five-year contract to play in Atlanta. The club also purchased the Atlanta Crackers, the city's International League franchise and speculation began that the franchise would be moved to Richmond. Although the National League owners approved the move, the Milwaukee County Board was able to secure a court order forcing the Braves to play the 1965 season in County Stadium.[21]

The county may have been able to delay the departure of the Braves from Milwaukee, but the lame-duck status did little to promote interest in the club. As of December 31, 1964, "only 28 season tickets had been sold and the team's radio-television sponsorship had been cancelled." Hopes were cast that a settlement between the franchise and the county would allow the team to move to Atlanta for the 1965 season. Speculation continued that the Braves would then move the Crackers IL franchise currently in Atlanta to Richmond. IL President Richardson encouraged Richmond hopes even more when he told reporters in Florida spring training that he believed that Richmond "positively will return to the International League" as the replacement for Atlanta when the Braves are finally able to move to that city.[22]

The optimism that Richmond would not endure an entire season without baseball was still alive on opening day. In the April 18, 1965, edition of the *Times-Dispatch* Shelley Rolfe's article headlined, "A Stillness at Parker Field," was printed on the same page as the article that recounted the Toledo Mud Hens' season opening victory. In Rolfe's article, it was noted that the Parker Field "grandstand had a green, clean look. Maintenance work had gone on, just as if everyone had been getting ready for an opener." Later in the week, sports editor Chauncey Durden reported that only 3,364 attended the Milwaukee Braves opener, and 2,804 was the reported paid attendance for the second game. With the feeble attendance at Braves games, he wrote that "faith, which moveth mountains and sometimes baseball franchises, remains strong in some of yesteryear's Parker Field faithful." Hope continued that the team could still move to Atlanta before long, thereby sending the IL to Richmond. But the Braves remained in Milwaukee all season, and Richmond was without baseball for 1965.[23]

For 1966, the Crackers, renamed Braves, were moved to Richmond. This move marked the second time that the Richmond ballclub was owned by a Major League franchise. Excitement was high, not only for the return of baseball to Richmond but for the return of a competitive team to represent the city. The Vees' highest season standing was a second place finish in 1960. During their eleven-year tenure in Richmond, the team had only two winning seasons (1957 and 1960) and qualified for the playoffs just three times (1957, 1959 and 1960). In the 1965 season, the Atlanta Crackers finished in second place, only two and a half games behind the International League season pennant winner Columbus Jets and one and a half games ahead of the third place and Governor's Cup champion Toronto Maple Leafs. Most members of the Crackers team were now on the Richmond roster.[24]

Richmond baseball fans enthusiastically welcomed the game back to the city. The stands and seats at Parker Field were painted "in aqua, orange, red and black colors," leading one fan attending a public workout of the Braves to quote, "I get a new feeling, a good feeling, just looking at the stands." Two days before the season's scheduled opener of Friday, April 22, 1966, Richmond Braves business manager, Lou Martin, reported to the *Times-Dispatch* that pre-game ticket sales were "the kind of advanced sales we used to have for Yankee exposition games." At the time of the interview, advanced tickets were "approaching 5,300," and game-day sales were expected to be about 3,000. The next day it was reported that "the boxes were sold out; some reserved seats available."[25]

On the day before the scheduled opening game, there was a parade that began at Parker Field, continued down Broad Street through downtown and wound its way to Willow Lawn. The players were then shuttled between an invitation-only, "Meet the Braves" party hosted by the Central Richmond Association and a radio "Meet the Braves" special broadcast on station WRNL. During the parade, Braves pitcher Pat Jarvis suffered a neck injury when the car he "was riding in made a sudden stop." The incident caused Jarvis to be placed on the ten-day disabled list.[26]

Friday, April 22, 1966, which was to have opened Richmond's new venture in the International League, was rainy. Team general manager, Hillman Lyons, officially announced the postponement an hour and half before the scheduled game time. With over 7,000 prepaid admissions, Lyons was hesitant to cancel the night's game, but, in the end, he felt it was the best thing for the team's fans: "We probably could have played and struggled and gotten five innings in (enough to invalidate rain checks). But we just couldn't do it... not as good as the people have been to us."[27]

On Saturday, the season officially began in Richmond. John McHale, president and general manager of the parent club Atlanta Braves, and John Mullen, Braves farm director, flew in for the game. Also on hand were local dignitaries. Governor Mills Godwin threw out the ceremonial first pitch to his "catcher," Richmond Mayor Morrill Crowe. The Acca Temple Shrine Band performed for the crowd. Official attendance was recorded at 7,411, the total number of tickets purchased for the rained-out opener from the night before. The actual attendance was estimated at slightly over 5,000 spectators. The *Times-Dispatch* reported that all was perfect, "only the score was wrong." The Rochester Red Wings, under the guidance of new manager Earl Weaver, defeated the Braves 3–2.

In the week leading to the season opener, the weather was not the only thing that threatened baseball's return to Richmond. On April 18, in a public hearing attended by about thirty-five persons before the State Alcoholic Beverage Control Board, spokesmen for Parker Field and the Braves urged approval of the license allowing the sale of beer during Braves games. Joseph E. Balducci, owner of Richmond Concessionaires, had applied for the license to sell beer at Parker in the newly constructed restaurant named the Teepee Room. The restaurant, located under the grandstand behind home plate and about fifty feet from the main entrance to the field, was build at a cost of about $18,000. The restaurant was the only planned location for beer sales. The Braves had made the sale of beer a condition of their contract in coming to Richmond. The license was opposed by two local Baptist ministers, the Rev. Manley W. Tobey, Jr., pastor of Bainbridge Baptist Church, and the Rev. John A.R. Godwin, pastor of Woodland Heights Baptist Church. The pastors were opposed to the sale of beer in "a recreational facility used by the entire city for all citizens." Robert J. Habenicht, city councilman and board member of the Greater Richmond Civic Recreation, operator of Parker Field under lease from the city, spoke on behalf of the license. He cited that the city should employ every means to keep baseball in Richmond "as a matter of economics." The control board delayed a decision until 5:00 p.m., Friday, April 22, just hours before the scheduled start of the season opener. The granted license specified that beer could be sold only during Braves "exhibitions" and excluded all high school events at Parker Field. Sale was limited to the Teepee Room, and guards were to be posted to prevent fans from carrying beer out of the restaurant.[28]

Despite losing the opener, the Braves, under manager Bill Adair, lived up to pre-season expectations. The Braves finished the season with a 75–72 record (.510) and secured a fourth place finish, eight games behind season pennant winner Rochester. That finish earned the Braves a playoff appearance in their first season in Richmond. The team defeated Weaver's Red Wings three games to one before losing the Governor's Cup Championship four games to one to the Toronto Maple Leafs, managed by Dick Williams. The Braves were led by outfielder and league All-Star Bill Robinson and first baseman Jim Beauchamp. Robinson had 159 total hits, still third on the Braves all-time hit list, and Beauchamp belted thirty-five homeruns with a .319 batting average, one point shy of the league title. GM Hillman Lyons was named the International League Executive of the Year. The season attendance of 234,005 exceeded league president George Sisler, Jr.'s expectations by 9,000 and surpassed the Atlanta Crackers' 1965 attendance by over 69,000[29]

Luman Harris was brought in to manage the 1967 Richmond Braves. Under Harris, the team earned Richmond its first International League season pennant by posting an 81–60 (.574) record. The Braves captured the season pennant by defeating Rochester in a one-game playoff on Tuesday, September 5. The two teams became deadlocked on Saturday, September 2, when the Braves defeated the Mud Hens to hold on to a half-game lead, and the Red Wings later won both ends of a double-header against Buffalo to eliminate the half game margin. Both teams lost on Sunday and then won their season finale on Monday, forcing the single game play-off. By virtue of a coin-toss, the Red Wings hosted the season championship game. The Braves, behind the three-hit, eight and one-third inning pitching performance of Mike Britton, a native of North Tonawanda, New York, a suburb of Buffalo, captured the flag with a 2–0 victory. The victory party was delayed by the heart attack death of Britton's father in the grandstand. Witnesses reported that as Britton stepped to bat in the ninth inning, his father standing to applaud began clutching his side. The person in the seat next to him began mouth-to-mouth, but Britton's father was pronounced dead by the time he was taken to a nearby hospital. The Braves went on to lose the opening round of the playoffs to Toledo, three games to two.[30]

The 1967 team featured four end-of-season all-stars: first baseman Jim Beauchamp, outfielder Tommie Aaron, second baseman Felix Millan and pitcher Ron Reed. Lyons was once again named IL Executive of the Year. He was also named Minor League Executive of the Year. Luman Harris was rewarded for guiding the AAA club to the pennant by being named the Braves Major League manager. Beauchamp, with thirty-three homeruns, won the IL home run title, despite playing in only ninety-six games for Richmond. Tommie Aaron, the younger brother of the Atlanta Braves Hank Aaron, was named the League MVP and was, by a fan vote, honored as the most popular Richmond Brave. On June 14, Ed Rakow set a single-game team record that still stands by striking out eighteen Toronto batters. The Braves won that game in 16 innings. Rakow pitched thirteen innings and gave up just five hits and four walks to accompany his eighteen strikeouts.[31]

Attendance in 1967 soared to 264,814. On Friday, September 1, a record crowd of 15,184 attended the Braves game against the visiting Columbus Jets at the 9,500 capacity Parker Field. The Braves 2–1 win was secured by solo homeruns by Mike Lum on the first pitch in the first inning and by Tommie Aaron in the ninth inning. The victory preserved the Braves half-game lead over Rochester going into the Braves final three games against Toledo. Before that game, the previous high attendance mark at Parker Field was 14,879 in 1954 for the first-ever game at the ballyard in the preseason exhibition game that featured the New York Yankees and the Vees. The September 1, 1967 single-game attendance record is the largest crowd recorded for a Braves' regular season game. The highest single-game record for the Braves was set on April 28, 1983, when 15,864 attended an exhibition game that pitted the R-Braves against the parent-club Atlanta Braves. While accurate attendance was not recorded, the 1908 Labor Day double-header, with an estimated attendance of over 15,000 and possibly as high as 19,000, is likely the largest crowd to witness a baseball game in Richmond.[32]

In 1967, Richmond was also host to the International League All-Star game on July 31. The 1967 game was the International League's twelfth annual mid-season all-star contest. In previous all-star games, the IL stars faced a Major League team. This game was the first to pair stars from the northern teams (Toronto, Rochester, Syracuse and Buffalo) against the southern teams' stars (Richmond, Jacksonville, Toledo and Columbus). The South squad featured Richmond manager Luman Harris and seven players: Ron Reed, Jim Beauchamp, Tommie Aaron, Felix Millan, Gil Garrido, Bobby Cox, and Del Bates. Beauchamp, Aaron, Millan and Cox were game starters. The South stars won 4–3.[33]

Richmond fans did not have much to celebrate in the next several seasons. The Braves did not return to playoffs until 1974. In that span, only the 1970 team that finished fifth, with a 73–67 (.521) record was above .500. In 1968, 1969 and 1973, the club finished last in the eight-team league. With many of its star players called up to Atlanta, the 1968 the Braves were twenty-three and a half games behind the pennant-winner Mud Hens. The season highlight was the August 15 exhibition game that brought the Atlanta Braves to Parker Field. In the third inning of the contest, Felix Millan, Hank Aaron and Tommie Aaron all hit home-runs for Atlanta. The big leaguers won 7–1. In 1969, the Richmond club finished twenty-two games behind the pennant winner. The August exhibition game with the Atlanta Braves was again a season highlight. In this game, Richmond fans were able to see the great Satchel Paige pitch part of the sixth and seventh innings, and Tommie Aaron belted two home-runs to lift the Atlanta club to an 8–7 victory. Despite the poor team performances, several players had strong individual seasons. Dave Nicholson won league homerun and RBI titles in 1968. Hal Breeden captured the homerun crown in 1970, and in both 1969 and 1970. Ralph Garr earned the IL batting title and led the league in stolen bases.[34]

As the team's performance plummeted, so did attendance. The 1968 figure dropped by over 100,000 to 151,617. After going from first to worst in 1967 and 1968, the 1969 attendance total again dropped significantly with only 80,477 spectators visiting Parker Field, despite the addition to the league of an instate rival. For the 1969 season, the New York Mets moved their IL affiliate from Jacksonville, Florida, to Norfolk/ Portsmouth, Virginia. The team began play as the Tidewater Tides and promptly won the pennant in its first season.[35]

The improved team performance in 1970 help boost Richmond attendance to 120,928 during the 1970 season. Attendance dropped slightly in 1971. Interest in the Braves and the International League should have increased. The Expos moved their IL franchise from Winnipeg, Canada, to the Newport News/Hampton, Virginia area. The team, playing as the Peninsula Whips, added a third Virginia franchise to the league. In 1973, when the Louisville Colonels were evicted from Fairgrounds Stadium when the Kentucky State Fair Board decided to redesign the facility, the Boston Red Sox moved the team to Pawtucket, Rhode Island. The International League decided to organize the clubs into an American and National division. The American division was comprised of Pawtucket, Toledo, Rochester and Syracuse. The National was made up of the three Virginia clubs and Charleston, West Virginia. Charleston and Tidewater represented the National division in the playoffs. Richmond was fourth in the National and had the worst record of the eight teams in the IL. Attendance had fallen to 72,156, the worst since the club moved to Richmond. To be fair to the Braves, attendance throughout the league was down. Total league attendance for 1973 fell below the one million mark, with only 978,811 spectators at IL ballgames. Attendance at the Peninsula Whips home park was only 45,356, and the team moved to Memphis after the season.[36]

In 1974, the Braves, under manager Clint Courtney, who took over the club in June of 1973 when Bobby Hoffman resigned due to health problems, had a winning record, finishing with 75 wins and 65 losses (.536). The league had replaced the American and National division format with Northern and Southern divisions. The Braves record earned second in the Southern division behind Memphis and third overall. The team then lost to Syracuse four games to one in the opening round of the playoffs. This winning season brought 93,679 spectators to Parker Field. During the season, Parker Field was once again host for the International League All-Star game. The game had returned to being a contest of IL stars playing against a major league club. In the 1974 game, the IL stars lost 2–1 to the New York Mets.[37]

In 1975, the International League eliminated the division format and returned to the traditional eight-team pennant race. After qualifying for the playoffs the season before, the Braves completed the 1975 season with a 62–75 record and were in sixth place, twenty-two games behind the pennant-winner Tidewater. The Tides won the pennant in a one-game playoff with Rochester. Attendance for the season still ranks as the lowest recorded during the Braves tenure in Richmond; only 68,348 spectators came to Parker Field. The final game of the season, a 5–1 loss to Norfolk, was played before only 994 spectators.[38]

The Braves 1975 season is best remembered for the tragic death of manager Clint "Scraps" Courtney. In mid–June, the team had completed a series in Toledo in which the second game of a Saturday double-header and the Sunday game were both rained-out. In the wee hours of the morning on Monday, June 16, after the team had completed the seven-hour bus ride to Rochester, New York, Courtney and several players were playing Ping-Pong in the motel's recreation area when the manger collapsed of a massive heart attack. Paramedics noted that he died almost immediately. He was officially pronounced dead at Gennesse Hospital, three blocks from the motel. Later Monday night, the Braves struggled through the Monday night game against the Red Wings and lost 1–0. Player-coach and interim manager, Al Gallagher, observed, "Everyone was trying too hard." The players had attempted to have the game postponed, but the Atlanta organization, Rochester and league officials felt it was best to play. Bob Lemon, who was later named to the Hall of Fame for his pitching career, managed the Braves for the remainder of the season.[39]

As if the dismal attendance and the untimely death of the manager weren't enough to make the 1975 season perhaps the worst in the Richmond Braves' history, it was also nearly the last season for the Braves. The Braves closed out the season on Monday, September 1, with the 5–1 loss to Tidewater. The day before, the parent club Atlanta Braves let the deadline expire for renewing the Braves one-year lease on Parker Field with the city of Richmond, and the Atlanta club was reported to be in a "state of turmoil." The Atlanta club was also suffering a significant decline in attendance. For the season, total attendance was only 534,672, one-third of what they drew in their first year in Atlanta and over 20,000 fewer patrons than their last season in Milwaukee. The low attendance and losing record prompted the team to replace manager Clyde King in early September and to put the team up for sale. Although the Braves and the city of Richmond were able to come to agreement on a one-year lease of Parker Field before the year was out, the long-term prospects for the relationship the city and ballclub remained in jeopardy. The city's refusal to make "much needed improvements" to the facility kept the Braves from extending the contract beyond a year.[40]

On January 14, 1976, baseball prospects in both Atlanta and Richmond were dramatically changed when R.E. "Ted" Turner III, a thirty-seven-year-old businessman, purchased the Braves organization from Atlanta LaSalle Corporation for a reported $11 million. Turner brought an enthusiasm to the organization that had been vacant for quite some time. "I think a lot of people, including myself, were getting frustrated....I'm going to aim for a winner and I think Richmond is going to be good this year...We're going to have a Little League spirit."[41]

Not only did the new ownership bring a renewed attitude to the clubhouse, he set about building a winning program. Jack McKeon was hired as the new Richmond manager. The *Times-Dispatch* reported that McKeon is "the most experienced manager the R-Braves have had. He knows what it takes and how to win in AAA baseball." McKeon's previous managing duties included fifteen years in the minor leagues with pennant-winning seasons in the American Association, another AAA league, and a couple seasons as manager with the major league Kansas City Royals. To assist McKeon, Johnny Sain was brought in as pitching coach. Sain was widely regarded as the best pitching coach in baseball. After completing his own pitching career, Sain began to develop a career as a coach that included working with the pitchers for five major league pennant-winning teams before he came to Richmond.[42]

The excitement created by the new owner and the presence of an experienced coaching staff carried over to the field. The R-Braves, a team expected to feature strong pitching and fielding with modest hitting ability, won the season opener against Syracuse by a score of 17–1 before a rousing crowd of 2,968. The momentum carried through the season. The club won eight of the last nine and twelve of the final sixteen games to capture a playoff spot by finishing fourth in the International League. The Braves record of 69–71 gave them a winning percentage of .49286; a mere .00011 points ahead of fifth place Rhode Island who finished 68–70 (.49275). The Braves moved into the fourth place slot with only two games remaining. They earned the playoff spot by twice defeating Tidewater. The Braves won 5–1 in the second to last game and won by the score of 5–2 in the last game of the season. After the final game, McKeon said, "This has to be one of the best and most satisfying finishes I have ever had."[43]

The Braves lost the opening game of the playoffs in Rochester 8–0 behind heavy hitting by Eddie Murray and Tom Kelly for the Red Wings. The Braves rebounded the next night and won game two. The teams then came to Richmond for game three, and the Braves won 5–4 behind a two-out ninth inning single by late season acquisition Dale Murphy that scored

Jeff Geach. In the clubhouse celebration after the win, Ted Turner gave his players increased incentive to win the Governor's Cup by announcing that the players would each receive a $1,000 bonus if they could claim the trophy. The Braves went out the next night and advanced to the championship series by defeating the season pennant-winning Red Wings 6–0 behind a complete game performance by pitcher Rick Camp. In the championship series, the Braves lost the first two games to Syracuse before holding off elimination by winning game three. The Chiefs claimed the 1976 Governor's Cup at their home park by defeating the Braves 8–3.[44]

The Braves season attendance for 1976 was 109,636. The final game of the regular season drew 3,159 fans. The playoff games against Rochester brought crowds of 3,386 and 4,010 to Parker Field. In his September 9, 1976 "Sportsview" column, Chauncey Durden concluded that "Richmonders will pay to see winning baseball." During their first two seasons in Richmond, the Braves enjoyed winning seasons and attracted over 535,000 fans for regular season, exhibition and playoff games, but "then came losing season after losing season as the Atlanta farm system became, perhaps the worst in baseball. Richmonders were turned off by an inferior baseball product. But the two playoff games against Rochester proved that they'll happily come running back to Parker Field to buy a good product." [45]

Durden's comments were in response to another lease dispute between the Braves business management and Richmond's city officials. On August 9, Atlanta Braves general manager John Alevizos was quoted as saying that the negotiations had "reached an impasse and that the team will be reluctantly relocated next year." The two sides continued the negotiations, with the city making small concessions, but Alevizos remaining firm that a better deal was needed. "The city had this old deal for 10 years because of the incompetence of my predecessors. They didn't know any different, why should they change?"[46]

Under the terms of the old deal, the city earned $15,000 a year rental or ten percent of gross, whichever was greater. The Braves also were responsible for maintenance expenses, security, trash removal and utilities. Alevizos said that the Braves lost $150,000 in 1975. According to figures released by the city council, the city of Richmond earned $82,198 from the lease during 1973–1975 and expected an estimated $27,760 in 1976. The terms of the lease nearly ended the baseball relationship in 1975, and, as the Braves were advancing into the second round of the playoffs in 1976, negotiations were not positive. City manager William Leidinger publicly felt that an agreement would be reached, but Alevizos was quotes as saying, "I have tried to make a compromise and it won't work.... Leidinger should stop wasting my time." While there was some public support for the ownership group, namely in the form of letters to the editor noting that concessions should be made to keep the Braves in Richmond, the impasse prompted Durden's diatribe on the support that the fans have given the Braves. He reasoned that "the community doesn't owe one thing to any sports promoter. The promoter offers a product for a price. If the product is an attractive one, the public will buy the product. If the product is inferior, there is sales resistance."[47]

After the game in which the Braves fell behind Syracuse two games to none in the Governor's Cup Championship, Alevizos and Leidinger were able to announce that an agreement had been reached. The Braves and the city signed a three-year deal that provided that the Braves pay $1,000 annual rent plus ten percent of gross ticket sales over $100,000, with the Braves receiving a "rebate of one-third the percentage not to exceed $4,500." Responsibility for utilities and two security policemen were overseen by the city. The Braves were still to maintain the field and arrange for cleanup of the stands. The team entered into contract with Richmond Concessionaire for the cleanup, with city trucks hauling away the trash. Emil Mosheim, director of community affairs for the city, said that the city would continue to make required structural improvements to the facility, but that the Braves were fiscally responsible for any improvements initiated by the club, unless special arrangement is made with the city. Alevizos said the deal was average in comparison to other International League arrangements but allowed "everyone to walk away happy."[48]

With the extended lease agreement in place, Turner followed through on his pledged to build a winning tradition. Beginning with the 1976 season, the Richmond Braves had eight consecutive seasons in which the club earned a playoff berth. In the thirteen year span of 1974–86, the R-Braves failed to qualify for the playoffs in only three seasons: 1975, 1984 and 1985. The team advanced to the Governor's Cup Championship in five of the ten playoff-seasons (1976, 1978, 1980, 1983 and 1986). The R-Braves captured their first Governor's Cup in 1978 and again won the Cup in 1986.[49]

In 1977, Tommie Aaron was brought back to Richmond, this time as manager. His club posted a 71–69 (.507) season record and claimed fourth place and the playoff berth. He returned to Richmond in 1978, and, despite repeating as fourth place finishers with a 71–68 (.511) record, the club defeated Charleston 3–1 in the first round and Rochester 4–3 to earn Richmond's first Governor's Cup Championship.[50]

The strongest seasons in the Braves eight-year playoff stretch were under the field management of Eddie Haas. Haas was Richmond manager for three and half seasons. From 1981–83, the club finished second, first and second and advanced to the Governor's Cup series in both 1981 and 1983. Although he had the three strong seasons, after posting a 47–49 record by late July 1984, Haas was called up to Atlanta to manage the major league club and was replaced as manager by Bobby Dews. The club ended the season in sixth place and posted a 66–73 final record. The poor showing that season can largely be attributed to an inexperienced pitching staff—for much of the season, four of the starting pitchers were AAA rookies—and a "constant state of flux that included 46 player moves" caused in large part to injuries on the Atlanta club.[51]

The R-Braves playoff run was possible because of some outstanding talent. Dale Murphy (1977), Glenn Hubbard (1978), Brook Jacoby (1982), and Brad Komminsk (1983) all earned International League Rookie of the Year honors. Eddie Haas was named the league's manager of the year in 1982 and 1983. Brett Butler was named the league's most valuable player in 1981, and Craig McMurty was the pitcher of the year in 1983. The R-Braves general managers garnered the International League Executive of the Year honors in 1974 (Roger Bartoff), 1981 and 1985 (Richard Anderson).[52]

As Chauncey Durden noted, the Richmond public will support a winning ball club. During the Braves eight-year playoff streak, the season attendance figure ranged from a low of 159,864 in 1974 to a high of 293,328 in 1983. Six of those seasons brought over 185,000 spectators at Parker Field, and four seasons brought over 200,000. The increased attendance in Richmond in the late 1970s and early 1980s was indicative of increased attendance throughout the International League and all of minor league baseball. In 1973, there were only eighteen leagues and 130 teams. Total minor-league attendance was about 10 million people, roughly a quarter of the attendance from the minor league glory days of the 1940s. By 1990, the number of minor league teams had increased to about 200, and attendance had surged to over 20 million. The International League teams in the early 1970s annually drew about one million spectators. Due to low attendance, two cities lost their franchises, and the Braves nearly left Richmond. However, by the early 1980s the league's franchises stabilized and total attendance pushed to two million spectators. By the end of the decade, Braves season attendance figures had eclipsed the 400,000 mark twice (1986 with 403,252 and 1989 with 455,686).[53]

While the Braves had winning ball clubs on the field, the stadium around them was beginning to fall apart. For years, the Parker Field facility had been in need of significant renovation. R-Braves general manager

Richard Anderson often spoke publicly about the poor conditions of the Braves homepark. *Times-Dispatch* columnist Bill Millsaps noted that "people have been coming out to Parker Field for more than 30 years and enduring its discomforts for the past 15 years." By 1983, the conditions were becoming so bad the Braves organization contemplated moving the AAA franchise to Greenville, South Carolina, where a new ballpark was being built for the their Class A franchise. The city wanted the Braves to build a new stadium in Richmond; the Braves thought that the city should build a new ballpark. "At that point, we were ready to leave, not because we wanted to. We didn't have much choice," said Anderson.[54]

In the spring of 1983, Anderson was able to convince the Richmond Chamber of Commerce and its president Carlton Moffatt that baseball was important to the "business and social health of the city." The chamber oversaw the formation of a Stadium Operating Committee (SOC), chaired by Dick Hollander, to investigate the possibilities of a new stadium. The SOC commissioned the consulting firm of Zuchelli, Hunter and Associates to conduct a feasibility study. Through the study, it was determined that a 12,500-seat stadium would cost roughly $8 million. All that was left to do was to create a cooperative agreement from the public and private sectors to fund the project.[55]

All parties agreed that the cooperation of the city of Richmond and the neighboring counties of Henrico and Chesterfield was the critical component to the project. In the early stages of the negotiations, Richmond city manager Manny Deese went on record as saying the he was committed to keeping the Braves in Richmond. The three jurisdictions worked together to pledge $4 million of public funding for a new stadium. With the unprecedented cooperation of the three civic organizations in place, the SOC was able to announce in March 1984 that a new ballpark was going to be built. The remaining $4 million was to be generated from the private sector. Robert S. "Bobby" Ukrop, a Richmond grocery executive, was perhaps the most influential person in garnering the private sector funding. Ukrop sought advice and cooperation from Richmond's corporate leaders. Significant assistance in the fund drive was provided by Lee Putney, Fenton Hord, Danny Williams, Charlie Tysinger, Bob Watts and E. Claiborne Robins, Sr., and the public relations firm of Finnegan & Agee. Much of that money came from corporations that purchased $250,000, ten-year leases on the new park's twelve super box suites. The corporate money and the support of the general public through T-shirt sales, buttons, badges and retail specials in a campaign built around a slogan of "pitch in to build a new ballpark," generated over $4 million to complete the project.[56]

Final home game at Parker Field, home of the Richmond Virginians (1854–64) and Richmond Braves (1966–84) (courtesy of Richmond Braves).

The Stadium Operating Committee decided that that an independent authority should operate the new stadium. The Richmond Metropolitan Authority (RMA) was the logical choice; however, that organization was only licensed to operate roads. Continuing in the spirit of cooperation that produce the necessary funding, the Virginia General Assembly quickly agreed to amend the RMA's powers and allowed it to operate the new stadium. Before construction began, a ten-year lease between the Braves and the RMA was agreed upon during an all-day negotiating session on August 31.[57]

Five design companies submitted bids for the stadium, and the contract was awarded to Baskerville and Son. McDevitt & Street was selected as the contractor. The stadium project was on a short time schedule. The new stadium was built on the site of the existing Parker Field. Demolition began on Tuesday, September 4, 1984, and had to be completed in time for opening day in April 1985. The Braves last game at Parker Field was marked by a celebration with balloons, bands and forty-one former Braves or Virginians, including Bob Beall, who came all the way from

Hillsborough, Oregon, for the festivities and Chico Ruiz, who has played in the most seasons for the Braves, is second in total games in a Braves uniform and is still in the top five in many career offensive categories for Richmond. Before 5,962 fans, the Braves defeated the Tidewater Tides 4–2 on Friday, August 31, 1984, to close out the stadium's history with a victory. After the game, many fans took home souvenirs of the stadium. People pulled out over 100 seats along the first baseline. Many tore up pieces of the grass field, one fan filled his pockets with infield dirt and another used a pocketknife to cut out a square of the backstop netting. The final event at Parker Field was a Labor Day concert featuring the Chairmen of the Board and the Drifters.[58]

The new stadium's name "the Diamond" was selected by the SOC on December 12, 1984. The committee wanted a name that would be reflective of the unique cooperation among the city, the counties, the fans and the team that was necessary to build the facility. They did not want to alienate any group by selecting the name of an individual but did want to honor certain people. The committee did make provisions for honoring the individuals that many felt the new park should be named after. The fountain near the main concourse bears the name of Dr. William H. Parker, namesake of the old stadium and a prominent figure in Richmond's athletic programs. The press box was named in honor of Frank Soden, the longtime radio voice of the Virginians and Braves, who retired in 1984. The home team dressing rooms and training facilities were named after Tommie Aaron, the popular former Braves player and later manager who died of leukemia early in 1984. The committee also recommended that a "Wall of Fame" be constructed to recognize individuals of "past, present and future" who have contributed to the area sports scene.[59]

The Diamond was built in seven months. The field dimensions were designed to be similar to Atlanta's Fulton County Stadium. The distance down the foul lines is 330 feet with the power alleys at 385 feet and 402 feet to straight away centerfield. The symmetrical design presented a playing field that was very different from the dimensions of Parker Field, where the left field line was only 325 feet, but the right field line was 370 feet with a distance of 400 feet in the right field power alley and 403 feet to center. Many of the Braves left-handed batters were excited by the changes, as 360-foot fly balls to right would now be homeruns and not routine outs.[60]

April 17, 1985, opening night at the Diamond, attracted a sell out crowd of 12,435 fans to the new ballpark. Unfortunately the hometown team lost 2–1 to Syracuse. The Braves were able to defeat the Chiefs the next night and captured their first victory at the Diamond by a score of

Opening night at the Diamond, April 17, 1985 (courtesy of Richmond Braves).

5–2. For seventy-four days during the season, the team led the International League standings. Three times, the Braves had six-game winning streaks. Several losses in the last month, including the season's longest streak of six straight losses, and the final game 7–6 loss to the Tides pushed the Braves into fifth and out of the playoffs. A win would have given the Braves a third place finish and playoff spot. Instead, the Tides shared third with Columbus, defeated Maine in the first round and then took three of four from Columbus to win the Governor's Cup.[61]

The one run loss was frustrating for Richmond fans, players and the media. Steve Shields, the R-Braves top starter, was scheduled to pitch the final game against the Tides. Early in the afternoon, the Atlanta club called up Shields and Dave Schuler, Richmond's best reliever. Matt West, on only two days rest, was forced into Shields' starting spot, and the Braves suffered the 7–6 loss, thereby missing the playoffs. Many felt that the Atlanta club, at the time twenty games out of the division lead with no real hope of playoff contention, should have left the pitchers on the Richmond squad to allow the club the opportunity to earn the cup. Manager Roy Majtyka said, "It's tough going into such a big game without your best pitcher, but that's a hazard of the game when you're managing in the minors. When the big club is having trouble, you expect callups." He was also quick to note that the club didn't lose the playoff berth in this one game; it was the long slump in August that cost the team opportunity for post-season play. "The toughest part to swallow was going so long in first place and then going from first to out of the playoffs. That will live with me as one of the toughest memories of my career."[62]

The Braves drew over 379,019 fans in the Diamond's first year. Ten times attendance was over 10,000. The season total set a franchise attendance record and ranked the Braves third in attendance in minor league baseball. The Braves accomplishments earned the franchise the Larry MacPhail Award, an award presented for the best front-office operation in the minor league baseball. General manager Richard Anderson was presented the award on December 9, 1985 at the National Association of Professional Baseball Leagues (NAPBL) annual winter meeting. Johnny Johnson, president of the NAPBL, praised the Braves: "The MacPhail trophy epitomizes what the Richmond Braves did during the past calendar year. ... Tales of Richmond's operation have spread throughout the country.[63]

The 1986 season marked the first time that a Richmond team captured both the season pennant and the Governor's Cup Championship. With the playing success, the season attendance continued to climb, crossing the 400,000 mark with 403,252. In his second season as manager, Roy Majtyka guided the club to an 80–60 record, four games ahead of second place Rochester Red Wings. Staff pitching ace Steve Shields earned the victory in the pennant clinching game on August 28, 1986, and the final Governor's Cup Championship on September 12, 1986. With the memory of the previous season finale firmly intact, the fact that Shields was still on the Richmond roster was significant. After the Braves 2–1 pennant-clinching victory over the Red Wings, Richmond general manager Richard Anderson said, "I think that this proves that the Atlanta organization is behind Richmond 100 percent." Hank Aaron, Atlanta's vice-president for player development said, "We want to develop players for the major leagues, but we think we have a good thing going in Richmond and want to keep it going. After all, they help pay some of the bills.... I think the feeling is that we won't tamper much with this team." Atlanta scouting director, Paul Snyder, noted that "there won't be a mass exodus, at least not until the regular season and the playoffs are over. A key to Richmond's championship title was Atlanta's restraint in roster shuffling. Second baseman Paul Runge noted, "We only lost one everyday player who was called up. Keeping everyone together helped an awful lot."[64]

On August 25, as the 1986 regular season was drawing to a close, Richmond general manager Anderson announced that he would be resigning from his position at the end of the season. On September 8, the Braves organization named Bruce Baldwin, as the new GM in Richmond. Baldwin had served the organization as a general manager of the Braves at Pulaski in the Appalachian Rookie League and in Greenville, South Carolina, in the Double A Southern League. Before becoming a baseball executive, Baldwin's previous experience included playing baseball while he was in the army, working as the sports information director at Oregon Tech, a television sports director, a public relations executive with the North American Soccer League, a minor-league umpire and a stand-up comedian. He began his baseball front office career with a five-year stint as the general manager in Eugene, Oregon, in the Northwest League (rookie classification). Before becoming the GM, he spent three seasons in the league as an umpire. While he was in Greenville, he was named the 1984 Sporting News Double A Executive of the Year and the Greenville Braves were the only team to have three years running with over 200,000 fans in attendance.[65]

After the excitement winning the pennant and the Governor's Cup in 1986, the 1987 season was huge disappointment for the Braves. The team finished in eighth place with a 56–83 record and was 24.5 games behind pennant-winner Tidewater. The Braves became the first International League team since the 1967–68 Braves to go from first to last in back-to-back seasons. The team hit the cellar position in mid–May and remained there for most of the season. The best run came in the stretch of June 21–August 11 in which the club went 30–24 and briefly pulled out of last position in early August. Many of the stars of the 1986 club were called up to the majors or traded. The club suffered several injuries and had players who just had poor seasons. Hank Aaron, the Atlanta vice-president and director of player personnel, noted that "our best prospects were at Greenville, but it wouldn't have been fair to force-feed those guys at Triple-A." During the season the Richmond team endured an eight-game losing streak and twice suffered seven-game and five-game losing streaks, while the best winning streak that could be put together was three games. Season attendance dropped to 332,436, a total that by far exceeds any season total from the Parker Field days but still registers as the lowest in Diamond history.[66]

After the 1987 season owners and executives of Organized Baseball's three Triple A leagues—the International League, the American Association and the Pacific Coast League—met in Hollywood, Florida. For more than a decade, the president's of the American Association and the International League had been discussing the idea of interleague play. The idea was originally proposed in 1917. For that season, the International League and the American Association had drafted a schedule that provided for each team to play forty-eight games with members of the other league. The United States entry into world war a week before the start of the season caused the idea to be abandoned. In the winter of 1987, the major leagues began contemplating the idea of interleague play, and the minor league presidents felt that it was time to explore the concept at the Triple A level.

Over the course of the Hollywood meetings, the American Association and the International League formed the Triple A Alliance and drafted plans for 1988 schedules with each team playing 142 games that included forty interleague games. The format gave teams in the eight member leagues five games against each of the teams in the other league. A post-season Alliance Classic, reviving the idea of the Junior World Series that was played sporadically until the 1970s, would feature the champion of each league. The Pacific Coast League, citing travel and cost constraints decided not to join the Alliance for interleague play. The leagues continued the Alliance schedule through the 1991 season when increased costs due to the professional baseball agreement with the major leagues rendered interleague play unprofitable.[67]

In creating the Triple A Alliance, the league presidents also introduced the Triple A All-Star game. In the all-star game, members of all three leagues formed two twenty-three man rosters representing the prospects for the National and American Leagues. National television broadcast arrangements for the all-star game were coordinated with ESPN. The first Triple A All-Star game was played in Buffalo's new Pilot Field on July 13, 1988, before a capacity crowd of 19,500.[68]

Also in 1988, the International League revived the divisional format with an East and a West division. The division winners competed for the Governor's Cup, and the winner advanced to the Alliance Classic. The teams in the East division were Maine, Pawtucket, Richmond and Tidewater. Columbus, Rochester, Syracuse and Toledo constituted the West division. Tidewater easily won the East division and then lost to Rochester in the cup series. The Braves, under first year manager Jim Beauchamp, were the runners up in the East, finishing at 66–73 and eleven games behind the Tides. The Braves were in fourth place at the all-star break but finished 31–21 after the break. They closed out the season with four straight victories and won nine of the final twelve games. Despite the fact that the Braves had an overall losing record, three of the final four home games of the season were near sell-outs. The season attendance was 355,704. The *Times-Dispatch* commended the Richmond fans' raucous support for the Braves: "One might have thought that this was the Seventh Game of the World Series, or at least the deciding game of the

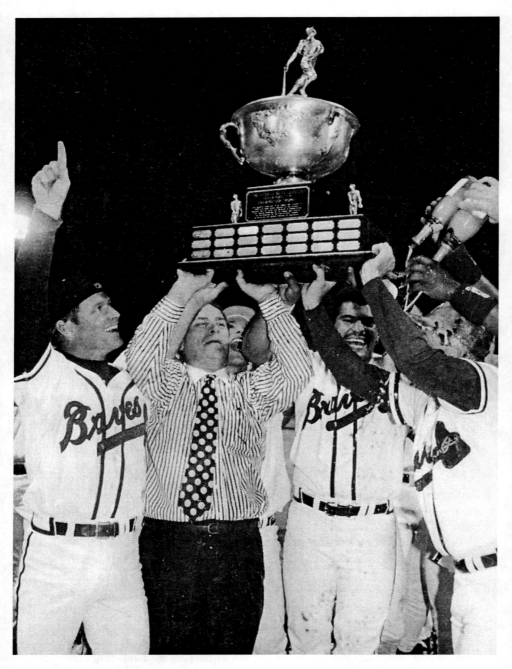

Pat Kelley, General Manager Bruce Baldwin, Eddie Perez and Manager Grady Little celebrate the 1994 Governor's Cup Championship (Courtesy of Richmond Braves).

Governor's Cup. In reality the fans were supporting a team that didn't make the playoffs and that has struggled to escape the cellar of the International League East for most of 1988."[69]

The momentum of the second half of 1988 carried over into 1989. The Braves won the West by a four game margin over the Tides with the pennant being earned in the final series of the season. Bruce Baldwin earned the International League Executive of the Year award. The league continued the East-West format, but, with the Maine Guides moving to Scranton/Wilkes-Barre, the league shuffled teams between divisions. The West division now comprised Columbus, Richmond, Tidewater and Toledo, while the teams in the East were Pawtucket, Rochester, Scranton/Wilkes-Barre and Syracuse. The Braves went on to beat Syracuse 3–1 in the Governor's Cup but were swept in four games by Indianapolis who captured its second Alliance Classic title.[70]

In his column in the September 7, 1989, edition of the *Richmond Times-Dispatch*, Jennings Culley noted that, despite the Richmond Braves three International League pennants and six playoff appearances in the 1980s, "none of that success has made a significant difference in Atlanta's position in the National League West. Not to date, at least. There is evidence that the young pitching talent from the farm may solidify the A-Braves once shaky rotation." Some of the players that were on the Richmond club in the late 1980s included pitchers John Smoltz, Kent Mercker, and Tom Glavine, and position players Dave Justice, Mark Lemke, and Jeff Blauser. All of them became critical components of the Atlanta Braves World Series teams in the early 1990s.[71]

The success of the Braves continued into the 1990s. In 1990, Bruce Baldwin and the front office staff earned the Braves its second Larry MacPhail Promotional Award for the best front-office operation in minor league baseball. The Braves then earned the Bob Frietas Award for outstanding long-term operation in 1993 and were the recipient of the John H. Johnson President's Trophy for outstanding minor league operation in 1997. On the field, the Braves earned playoff berths in four consecutive years, 1992–1995. The 1994 club earned Richmond its fourth Governor's Cup Championship. Chris Chambliss managed the first team in Richmond's playoff run. Grady Little, a future major league manager, was at the helm for the 1993–1995 teams.[72]

The Braves sweep of the Syracuse in the 1994 Governor's Cup championship series was broadcast on ESPN/ESPN 2 as minor league baseball stepped into the national spotlight while the major league players and owners were locked in a bitter labor battle. The dispute triggered a major league players' strike that began in early August and culminated with the owners terminating the remainder of the season in early September. The minors benefited from the strike with an overall attendance increase of fourteen percent.[73]

The Richmond Braves teams of the 1990s continued to produce major league prospects. The opening day roster of the 1992 Richmond Braves included seven future major league players: Ryan Klesko, David Nied, Mark Wohlers, Billy Taylor, Vinnie Castilla, Armando Reynosa and Jeff Manto. The 1993 starting squad of Mike Kelly, Melvin Nieves, Tony Tarrasco, Klesko, Ramon Caraballo, Chipper Jones, Jose Oliva and Javy Lopez earned the nickname the Great 8. Other notable Richmond Braves from the 1990s that have contributed to the Atlanta club or have earned major league success include Steve Avery, Deion Sanders, Mike Mordecai, Eddie Perez, Tony Graffanino, Andruw Jones (who spent only two weeks with Richmond on his meteoric rise to the major leagues and at age nineteen is the youngest R-Braves player), Kevin Millwood, Randall Simon, Bruce Chen, and Wes Helms.[74]

There have also been some significant individual performances in the recent decade. On May 3, 1992, Pete Smith, in the second game of a double header at Rochester, threw a complete game seven-inning perfect game. Smith's perfect game is the only one in Braves history. The club only has two no-hitters thrown by Braves pitchers; one was by Mickey Mahler against Toledo on June 1, 1977, and the other was a combined effort by Charlie Puleo and Steve Ziem at Oklahoma City on June 27, 1989. Kevin Millwood pitched 8.2 no-hit innings in a 9–0 victory against Syracuse on June 22, 1997. With ten RBI's in a June 27, 1998 game against Charlotte, Randall Simon set the team single game record. Three times in the 1990s a player earned seven RBI's in a game. Ryan Klesko did so on July 27, 1993. In 1999, the feat was accomplished twice: once by Howard Battle on April 10 at Durham and once by Brad Tyler on June 13 at Pawtucket.[75]

With the success on the field, it is no surprise that the Braves are continually one of the league leaders in attendance. In the 1990s, the lowest season attendance was 427,552 in 1990. Even in the later half of the decade, when the Braves finished with a five-straight losing seasons and fourth place finishes in the division, the attendance has continued to be over 450,000. The team even had seven consecutive seasons with over 500,000 fans. The all-time high was set in 1993 when 540,489 came out to the Diamond. In a 1990 column, Bill Milsaps, of the *Richmond Times-Dispatch*, noted that much of the Braves success at the ticket booth is directly attributed to the "customer- and community-oriented" family atmosphere that the Braves front office has created at the Diamond. He quoted general manager Bruce Baldwin: "We want the Diamond to be a happy place and for kids and their parents to take away nothing but good memories."[76]

The Braves lease on the Diamond extends until the end of the 2004 season. The Atlanta organization has expressed concerns about the condition of the aging facility. Since the Diamond's construction in 1985, it has widely been described as one of the minor leagues' finest ballparks. However, with the building boom of he 1990s, the Braves now have one of the oldest stadiums in the league. The Richmond Metropolitan Authority received proposals from several design firms that specialize in stadiums and selected Dallas-based HKS, Inc. to perform design renovations to the facility. The target date for the renovation is planned to coincide with the expiration of the current lease between the Braves and the RMA.[77] Richmond fans hope that a renewed ballpark will help to rejuvenate the Braves and that the team will soon return to its winning ways of the past.

Appendix A.
Ballparks Where
Richmond Professional Clubs
Played Home Games

1. The Fair Grounds (currently Monroe Park)

2. Virginia Park, west end of Franklin Street, later site of statue of Robert E. Lee

3. Mayo Island Park/Tate Field, on east side of 14th Street, adjacent to Southern Railway tracks and the Virginia Boat Club

4. West End Park, corner of Vine and Main streets

5. Broad Street Park (I), where Allen Avenue dead ends with Broad Street

6. Broad Street Park (II), where Broad Street intersects with Addison Street

7. Lee Park, North Boulevard at Moore Street

8. City Stadium, bordered by McCloy Street, Freeman Road and Maplewood Ave.

9. Mooers Field, at Roseneath and Norfolk streets, near 3400 West Broad Street

10. Parker Field/The Diamond, 3001 North Boulevard

Appendix B. Names Assumed by Richmond's Professional Baseball Club

1. Virginians—1884, 1915, 1954
2. Colts—1894, 1906, 1912, 1918
3. Richmond Reds—1894
4. Legislators—1895
5. Crows—1895
6. Bluebirds—1895, 1898, 1900
7. Johnny Rebs—1896
8. Giants—1896
9. Grays—1901
10. Lawmakers—1906
11. Rebels—1912
12. Climbers—1915
13. Braves—1966

Appendix C. Professional Baseball in Richmond, Year by Year, 1884–2000

Year	Name	League	Record	Pct.	Finish	Notes
1884	Virginias	Eastern	30-28	.517	7	Left league to join AA
		American Association	12-30	.286	10	Joined AA on August 5, 1884
1885	Virginias	Eastern	67-26	.720		League disbanded on Sept. 21
1886-1893	No pro team					
1894	Reds, Legislators Colts and Crows	Virginia State	67-48	.582	3	
1895	Bluebirds	Virginia State	78-45	.634	1	Nowlan Cup Champions
1896	Bluebirds	Virginia State split schedule	35-29 36-26	.547 .581	1 2	Nowlan Cup Champions
1897	Johnny Rebs/ Giants	Atlantic	73-58	.557	4	
1898	Bluebirds	Atlantic	78-43	.644	1	Atlantic League pennant
1899	Bluebirds	Atlantic	50-16	.758	1	Atlantic League pennant
		split schedule	13-9	.590	1	League disbanded August 6

Year	Name	League	Record	Pct.	Finish	Notes
1900	Bluebirds	Virginia State	21-13	.600		League disbanded June 12
1901	Grays	Virginia–North Carolina	19-38	.333	5	Richmond withdrew July 6 and the league folded
		split schedule	7-5	.583	4	August 17
1902-1905	No pro team					
1906	Lawmakers	Virginia State	57-54	.513	3	
1907	Colts	Virginia State	62-62	.500	4	
1908	Colts	Virginia State	87-41	.680	1	VSL pennant winner
1909	Colts	Virginia State	63-61	.508	3	
1910	Colts	Virginia State	50-67	.427	5	
1911	Colts	Virginia State	56-62	.475	4	
1912	Colts	Virginia State	77-56	.579	3	
	Rebels	United States	22-13	.629	2	Outlaw "major league" that folded on June 24
1913	Colts	Virginia State	74-60	.552	3	
1914	Colts	Virginia State	78-56	.582	2	
1915	Virginians/Climbers	International	59-81	.422	7	
1916	Climbers	International	64-75	.460	6	
1917	Climbers	International	53-94	.386	8	
1918	Colts	Virginia	29-21	.586	1	Season ended July 20; World War I
1919	Colts	Virginia	20-31	.392	5	Championship series with Petersburg cancelled
		split schedule	40-19	.678	1	
1920	Colts	Virginia	43-14	.754	1	Lost playoffs to Portsmouth
		split schedule	33-25	.569	3	
1921	Colts	Virginia	31-30	.508	4	
		split schedule	44-29	.603	3	
1922	Colts	Virginia	49-68	.419	6	
1923	Colts	Virginia	71-53	.573	2	
1924	Colts	Virginia	76-59	.563	1	Pennant winner
1925	Colts	Virginia	79-54	.594	1	Pennant winner
1926	Colts	Virginia	83-68	.556	1	Pennant winner

Year	Name	League	Record	Pct.	Finish	Notes
1927	Colts	Virginia	65-65	.500	3	
1928	Colts	Virginia	15-27	.357	3	Tied in last; league folded June 3
1929-1930	No pro team					
1931	Colts	Eastern split schedule	24-39 31-38	.381 .449	8 7	
1932	Colts	Eastern	45-37	.549	3	League disbanded July 17
1933	Colts	Piedmont split schedule	39-31 34-36	.557 .486	2 5	
1934	Colts	Piedmont split schedule	29-41 31-37	.414 .456	5 4	
1935	Colts	Piedmont split schedule	30-41 40-25	.423 .615	5 1	Pennant winner in playoff with Asheville
1936	Colts	Piedmont	76-66	.535	3	Lost 1st round playoffs—Norfolk
1937	Colts	Piedmont	72-66	.522	4	Lost 1st round playoffs—Norfolk
1938	Colts	Piedmont	66-72	.478	5	
1939	Colts	Piedmont	70-71	.496	4	Lost 1st round— Asheville
1940	Colts	Piedmont	77-59	.566	1	Lost 1st round— Durham Bulls
1941	Colts	Piedmont	67-71	.486	5	
1942	Colts	Piedmont	74-60	.522	3	Lost 1st round— Portsmouth
1943	Colts	Piedmont	72-57	.558	2	Lost 1st round— Norfolk
1944	Colts	Piedmont	67-72	.482	4	Lost 1st round— Lynchburg
1945	Colts	Piedmont	76-60	.559	2	Won 1st round— Newport News Lost championship—Portsmouth
1946	Colts	Piedmont	60-80	.429	5	
1947	Colts	Piedmont	68-71	.489	4	Lost 1st round— Roanoke
1948	Colts	Piedmont	64-75	.460	6	
1949	Colts	Piedmont	71-68	.511	3	Lost 1st round— Portsmouth

Year	Name	League	Record	Pct.	Finish	Notes
1950	Colts	Piedmont	63-76	.453	4	Lost 1st round—Portsmouth
1951	Colts	Piedmont	77-63	.550	2	Won 1st round—Newport News Lost championship—Norfolk
1952	Colts	Piedmont	69-66	.511	3	Won 1st round—Norfolk Won championship—Portsmouth
1953	Colts	Piedmont	45-86	.343	7	
1954	Virginians (Vees)	International	60-94	.390	7	
1955	Virginians (Vees)	International	58-95	.379	8	
1956	Virginians (Vees)	International	74-79	.484	5	
1957	Virginians (Vees)	International	81-73	.526	3	Lost 1st round—Buffalo
1958	Virginians (Vees)	International	71-82	.464	6	
1959	Virginians (Vees)	International	76-78	.494	4	Won 1st round—Buffalo. Lost championship—Havana
1960	Virginians (Vees)	International	82-70	.539	2	Lost 1st round—Rochester
1961	Virginians (Vees)	International	71-83	.461	6	
1962	Virginians (Vees)	International	59-95	.383	7	
1963	Virginians (Vees)	International	66-81	.449	7	
1964	Virginians (Vees)	International	65-88	.425	7	
1965	No pro team					
1966	Braves	International	75-72	.510	4	Won 1st round-Rochester Lost championship—Toronto
1967	Braves	International	81-60	.574	1	Lost 1st round—Toledo
1968	Braves	International	59-87	.404	8	
1969	Braves	International	56-83	.403	8	
1970	Braves	International	73-67	.521	5	
1971	Braves	International	69-71	.493	6	
1972	Braves	International	65-78	.455	6	

Year	Name	League	Record	Pct.	Finish	Notes
1973	Braves	International	53-93	.363	4 S*	
1974	Braves	International	75-65	.536	2 S	Lost 1st round—Syracuse
1975	Braves	International	62-75	.453	6	
1976	Braves	International	69-71	.493	4	Won 1st round—Rochester Lost championship—Syracuse
1977	Braves	International	71-69	.507	4	Lost 1st round—Pawtucket
1978	Braves	International	71-68	.511	4	Won 1st round—Charleston Won championship—Pawtucket Governor's Cup Champions
1979	Braves	International	76-64	.543	3	Lost 1st round—Syracuse
1980	Braves	International	69-71	.493	4	Lost 1st round—Columbus
1981	Braves	International	83-56	.597	2	Won 1st round—Tidewater Lost championship—Columbus
1982	Braves	International	82-57	.590	1	Lost 1st round—Syracuse
1983	Braves	International	80-59	.576	2	Won 1st round—Charleston Lost championship—Tidewater
1984	Braves	International	66-73	.475	6	
1985	Braves	International	75-65	.536	5	
1986	Braves	International	80-60	.571	1	Won 1st round—Tidewater Won championship—Rochester Governor's Cup Champions
1987	Braves	International	56-83	.403	8	
1988	Braves	International	66-75	.468	2 E†	

*Fourth place, Southern Division. The International League adopted divisional play in 1973, sorting its eight teams evenly into Northern and Southern divisions. The experiment was abandoned after the 1974 season.

†Second place, Eastern Division. In 1988, the IL was again split, this time into Eastern and Western divisions. After a season in the East, the Braves moved in 1989 to the West, where the club remained until 1998. That year, the IL took in three teams from the newly dissolved American Association and reorganized again, creating Northern, Southern, and Western divisions. The Braves joined the Southern Division, where they remain.

Year	Name	League	Record	Pct.	Finish	Notes
1989	Braves	International	81-65	.555	1 W	Won Championship—Syracuse Governor's Cup Champions Lost Triple A Classic-Indianapolis
1990	Braves	International	71-74	.490	3 W	
1991	Braves	International	65-79	.451	4 W	
1992	Braves	International	73-71	.507	2 W	Lost 1st round—Columbus
1993	Braves	International	80-62	.563	2 W	Lost 1st round—Charlotte
1994	Braves	International	80-61	.567	1 W	Won 1st round—Charlotte Won championship—Syracuse Governor's Cup Champions
1995	Braves	International	75-66	.532	2 W	Lost 1st round—Norfolk
1996	Braves	International	62-79	.440	4 W	
1997	Braves	International	70-72	.493	4 W	
1998	Braves	International	64-80	.444	4 S	
1999	Braves	International	64-78	.451	4 S	
2000	Braves	International	51-92	.357	4 S	

Notes

Chapter I. Baseball Beginnings
in Richmond, Virginia, 1866–1883

1. Bell I. Wiley, *Life of Johnny Reb, the Common Soldier of the Confederacy* (Indianapolis: Bobbs-Merrill Company, 1943), p. 159; *Richmond Daily Dispatch* (Richmond, Virginia), August 31, 1866, hereafter cited as *Daily Dispatch*.

2. Daily *Dispatch*, September 12, 1866.

3. *Ibid.*, July 12, August 4, 15, 25, September 25, October 10, 29, November 11, 1866.

4. *Ibid.*, July 12, December 13, 1866.

5. *Ibid.*, October 29, November 9, 1866.

6. *Ibid.*, October 29, 1866, August 9, 1867, August 8, 1868.

7. *Ibid.*, November 6, December 22, 1866.

8. *Ibid.*, February 5, 1867.

9. *Ibid.*, July 31, 1867.

10. *Ibid.*, July 23, 31, October 9, 16, 26, 1867.

11. *Ibid.*, September 12, 24, 1867.

12. *Ibid.*, February 25, August 6, December 20, 1867.

13. *Ibid.*, May 6, July 3, August 17, 1868.

14. *Ibid.*, August 23, September 22, 28, October 7, 1869.

15. *Ibid.*, July 6, 1872, March 23, 1874.

16. *Ibid.*, May 7, June 2, July 2, August 28, 1875.

17. *Ibid.*, April 28, 30, May 3, October 9, 1875, May 9, July 3, August 18, September 14, 26, 1876.

18. Virginius Dabney, Richmond, The Story of A City (*Garden City*: Doubleday, 1976), p. 241; Daily Dispatch, September 5, 1876.

19. *Daily Dispatch*, September 27, 28, 1877.

20. *Ibid.*, May 10, 25, 27, July 1, 3, 6, August 7, September 15, 1878.

21. *Ibid.*, June 21, 1878; *Religious Herald* (Richmond, Virginia), May 20, 1875.

22. *Daily Dispatch*, March 11, April 8, May 5, September 6, 18, 1878.

23. *Ibid.*, April 3, May 10, June 11, 1879.

24. *Ibid.*, July 5, 1880.

25. *Ibid.*, March 11, July 6, 10, 31, August 25, 1881.

26. *Ibid.*, July 15, August 3, 10, 17, 31, 1882.

27. *Ibid.*, September 19, October 1, 1882.

28. *Ibid.*, July 19, 22, 27, 28, 30, August 5, 9, 10, 19, 20, September 21, 29, October 3, 5, 11, 1982; February 20, 1883.

29. *Ibid.*, November 22, 1882.

30. *Ibid.*, February 20, July 14, 23, August 5, 17, 28, 1883.

31. *Ibid.*, June 24, July 5, 11, August 15, September 14, October 28, 1883.

32. *Ibid.*, August 2, 15, September 8, October 11, 1883.

33. *Ibid.*, July 8, 1883.

34. *Ibid.*, September 14, 1883.

Chapter II. Professional Baseball Comes to Richmond, 1884

1. *Daily Dispatch*, January 6, 1884; Bill O'Neal, *The International League, A Baseball History, 1884–1991* (Austin, Texas: Eakins Press, 1992), p.3.

2. *Daily Dispatch*, January 6, 1884.

3. *Ibid.*, March 4, April 4, 11, 14, 1884.

4. *Ibid.*, April 13, July 8, 1884.

5. *Ibid.*, April 4, May 31, 1884.

6. *Ibid.*, April 20, 1884.

7. *Ibid.*, May 30, 1884.

8. *Ibid.*, May 27, 1884; July 5, 18, 1884.

9. O'Neal, *The International League*, pp. 4–5.

10. David Nemac, *The Beer and Whiskey League: The Illustrated History of the American Association-Baseball's Renegade Major League* (New York: Lyons and Burford, 1994), pp. 40, 57, 60.

11. *Daily Dispatch*, August 5, 1884.

12. *Ibid.*, August 9, 1884.

13. *Ibid.*, August 9, 26, 1884.

14. Nemec, *Beer and Whiskey League*, p. 73; O'Neal, *International League*, p. 340; *Daily Dispatch*, October 24, 1884.

15. Michael Benson, *Ballparks of North America* (Jefferson, North Carolina: McFarland, 1989), p. 330.

16. *Daily Dispatch*, August, September 28, 30, 1884.

17. *Ibid.*, September 2, 1884; Nemec, *Beer and Whiskey League*, pp. 68–69.

18. *Daily Dispatch*, April 20, May 1, 1884.

19. *Ibid.*, December 14, 1884; March 14, April 4, 1885.

20. *Ibid.*, December 13, 14, 1885.

21. *Ibid.*, March 8, 24, July 21, 1885
22. *Ibid.*, April 5, 7, May 3, 1885.
23. *Ibid.*, June 21, 24, 25, 1885.
24. *Ibid.*, June 30, July 1, 1885.
25. *Ibid.*, July 9, August 13, 1885.
26. *Ibid.*, May 28, 31, 1885.
27. *Ibid.*, July 1, 9, 25, 1885.
28. *Ibid.*, July 21, 26, August 22, 1885.
29. *Ibid.*, August 8, 9, 1885.
30. *Ibid.*, August 15, 16, 18, 1885.
31. *Ibid.*, August 28, 29, September 1, 1885; Hiram T. Askew, "Billy Nash: First Richmond Baseball Great," *Richmond Quarterly*, Spring, 1981, pp. 34–36.
32. *Ibid.*, August 28, 29, September 1, 1885.
33. *Ibid.*, September 18, 19, 20, 22, 1885, and September 16, 1894.

Chapter III. Richmond's Second
Venture into Professional Baseball

1. *Richmond Dispatch*, April 18, 20, 1886.
2. Harold Seymour, *Baseball: The Early Years* (New York: Oxford University Press, 1960), pp. 182–185.
3. *Richmond Dispatch*, March 9, 1890; Seymour, *The Early Years*, p. 184.
4. Harold Seymour, *Baseball: The People's Game* (New York: Oxford University Press, 1990), pp. 131–143.
5. *Richmond Dispatch*, April 18, 1886.
6. *Ibid.*, March 2, 1890.
7. The city of Manchester became independent from Chesterfield County in 1874 and was annexed by the city of Richmond in 1910.
8. *Richmond Dispatch*, March 2, 23, 1890.
9. *Ibid.*, March 2, 7, 21, 22, 23, 25, 1890.
10. *Ibid.*, March 23, 1890.
11. *Ibid.*, March 7, 23, 1890.
12. *Ibid.*, March 22, 1890.
13. *Ibid.*, March 25, 29, 1890.
14. *Ibid.*, April 29, May 2, 3, 1890.
15. *Ibid.*, September 4, 1883; May 18, 1890.
16. *Ibid.*, May 18, 1890; E.R. Chesterman, "Ball in Other Days: History of the Game as Played in Richmond," *Richmond Dispatch*, September 16, 1894; Ben Blake, "Parks, Leagues, Names Are All That Change," *Richmond Dispatch*, April 16, 1895.
17. *Ibid.*, March 3, 4, 7; September 16, 1894.
18. *Ibid.*, March 3, 4, 1894.
19. Bill O'Neal, *The Southern League: Baseball in Dixie, 1885–1994* (Austin, Texas: Eakin Press, 1994), p. 15; *Richmond Dispatch*, March 7, 1894.
20. The National Agreement was essentially the peace agreement that settled the baseball war of the American Association and the National League started

in 1883. The agreement, crafted in 1884, provided regulations for teams and leagues for players and territories. Seymour, *The Early Years*, pp. 144–148.

21. *Richmond Dispatch*, March 14, 18, 1894; April 12, 1894; April 7, 1895.

22. Michael Benson, *Ballparks of North America: A Comprehensive Historical Reference to Baseball Grounds, Yards and Stadiums, 1845 to the Present* (Jefferson, North Carolina: McFarland, 1989), p. 332; *Richmond Dispatch*, March 14, April 22, June 12, 1894.

23. Peter Filichia, *Professional Baseball Franchises: From the Abbeville Athletics to the Zanesville Indians* (New York: Facts on File, 1993), pp. ix–x.

24. *Richmond Dispatch*, April 29, May 2, 3, June 5, 13, 23, 24, 26, 28, September 15, 1894; April 14, 1895, March 15, 1896.

25. *Ibid.*, July 1, September 2, 16, 1894.

26. *Ibid.*, July 17, 20, September 1, 2, 1894.

27. *Ibid.*, July 19, 1894.

28. A. Woolner Calisch, "The Birth of Baseball in Richmond: Game's Earliest Days Is Recalled," *Richmond Times-Dispatch Magazine*, September 10, 1939, p. 3; *Richmond Dispatch*, April 22, 1894

29. *Richmond Dispatch*, September 16, 1894.

30. *Ibid.*, September 9, 16, 1894.

31. *Ibid.*, April 14, 1895.

32. *Ibid.*, April 16, 17, 19; September 3, 15, 1895.

33. David F. Chrisman, *History of the Virginia League: 1900–1928; 1939–51* (Bend, Oregon: Maverick Press, 1988), pp. 1–2; Mike Shatzkin, ed., *The Ballplayers: Baseball's Ultimate Biographical Reference* (New York: William Morrow, 1990), p. 1068; *Richmond Dispatch*, April 14, 1895.

34. *Richmond Dispatch*, August 30, September 15, 22, 1895.

35. *Ibid.*, September 19, 25–29, 1895.

36. *Ibid.*, October 15, 1895; February 11, 1896.

37. *Ibid.*, July 2, August 12, 1896.

38. *Ibid.*, August 12, 13, 1896.

39. *Ibid.*, August 21–23, 25, 1896.

40. *Ibid.*, September 13, 16, 17, 23, 1896.

41. Ed Barrow with James M. Kahn, *My Fifty Years in Baseball* (New York: Coward-McCann, 1951), pp. 27–39.

42. O.P. Caylor, "Baseball Outlook for 1897," *Richmond Dispatch*, March 21, 1897.

43. Ira Smith, *Baseball's Famous Pitchers* (New York: A.S. Barnes, 1954), pp. 59–63; Mike Shatzkin, ed., *The Ballplayers*, pp. 182, 613; *Richmond Dispatch*, March 28, May 2, 1897.

44. Benson, *Ballparks of North America*, p. 332; *Richmond Dispatch*, March 28, 1897.

45. *Richmond Dispatch*, May 8, September 4, 5, 11, 1897.

46. *Ibid.*, April 27, May 9, July 6, September 7, 19, 1897.

47. *Ibid.*, September 21, 22, 1897.

48. *Ibid.*, September 24, 1897.

49. *Ibid.*

50. *Ibid.*, November 27, 28, 1897; February 27, March 13, 1898.

51. *Ibid.*, February 13, 1898.

52. Nemec, *Beer and Whiskey League*, p. 15; Seymour, *Baseball: The Early Years*, pp. 201–205. Another interesting exploration of the business aspect of baseball can be found in Robert F. Burk, *Never Just a Game: Players, Owners and American Baseball to 1920* (Chapel Hill: University of North Carolina Press, 1994).

53. *Richmond Dispatch*, April 17, 24, 1898.

54. *Ibid.*, February 16, April 17, 24, 26, 1898.

55. Barrow, *My Fifty Years in Baseball*, pp. 40–41; Shatzkin, ed., *The Ballplayers*, p. 52; Joel Zoss and John Bowmen, *Diamonds in the Rough: The Untold History of Baseball* (Chicago: Contemporary Books, Inc., 1996), p. 87; *Richmond Dispatch*, September 11, 1898.

56. *Richmond Dispatch*, September 18, 20; October 13, 14, 16; November 25, 27, 1898.

57. *Ibid.*, October 16, 1898; March 5, April 9, 1899.

58. *Ibid.*, April 27, May 7, 9, July 1, 1899.

59. *Ibid.*, July 6, 1899.

60. *Ibid.*, July 9, August 8, 1899.

61. Edward Barrow, *My Fifty Years in Baseball*, pp. 47, 48; *Richmond Dispatch*, August 8, 1899; March 21, April 6, 15, 1900.

62. *Richmond Dispatch*, April 22, 29, 1900.

63. *Ibid.*, May 1, 2, 9, June 1, 1900.

64. *Ibid.*, June 1, 8, 12, 1900.

65. *Ibid.*, June 12, 1900.

66. Jim L. Sumner, "Virginia–North Carolina League: A Fascinating Failure," *Baseball Research Journal*, 18 (1989), p. 38; *Richmond Dispatch*, June 12, 1900.

67. *Richmond Dispatch*, April 14, 16, 17, June 22, 1901.

68. Sumner, "Virginia-North Carolina League," pp. 39–40; *Richmond Dispatch*, June 23, July 6, 7, 1901; Calisch, "The Birth of Baseball in Richmond," p. 3.

Chapter IV. The Revival and Demise of the Virginia State League, 1906–1914

1. Pietrusza, *Major Leagues*, p. 134.

2. Sullivan, *The Minors*, pp. 35–41; Pietrusza, *Major Leagues*, pp. 127–140, 145–182; Obojski, *Bush League*, pp. 13–17; Seymour, *Baseball, the Early Years*, pp. 293–324.

3. Obojski, *Bush League*, pp. 13–14; Sullivan, *The Minors*, pp. 44–46.

4. Obojski, *Bush League*, pp. 14–15.

5. *Ibid.*, p. 16.

6. *Ibid.*, pp. 16–17; Pietrusza, *Major Leagues*, pp. 178–183.

7. *Richmond Times-Dispatch*, April 16, 19, 20, 23, August 19, 20, 1905.

8. *Ibid.*, April 23, August 20, 1905.

9. *Ibid.*, August 20, 22, 1905.

10. *Ibid.*, September 3, 15, 1905.

11. *Ibid.*, October 26, 1905; March 11, 17, April 4, 1906.

12. *Ibid.*, March 8, 11, April 6, 1906.

13. *Ibid.*, June 30, July 23, 1907; September 20, 1908; William S. Simpson, Jr., "1908, the Year Richmond Went 'Baseball Wild,'" *Virginia Cavalcade* (Spring, 1977), pp. 184–191.

14. *Richmond Times-Dispatch*, April 26, 27, 1906.

15. *Ibid.*, April 27, September 4, 9, 1906.

16. *Ibid.*, September 9, 1906.

17. Chrisman, *History of the Virginia League (1900–28; 1939–51)* (Bend, Oregon: The Maverick Press, 1988), p. 3; *Richmond Times-Dispatch*, June 30, July 3, 23, September 22, 23, 1907.

18. Simpson, "1908, The Year Richmond Went Baseball Wild," pp. 184–191; O'Neal, *International League*, p. 335; *Richmond Times-Dispatch*, September 20, 21, 1908.

19. Paul Dickson, *The New Dickson Baseball Dictionary* (New York: Harcourt Brace and Company, 1999), p. 468; Simpson, "1908, The Year Richmond Went Baseball Wild," p. 191; *Richmond Times-Dispatch*, September 20, 1908.

20. *Richmond Times-Dispatch*, September 12, 13, 1909.

21. *Ibid.*, September 13, 14, 1909.

22. *Ibid.*, September 7, 10, 11, 1910.

23. *Ibid.*, September 10, 1910.

24. *Ibid.*, August 14, September 10, 14, 15, 1910.

25. *Thirteenth Census of the United States: Taken in the Year 1910*, Vol. III; Population, 1910 (Washington: Government Printing Office, 1913), p. 946.

26. *Richmond Times-Dispatch*, September 11, 14, 15, 1910.

27. *Ibid.*, October 9, 11, 12, 16, 28, 1910.

28. *Ibid.*, October 23, 1910.

29. *Ibid.*, April 20, September 7, 9, 19, 1911.

30. *Ibid.*, September 18, 25, 1911.

31. *Ibid.*, October 11, 14, 15, 18, 1911.

32. *Ibid.*, September 25, 27, November 5, 1911.

33. Pietrusza, *Major Leagues*, pp. 193–201; *Richmond Times-Dispatch*, December 22, 1911.

34. Pietrusza, *Major Leagues*, p. 197; *Richmond Times-Dispatch*, January–March, 1912.

35. *Richmond Times-Dispatch*, September 24, 1911; January 10, 1912.

36. Benson, *Ballparks of North America…*, p. 132; Pietrusza, *Major Leagues…*, p. 198; *Richmond Times-Dispatch*, April 14, 30, 1912.

37. *Richmond Times-Dispatch*, April 19, May 2, 12, 1912.

38. Pietrusza, *Major Leagues…*, pp. 202–205; *Richmond Times-Dispatch*, May 3, 24, 1912.

39. Pietrusza, *Major Leagues…*, pp. 205–207; *Richmond Times-Dispatch*, June 4, 8, 9, 11, 20, 23, 24, 1912.

40. *Richmond Times-Dispatch*, June 5–13, 1912.

41. *Ibid.*, May 1, June 5, 24, August 29, 31, September 8, 1912.

42. *Ibid.*, January 7, June 15, 1912.

43. *Ibid.*, April 12, 1913; Benson, *Ballparks of North America…*, p. 332.

44. *Richmond Times-Dispatch*, April 18, September 13, 14, 1913.

45. *Ibid.*, March 8, 15, 29, April 2, 5, 1914.

46. *Ibid.*, July 2, 4, 1914.

47. *Ibid.*, September 12, 13, 1914.

48. *Ibid.*, September 12, 13, 1914; Ira L. Smith, *Baseball's Famous Pitchers* (New York: A.S. Barnes, 1954), pp. 166–170.

49. *Richmond Times-Dispatch*, September 14, 1913; March 15, April 12, 1914.

50. *Ibid.*, June 26, 1914.

51. Mark Okkonen, *The Federal League of 1914–1915: Baseball's Third Major League* (Garret Park, Maryland: Society for American Baseball Research, 1989), pp. 3–5; Pietrusza, *Major Leagues...*, pp. 209–212.

52. Benson, *Ballparks...*, p. 24; Okkonen, *Federal League...*, pp. 5–9; Pietrusza, *Major League...*, pp. 212–227.

53. O'Neal, *The International League*, pp. 236–239; Sullivan, *The Minors...*, pp. 71–73.

54. Benson, *Ballparks...*, p. 24; Okkonen, *Federal League...*, pp. 11–13; Pietrusza, *Major Leagues...*, p. 229; Sullivan, *The Minors...*, pp. 75–76.

55. *Richmond Times-Dispatch*, June 26, 1914; Neil J. Sullivan, *The Minors...*, pp. 75–76; Okkonen, *Federal League...*, pp. 11–13.

56. *Richmond Times-Dispatch*, June 26, 27, 29, 1914.

57. Sullivan, *The Minors...*, p. 76; *Richmond Times-Dispatch*, July 3, 1914.

58. Pietrusza, *Major Leagues...*, p. 243; O'Neal, *The International League*, p. 244; Sullivan, *The Minors...*, pp. 76–77.

59. *Richmond Times-Dispatch*, December 6–10, 12, 1914; April 4, 1954; Robert L. Scribner, "Two Out, and —? The Richmond 'Virginians' Need Not Feel Unfamiliar in the International League, They Have Been There Twice Before," *Virginia Cavalcade* (Spring, 1954), pp. 18–22.

60. Benson, *Ballparks...*, p. 333; *Richmond Times-Dispatch*, December 9, 1914; March 23, 1915.

61. *Richmond Times-Dispatch*, April 25, 28, 1915.

62. *Ibid.*, April 28, 1915..

63. *Ibid.*, September 14, 19, 1915; O'Neal, *The International League...*, p. 336.

64. *Richmond Times-Dispatch*, December 12, 14, 16, 19, 20, 23, 24, 28, 1915.

65. Scribner, "Two Out, and...?," p. 21.

66. *Richmond Times-Dispatch*, September 17–18, 1916.

67. Benson, *Ballparks...*, p. 332; Ben W. Blake, "Roots: Parks, League, Names are all that change," *Richmond Times-Dispatch*, April 6, 1985, Section C-10; *Richmond Times-Dispatch*, February 2, 1917.

68. O'Neal, *International League*, pp. 65–68; Richmond *Times-Dispatch*, September 16, 1917.

69. *Richmond Times-Dispatch*, April 18, 1917.

70. *Ibid.*

71. *Ibid.*, May 25, 1917.

72. O'Neal, *International League*, pp. 67–68; Richmond *Times-Dispatch*, September 16, 1917.

73. O'Neal, *The International League...*, p. 68.; Scribner, "Two out, and...?", p. 22: Joel Zoss and John Bowman, *Diamonds in the Rough, the Untold History of Baseball* (New York: Macmillan, 1989), pp. 88–93; *Richmond Times-Dispatch*, September 16, 1917.

74. O'Neal, *The International League…*, pp. 68–69; Zoss and Bowman, *Diamonds in the Rough…*, p. 91; *Richmond Times-Dispatch*, April 4, 1954.

Chapter V. The Virginia League Again, 1918–1928, and the Eastern League, 1931–1932

1. *Richmond Times-Dispatch*, March 27, 28, 29, April 1, 7, 1918.
2. *Ibid.*, March 24, 27, 28, 1918; Scribner, "Two Out and…?", p. 22.
3. *Richmond Times-Dispatch*, March 27, 28, 1918; April 4, 1954; O'Neal, *International League*, p. 69.
4. *Richmond Times-Dispatch*, April 4, 1954.
5. *Ibid.*, March 29, 1918.
6. *Ibid.*, March 29, April 3, 4, 5, 7, 9, 10, 26, May 3, 1918.
7. *Ibid.*, April 3, 8, 1918; O'Neal, *International League*, p. 69; Zoss and Bowman, *Diamonds in the Rough*, p. 91.
8. *Richmond Times-Dispatch*, April 4, 5, 7, 9,10, 13, 26, May 3, 22, 1918.
9. *Ibid.*, May 22, 23, 1918.
10. *Ibid.*, May 23, 1918.
11. *Ibid.*, July 20, 1918; Zoss and Bowman, *Diamonds in the Rough*, p. 91.
12. *Richmond Times-Dispatch*, July 21, 1918.
13. Seymour, *Golden Age…*, p. 255; Zoss and Bowman, *Diamonds in the Rough*, p. 93; Richmond *Times-Dispatch*, November 11, 17, 1918; April 16, 1919.
14. *Richmond Times-Dispatch*, May 9, 10, 24, 26, 1919.
15. Lee Allen and Tom Meany, *Kings of the Diamond: The Immortals in Baseball's Hall of Fame* (New York: G.P. Putnam's Sons, 1965), pp. 50–52; Shatzkin, ed., *The Ballplayers…*, p. 68; Ira Smith, *Baseball's Famous Pitchers*, pp. 93–99; *National Baseball Hall of Fame and Museum 1999 Yearbook* (Cooperstown, New York; National Baseball Hall of Fame and Museum, 1999), p. 93; *Richmond Times-Dispatch*, May 26–30, 1919.
16. *Richmond Times-Dispatch*, May 30, July 8, September 3, 7, 11, 1919.
17. *Ibid*, September 4, 5, 6, 1919.
18. *Ibid.*, April 22, 23, July 4–5, September 5, October 14, December 4, 1920; January 10, 1921.
19. *Ibid.*, September 13, 14, 1920.
20. *Ibid.*, September 14–22, 1920.
21. *Ibid*, September 23, 24, 25, 1920.
22. *Ibid.*; Sullivan, *The Minors…*pp. 97–101.
23. *Richmond Times-Dispatch*, October 29, November 6, 9, 1920.
24. *Ibid.*, November 6, 1920.
25. *Ibid.*
26. *Ibid.*, January 11, 13, 14, 16, February 11, 17, 1921.
27. *Ibid.*, December 31, 1920; February 11, 12, 1921.
28. Benson, *Ballparks…*, pp. 331–332; Harry M. Ward, "Richmond Sports at Flood Tide: Mayo Island, 1921–1941," *Virginia Cavalcade* (Spring 1985), pp. 182–84; *Times-Dispatch*, February 12, 1921; March 4, 14, 21, 1922; April 16, 1985.
29. *Richmond Times-Dispatch*, February 10, March 12, 27, 28, 29, 1921.

30. *Ibid.*, January 16, April 7, 1921.
31. *Ibid.*, April 12, December 16, 1921; May 30, 1922.
32. *Ibid.*, February 18, 19, April 29, 1921.
33. *Ibid.*, April 21, 22, 23, 24, May 13, 14, 15, 22, July 1, 3, 19, 1921.
34. *Ibid.*, July 1, August 2, September 10, 1921.
35. *Ibid.*, September 10, 11, 18, 20, 21, 24, 25, 1921.
36. *Ibid.*, October 4, 9, 1921.
37. *Ibid.*, October 1, 3, November 17, 21, 1921.
38. *Ibid.*, November 17, 21, 1921; February 3, 1922.
39. *Ibid.*, February 3, 4, 5, 7, 11, 16, 24, March 2, 1922.
40. *Ibid.*, April 21, 1922.
41. *Ibid.*, April 27, 28, May 29, 30, 1922.
42. *Ibid.*, April 29, 1919; May 30, June 1, 6, 8, 30, July 1, 9, September 7, 1922.
43. *Ibid.*, May 30, June 4, September 7, 1922.
44. *Ibid.*, July 20, 21, 1922.
45. *Ibid.*, August 2, 1922.
46. *Ibid.*, July 9, 11, September 6, 7, 12, November 22, 26, December 12, 19, 1922; January 2, 1923.
47. *Ibid.*, July 21, November 2, 9, 10, 26, December 8, 12, 19, 1922; January 2, 3, 4, 7, 9, 13, 14, 1923.
48. *Ibid.*, November 19, December 20, 1922; January 13, 14, 1923.
49. *Ibid.*, September 3–14, 1923.
50. *Ibid.*, September 13, 20, 21, 1923.
51. *Ibid.*, December 14, 31, 1923; January 6, 7, 1924.
52. *Ibid.*, October 14, 1920; February 20, March 2, April 7, 17, 18, September 16, 18, 20, 1924.
53. *Ibid.*, September 14–21, 1924.
54. *Ibid.*, December 13, 14, 15, 17, 18, 21, 22, 1924.
55. *Ibid.*, September 13, December 27, 1925.
56. *Ibid.*, September 13, December 27, 1925; February 16, 1927.
57. *Ibid.*, January 6, April 1, July 20, 21, 22, September 16, 19, 26, December 26, 1926.
58. *Ibid*, September 20, 1907; August 14, 1910; December 30, 1923; March 28, April 4, 1926.
59. *Ibid.*, April 15, 1925; April 13, December 26, 1926.
60. *Ibid.*, November 10, 17, 20, December 26, 1926; January 16, 1927.
61. *Ibid.*, December 17, 1926; January 23, 25–28, February 4–8, 12, 14, March 7, 14, 17, 18, 1927.
62. *Ibid.*, January 16, February 16, April 14, July 1, 2, September 4, 11, 1927.
63. *Ibid.*, September 12, 14, November 27, December 5, 6, 7, 13, 16, 18, 25, 26, 1927; January 10, March 11, 15, April 15, 18, 19, 1928.
64. *Ibid.*, April 18, June 4, 5, 1928.
65. *Ibid.*, May 22, 23, 27, 28, 30, June 3, 4, 5, 6, 1928.
66. *Ibid.*, June 3, 4, 5, 6, 1928; September 10, 1939; April 16, 1985.
67. *Ibid.*, January 3, 1932.
68. *Ibid.*, April 26, 27, 28, 1931.

69. *Ibid.*, June 6, 8, 11, 1931.

70. *Ibid.*, June 11, 1931.

71. *Ibid.*, June 26, 27, July 2, 1931.

72. *Ibid.*, April 27, June 26, 1931.

73. *Ibid.*, June 29, September 3, 4, 13, 1931.

74. *Ibid.*, December 26, 31, 1931; January 4, 5, 6, July 17, 18, 1932; February 27, 1933.

Chapter VI. The Richmond Colts and the Piedmont League, 1933–1953

1. *Times-Dispatch*, February 27, 1933.

2. Harry M. Ward, *Richmond: An Illustrated History* (Northridge, California: Windson Publications, Inc., 1985), p. 250. In 1901, at the suggestion of T.J. Hickey, president of the Western League, representatives of each of the minor leagues met in Chicago and formed the National Association of Baseball Leagues. The association established rules and regulations to stabilize minor league baseball and adopted a classification system for the minor leagues. Under this system minor leagues were divided into four classes: A, B, C, and D. This system was designed to provide equal competition among teams in a given league. Leagues composed of smaller cities and with lower operating budgets were labeled as Class D. The team rosters were to be composed of players with limited experience. Class A, the highest classification, contained the most experienced minor league players. In 1908, the classification was altered to include AA rating, and, in 1946, AAA ratings were introduced. In 1963 the B, C, and D ratings were discontinued and "rookie league" and "instructional league" circuits were formed for the less experienced players. See Obojski, *Bush League*, p. 14–15.

3. *Times-Dispatch*, March 5, 18, 1933.

4. *Ibid.*, March 31, April 13, 25, 1933.

5. *Ibid.*, August 30, 1933.

6. *Ibid.*, April 1, 1934; March 13, 1935; April 2, 1936; May 4, 1937. Also see Harry M. Ward, "Richmond Sports at Flood Tide: Mayo Island, 1921–41," *Virginia Cavalcade* (Spring 1985), p. 189.

7. *Times-Dispatch*, April 7, 1934.

8. *Ibid.*, April 30, 1934.

9. *Ibid.*, March 24, April 1, 6, 1934.

10. *Ibid.*, May 17, 21, 1934.

11. *Ibid.*, June 2, 1934.

12. *Ibid.*, September 16, 1934.

13. *Ibid.*, September 19, 1934.

14. *Ibid.*, March 13, 24, April 2, 1935.

15. Mike Shatzkin, editor, *The Ballplayers: Baseball's Ultimate Biographical Reference* (New York: William Morrow, 1990), p. 935.

16. *Times-Dispatch*, March 26, April 19, 1935.

17. *Ibid.*, April 26, 30, 1935.

18. *Ibid.*, September 8, 19, 1935.

19. *Ibid.*, September 17, 1935.
20. David F. Chrisman, *The History of the Piedmont League (1920–1955)* (Bend, Oregon: Maverick Publications, 1986), pp. 83–84.
21. *Times-Dispatch*, July 25, August 8, 9, 1935.
22. *Ibid.*, September 8, 1935.
23. *Ibid.*, September 20, 1935.
24. *Ibid.*, March 27, 29, 1936.
25. *Ibid.*, April 5, 24, May 5, 1936.
26. Shatzkin, editor, The *Ballplayers...*, p. 990.
27. *Times-Dispatch*, April 1, 2, September 10, 1936.
28. *Ibid.*, May 22, 1936; March 2, April 24, August 21, 1937.
29. *Ibid.*, September 9, 1936; Chrisman, *History of the Piedmont League*, p. 90.
30. *Times-Dispatch*, September 13, 18, 1936.
31. *Ibid.*, May 19, 1936.
32. *Ibid.*, June 20, 1936.
33. *Ibid.*, March 8, 21, April 1, 15, 21, 1937.
34. *Ibid.*, April 23, May 1, 1937; September 6, 1937.
35. *Ibid.*, June 1, 1937.
36. *Ibid.*, July 15, August 9, 21, 1937.
37. Chrisman, *History of the Piedmont League*, p. 98; *Times-Dispatch*, August 17, September 9, 11, 17, 1937.
38. *Times-Dispatch*, April 4, 17, 21, 25, 1938.
39. *Ibid.*, August 25, September 8, 1938.
40. *Ibid.*, July 27, August 24, 27, 30, 1938.
41. *Ibid.*, July 15, 1938.
42. *Ibid.*, February 28, March 29, 31, 1939.
43. Chrisman, *History of the Piedmont League*, p. 109; *Times-Dispatch*, April 6, 20, May 12, July 31, August 2, 12, 17, 1939.
44. *Times-Dispatch*, July 25, 26, August 13, 1939.
45. *Ibid.*, September 19, 23, 1939.
46. *Ibid.*, March 11, 22, 27, 28, April 1, 1940.
47. Chrisman, *History of the Piedmont League*, pp. 114–115; *Times-Dispatch*, June 20, September 3, 1940.
48. *Times-Dispatch*, September 3, 10, 12, 18, 1940.
49. *Ibid.*, May 21, July 29, 1940.
50. *Ibid.*, June 4, July 2, 3, 20, August 12, 1940.
51. *Ibid.*, March 27, 29, April 25, 26, 1941.
52. *Ibid.*, June 25, July 2, 26, 1941.
53. *Ibid.*, February 16, 25, 1938.
54. *Ibid.*, July 17, 19, 1941.
55. *Ibid.*, July 10, 1941.
56. *Ibid.*, April 12, 15, 1941.
57. *Ibid.*, August 17, September 7, 1941.
58. *Ibid.*, July 21, August 30, 1941.
59. *Ibid.*, August 11, 1941.
60. *Ibid.*, September 1, 1941.

61. *Ibid.*, September 15, 19, 1941.

62. *Ibid.*, March 31, 1942.

63. *Ibid.*, February 22, March 30, August 2, 15, September 17, 1942.

64. *Ibid.*, February 22, April 18, 19, 23, 1942.

65. *Ibid.*, April 26, 1942.

66. *Ibid.*, May 14, 15, 1942.

67. *Ibid.*, June 11, 13, July 9, 14, 1942.

68. *Ibid.*, July 3, July 21, August 2, 3, 1942.

69. *Ibid.*, June 17, 18, 1942.

70. *Ibid.*, August 16, September 17, 23, 1942; Chrisman, *History of the Piedmont League*, pp. 130–131.

71. *Times-Dispatch*, March 25, April 3, 12, 17, 1943.

72. *Ibid.*, March 18, June 19, 1943.

73. *Ibid.*, May 8, September 5, 1943; Chrisman, *History of the Piedmont League*, p. 137.

74. *Times-Dispatch*, August 29, September 13, 14, 20, 1943.

75. *Ibid.*, March 26, 1943; William Mead, *Baseball Goes to War* (Washington: Farragut Publishing Company, 1985), p. 38; Richard Goldstein, *Spartan Seasons: How Baseball Survived the Second World War* (New York: Macmillan, 1980), pp. 124–125.

76. *Times-Dispatch*, July 29, August 23, 1943.

77. *Ibid.*, April 4, 1943.

78. *Ibid.*, March 1, 27, August 20, 1944.

79. *Ibid.*, April 3, 4, 10, 17, 22, 1944.

80. *Ibid.*, April 29, 30, September 11, 1944.

81. *Ibid.*, May 18, 27, July 27, 1944.

82. *Ibid.*, August 2, 1944.

83. *Ibid.*, September 8, 22, 23, October 3, 1944; Hamner had a sixteen-year career with the Philadelphia Phillies, Shatzkin, *The Ballplayers...*, p. 438.

84. *Ibid.*, September 10, 1944.

85. *Ibid.*, June 27, 1944.

86. *Ibid.*, July 12, September 9, 1944.

87. *Ibid.*, March 12, 16, May 6, 1945.

88. *Ibid.*, March 29, April 16, 19, 23, 27, 29, 1945.

89. Chrisman, *History of the Piedmont League*, pp. 150–151; *Times-Dispatch*, September 9, 1945.

90. *Times-Dispatch*, August 27, 1945.

91. *Ibid.*, September 14, 20, 26, 1945.

92. *Ibid.*, March 15, 1946.

93. *Ibid.*, March 21, 1946.

94. *Ibid.*, April 7, 15, 21, 24, 1946.

95. *Ibid.*, April 28, May 6, 8, 1946.

96. *Ibid.*, May 12, 1946.

97. *Ibid.*, September 1, 27, 1946.

98. *Ibid.*, March 1, 12, 1947.

99. *Ibid.*, April 11, 16, 19, 1947.

100. *Ibid.*, April 25, June 22, July 12, 1947.

101. *Ibid.*, May 4, June 16, August 14, September 18, 19, 1947.

102. Chrisman, *History of the Piedmont League*, p. 164; *Times-Dispatch*, August 31, 1947.

103. *Times-Dispatch*, September 12, 15, 24, 1947.

104. *Ibid.*, March 12, 1948.

105. *Ibid.*, March 25, 29, September 8, 1948.

106. *Ibid.*, April 24, 1948.

107. *Ibid.*, May 7, September 8, 1948; Chrisman, *History of the Piedmont League*, pp. 169–170.

108. *Times-Dispatch*, August 18, 1948.

109. *Ibid.*, April 5, 1950.

110. *Ibid.*, March 18, 21, April 8, July 31, 1949.

111. *Ibid.*, March 21, June 22, 1949.

112. *Ibid.*, April 11, 13, 15, 18, 1949.

113. *Ibid.*, April 22, September 6, 1949.

114. Chrisman, *History of the Piedmont League*, p. 174; *Times-Dispatch*, September 14, 18, 26, 1949.

115. *Times-Dispatch*, May 29, 1949.

116. *Ibid.*, June 20, 1949.

117. *Ibid.*, March 6, April 6, 1950.

118. *Ibid.*, March 18, April 13, 14, 18, 20, 22, 1950.

119. *Ibid.*, April 27, 1950.

120. *Ibid.*, September 10, 17, 18, October 1, 1950.

121. *Ibid.*, July 12, 13, 14, September 3, 1950.

122. *Ibid.*, August 1, 1950.

123. *Ibid.*, September 19, 1950.

124. *Ibid.*, March 17, 19, 26, 1951.

125. *Ibid.*, April 12, 15, 18, 1951.

126. *Ibid.*, April 22, July 17, 1951; April 2, 1952.

127. *Ibid.*, September 9, 10, 11, 18, 1951.

128. *Ibid.*, May 28, 1951.

129. *Ibid.*, July 23, 24, 1951.

130. *Ibid.*, June 5, 1951; May 23, 1952.

131. *Ibid.*, February 27, March 30, 1952.

132. *Ibid.*, April 13, 15, 17, 1952.

133. *Ibid.*, April 19, 30, 1952.

134. *Ibid.*, June 20, 21, 22, 26, 1952.

135. *Ibid.*, July 13, 1952.

136. *Ibid.*, August 24, September 3, 1952. Chrisman, *History of the Piedmont League*, p. 192.

137. *Times-Dispatch*, July 11, 1952.

138. *Ibid.*, September 9, 10, 14, 15, 1952.

139. *Ibid.*, March 24, 1953.

140. *Ibid.*

141. *Ibid.*, March 29, 1953.

142. *Ibid.*, March 22, 1953.

143. *Ibid.*, April 20, 1953.

144. *Ibid.*, April 15, September 13, 1953.

145. *Ibid.*, April 23, 24, 27, 1953.

146. *Ibid.*, June 2, 1953.

147. *Ibid.*, June 8, 1953.

148. *Ibid.*, June 25, 1953.

149. *Ibid.*, July 21, 1953.

150. *Ibid.*, September 6, 1953.

151. *Ibid.*, September 12, 13, 18, 1953.

152. *Ibid.*, August 26, 1953.

Chapter VII. Richmond and the International League

1. *Times-Dispatch*, December 18, 1953.

2. *Ibid.*, October 15, December 23, 1953; January 4, 6, 1954.

3. *Ibid.*, December 20, 1953.

4. *Ibid.*, December 31, 1953.

5. *Ibid.*, March 8, 1954.

6. *Ibid.*, February 7, 1954.

7. *Ibid.*, September 13, 1954.

8. Irving, Elliott, *Remembering the Vees* (Farmville, Virginia: Cumberland Press, 1979), p. 13.

9. *Times-Dispatch*, November 2, 1955.

10. *Ibid.*, November 3, 1955.

11. *Ibid.*, November 15, 1955.

12. *Ibid.*, September 14, 1956.

13. Irving, *Remembering the Vees*, p. 15.

14. *Times Dispatch*, January 22, 1959.

15. Irving, *Remembering the Vees*, pp. 18, 19.

16. *Ibid.*, pp. 21, 22.

17. *Times-Dispatch*, November 15, 1964.

18. Irving, *Remembering the Vees*, p. 25.

19. *Times-Dispatch*, December 1 and 20, 1964.

20. *Ibid.*, December 1 and 2, 1964.

21. *Ibid.*, December 20 and 31, 1964; "The Story of the Braves," found in the "History" section of the *Atlanta Braves official website* (www.braves.mlb.com), accessed on January 13, 2002.

22. *Times-Dispatch*, December 31, 1964, and April 7, 1965.

23. *Ibid.*, Rolfe, April 18, 1965; Durden, April 23 and 25, 1965.

24. *Times-Dispatch*, April 17, 19, 22, 1966. The Governor's Cup Championship series is the final round of playoffs in the International league. The league follows the Shaughnessty Plan. Proposed in 1932 by Montreal Royals general manager, Frank Shaughnessy, and enacted by the International league for the 1933 season, the plan provides for a playoff system in which the top four teams earn playoff berths. The team that finished in first place is named the season pennant winner. The first round of the playoffs features a best 3-of-5 series. The first round winners compete in the best 4-of-7 games second round with the series

champion winning a trophy names the Governor's Cup. The cup earned its name from its sponsorship by the Governors of Maryland, New Jersey, New York and the Lieutenant Governors of the Canadian Provinces of Quebec and Ontario. The playoff system, modeled after a Canadian hockey system, was created to sustain fan interest, even if one or two teams were able to significantly pull away from the other teams, as the Newark Bears were able to do in the early 1930s. Shortly after the International League began using the Shaughnessy playoffs, most other minor league teams began their own versions of the system. (International league Official Website, Governor's Cup History section, accessed on November 25, 2001; O'Neal, *International League*, pp. 113–116.)

25. *Times-Dispatch*, April 20–22, 1966.

26. *Ibid.*, April 21–22, 1966.

27. *Ibid.*, April 23, 1966.

28. *Ibid.*, April 19 and 23, 1966.

29. O'Neal, *International League*, pp. 174–175 and 338; *Richmond Braves 2001 Media Guide*, CD-ROM edition, "History" Section; *Times-Dispatch*, April 20, 1966.

30. *Braves 2001 Media Guide*, "History"; *Times-Dispatch*, September 2–6, 1967.

31. *Braves 2001 Media Guide*, "History"; O'Neal, *International League*, p. 338; *Times-Dispatch*, June 15 and September 5, 1967.

32. *Braves 2001 Media Guide*; *Times-Dispatch*, Septemaber 2, 1967; O'Neal, *International League*, p. 335.

33. *Times-Dispatch*, July 31, and August 1, 1967.

34. *Braves 2001 Media Guide*; *Times-Dispatch*, August 15, 16, 1968; June 5, 6, 1969; O'Neal, *International League*, pp. 177–178 and 338–341; *Richmond Braves 2000 Yearbook*, "Memory Lane: Richmond Baseball makes the Trip Through the Years," p. 38–40.

35. *Braves 2001 Media Guide*; O'Neal, *International League*, pp. 177–178 and 338–341.

36. *Braves 2001 Media Guide*; O'Neal, *International League*, pp. 177–181 and 338–341.

37. *Braves 2001 Media Guide*; *Richmond Braves 2000 Yearbook*, "Memory lane: Richmond Baseball Makes the Trip Through the Years, p. 40.

38. *Braves 2001 Media Guide*; O'Neal, *International League*, pp. 187–88; *Richmond Times-Dispatch*, September 2, 1975.

39. *Richmond Times-Dispatch*, June 15–17, 1975.

40. *Ibid.*, September 2, December 30, 1975; April 4, 1976.

41. *Ibid.*, April 4, 15, 1976.

42. *Ibid.*, April 16, 1976.

43. *Ibid.*, April 16, 17, September 2–5, 1976.

44. *Ibid.*, September 6–12, 1976.

45. *Braves 2001 Media Guide*: *Times-Dispatch*, September 9, 1976.

46. *Times-Dispatch*, September 10, 1976.

47. *Ibid.*, September 8–11, 1976.

48. *Ibid.*, September 10–11, 1976.

49. *Braves 2001 Media Guide*.

50. *Ibid.*

51. *Braves 2001 Media Guide*, *Times-Dispatch*, September 2, 1984.

52. *Braves 2001 Media Guide.*

53. *Braves 2001 Media Guide*; O'Neal, *International League*, pp. 184–85; Sullivan, *The Minors*, pp. 256–57.

54. Bill Millsap's column, *Richmond Times-Dispatch*, September 1, 1984; *Times-Dispatch* special supplement, *Anderson's Lobbying Led to New Stadium* by Bill Millsaps and *The Diamond Trail: How Teamwork Created a New Stadium* by Tom Haudricourt, April 16, 1985.

55. Haudricourt, *Times-Dispatch*, April 16, 1985.

56. *Ibid.*; *Braves* 2001 Media Guide.

57. Haudricourt, *Times-Dispatch*, April 16, 1985.

58. *Ibid.*, *Times-Dispatch*, September 1, 4, 1984; *Braves 2001 Media Guide.*

59. *Times-Dispatch*, September 13, 19, 1984.

60. Tom Hardicourt, *Richmond Times-Dispatch* supplement issue, *Don't Fence me In: Diamond Should Aid Lefty Power Hitters*, April 16, 1985; Richmond Braves 1983 Media Guide, p. 3.

61. *Braves 1983 Media Guide*, pp. 3, 72, 73, 91.

62. *Times-Dispatch*, September 3, 1985.

63. *Braves 1986 Media Guide*, p. 5; *Media Guide 2001*; *Times-Dispatch*, November 19, 29, 1985.

64. *Braves 1987 Media Guide*, pp. 6, 7;, 18, 26. *Times-Dispatch*, August 29-September 3, 1986.

65. *Times-Dispatch*, September 8–13, 1986.

66. *Braves 1988 Media Guide*, pp. 28–29; *Braves 2001 Media Guide*; *Times-Dispatch*, September 1, 2, 14, 30, 1987.

67. O'Neal, *International League*, pp. 205–207, 216; *Braves 1988 Media Guide*, pp. 30–31, 39–42, 46; *Braves 1996 Media Guide*, p. 80.

68. O'Neal, *International league*, p. 206.

69. *Braves 2001 Media Guide*; O'Neal, *International League*, p. 207; *Times-Dispatch*, August 30, 1988.

70. *Braves 2001 Media Guide*; *Braves 1991 Media Guide*, p. 41; O'Neal, *International League*, p. 209–211.

71. *Braves 2001 Media Guide*; *Times-Dispatch*, September 7, 1989.

72. *Braves 2001 Media Guide.*

73. *Richmond Braves 2000 Yearbook*, "Memory Lane: Richmond Baseball Makes the Trip Through the Years," p. 46; Robert F. Burk, *Players, Owners and American Baseball Since 1921: Much More Than Just a Game* (Chapel Hill: University of North Carolina Press, 2001) pp. 288–289.

74. *Braves 2001 Media guide*; *Richmond Braves 2000 Yearbook*, "Memory Lane: Richmond Baseball Makes the Trip Through the Years," pp. 44–46.

75. *Braves 2001 Media Guide*; *Braves 2000 Media Guide*, pp. 64–65; *Richmond Braves 2000 Yearbook*, "Memory Lane: Richmond Baseball Makes the Trip Through the Years," p. 44–46.

76. Braves *2001 Media Guide*; *Times-Dispatch*, August 30, 1990.

77. Richmond Braves official team website, "HKS Inc. to plan the Diamond Face-Lift" section (www.rbraves.com/hks.asp) accessed on October 30, 2001; Richmond Metropolitan Authority website, "The Diamond" section (www.rmaonline.org/Facilities/diamond.htmal), accessed on February 24, 2002.

Bibliography

Newspapers

Richmond Daily Dispatch, 1861-1903
Richmond Times, 1886-1903
Richmond Times-Dispatch, 1903-2001
Richmond News Leader, 1903-1992

Articles

Askew, Hiram T. "Billy Nash: First Richmond Baseball Great," *Richmond Quarterly* (Spring 1981).

Chadwick, Henry. "Baseball in the South," in Gerald R. Gems, ed., *Sports in North America: A Documentary History*, vol. 5, Sports Organized: 1880-1900 (Gulf Breeze, Florida: Academic International Press, 1996).

Gudmasted, Robert H. "Baseball, the Lost Cause, and the New South in Richmond, Virginia, 1883-1890," *Virginia Magazine of History and Biography* (Summer, 1998).

Henley, Bernard J. "The Early Years of Baseball in Richmond," *Richmond Quarterly* (Winter, 1978).

Scribner, Robert L. "Two Outs and—?" *Virginia Cavalcade* (Spring, 1954).

Simpson, William S., Jr. "1908: The Year Richmond Went Baseball Wild," *Virginia Cavalcade* (Spring 1977).

Sumner, Jim L. "Virginia–North Carolina League: Fascinating Failure," *Baseball Research Journal* (1986).

Ward, Harry M. "Richmond Sports at Flood Tide: Mayo Island, 1921-41," *Virginia Cavalcade* (Spring, 1985).

Books

Allen, Lee, and Thomas Meany. *Kings of the Diamond* (New York: G.P. Putnam, 1965).

Barrow, Ed, and Khan, James H. *My Fifty Years in Baseball* (New York: Coward-McCann, 1951).

Benson, Michael. *Baseball Parks of North America: A Comprehensive Historical Reference to Baseball Grounds, Yards and Stadiums, 1845 to the Present* (Jefferson, North Carolina: McFarland, 1989).

Burk, Robert F. *Never Just a Game: Players, Owners and American Baseball to 1920* (Chapel Hill: The University of North Carolina Press, 1994).

_____. *Players, Owners and American Baseball Since 1921: Much More Than Just a Game* (Chapel Hill: University of North Carolina Press, 2001).

Chrisman, David F. *The History of the Piedmont League, 1925-1955* (Bend, Oregon: Maverick Publications, 1987).

_____. *The History of the Virginia League (1900-1928, 1939-1951)* (Bend, Oregon: Maverick Publications, 1988).

Dabney, Virginius. *Richmond: The Story of A City* (Charlottesville: University of Virginia Press, 1976).

Dickson, Paul. *The New Dickson Baseball Dictionary* (New York: Harcourt Brace, 1989. Revised 1999).

Feagans, Todd, editor. *Richmond Braves 2000 Yearbook* (Richmond: Cadmus Communications, 2000).

Filichia, Peter. *Professional Baseball Franchises: From the Abbeville Athletics to the Zanesville Indians* (New York: Facts on File, Inc., 1993).

Finch, Robert L. *The Story of Minor League Baseball* (Columbus, Ohio: Stoneham, 1953).

Goldstein, Richard. *Spartan Seasons: How Baseball Survived the Second World War* (New York: Macmillan, 1980).

Irving, Elliott. *Remembering the Vees* (Farmville, Virginia: Cumberland Press, 1979).

Mead, William. *Baseball Goes to War* (Washington: Farragut Publishing Company, 1985).

Nemec, David. *The Beer and Whiskey League: The Illustrated History of the American Association—Baseball's Renegade Major League* (New York: Lyons Printing, 1994).

Obojski, Robert. *Bush League: History of Minor League Baseball* (New York: Macmillan, 1975).

Okkonen, Mark. *The Federal League of 1914-1915: Baseball's Third Major League* (Garret Park, Maryland: Society for American Baseball Research, 1989).

O'Neal, Bill. *The International League: A Baseball History, 1884-1991* (Austin, Texas: Eakin Press, 1992).

_____. *The Southern League: Baseball in Dixie, 1885-1994* (Austin, Texas: Eakin Press, 1994).

Pietrusza, David. *Major Leagues: The Formation, Sometimes Absorption and Mostly Inevitable Demises of 18 Professional Baseball Organizations, 1871 to Present* (Jefferson, North Carolina: McFarland, 1991).

Ralph, John J. *National Baseball Hall of Fame and Museum 1999 Yearbook* (Cooperstown, New York: National Baseball Hall of Fame and Museum, 1999).

Richmond Braves Media Guide (1983, 1986, 1987, 1988, 1991, 1996, and 2001).

Riley, James A. *The Biographical Encyclopedia of the Negro Baseball Leagues* (New York: Carroll and Graf, 1994).

Seymour, Harold. *Baseball: The Early Years* (New York: Oxford University Press, 1960).

_____. *Baseball: The Golden Age* (New York: Oxford University Press, 1971).

_____. *Baseball: The People's Game* (New York: Oxford University Press, 1971).

Shatzkin, Mike, editor. *The Ballplayers: Baseball's Ultimate Biographical Reference* (New York: William Morrow, 1990).

Smith, Ira L. *Baseball's Famous Pitchers* (New York: A.S. Barnes, 1954).

Sullivan, Neil J. *The Minors: The Struggle and Triumph of Baseball's Poor Relations from 1876 to the Present* (New York: St Martin's Press, 1990).

United States Government Papers. *Thirteenth Census of the United States: Taken in the Year 1910, Vol. III: Population, 1910* (Washington, D.C.: U.S. Government Printing Office, 1913).

Voigt, David Q. *America Through Baseball* (Chicago: Nelson Hall, 1976).

White, G. Edward. *Creating the National Pastime: Baseball Transforms Itself, 1903–1953* (Princeton, New Jersey: Princeton University Press, 1996).

Zoss, Joel, and John Bowman. *Diamonds in the Rough: The Untold History of Baseball* (New York: Macmillan; London: Collier Macmillan, 1989. Reprint, Chicago: Contemporary Books, 1996).

Websites

Atlanta Braves official website (www.braves.mlb.com). Accessed on January 13, 2002.

Richmond Braves official website (www.rbraves.com). Accessed on October 30, 2001.

Richmond Metropolitan Authority website (www.rmaonline.org). Accessed on February 24, 2002.

Index